FESTIVE

BAKING

HOLIDAY CLASSICS IN THE SWISS GERMAN AND AUSTRIAN TRADITION

DOUBLEDAY

New York London Toronto Sydney

FESTIVE

BAKING

SARAH KELLY IAIA

Published by Doubleday, a division of Bantam Doubleday Dell Publishing Group, Inc., 666 Fifth Avenue, New York, New York 10103

Doubleday and the portrayal of an anchor with a dolphin are trademarks of Doubleday, a division of Bantam Doubleday Dell Publishing Group, Inc.

Published in an earlier form in the United Kingdom by Penguin under the title *Festive Baking in Austria, Germany and Switzerland*

Library of Congress Cataloging-in-Publication Data

Iaia, Sarah Kelly, 1943–
    Festive baking : classic holiday recipes in the Swiss, German, and Austrian tradition / Sarah Kelly Iaia.
    — 1st U.S. ed.
        p.   cm.
    Revision of : Festive baking in Austria, Germany, and Switzerland/ Sarah Kelly. Harmondsworth, Middlesex, England : Penguin Books, 1985. (Penguin handbooks).
    Includes index.
    1. Baking. 2. Confectionery. 3. Cookery, Swiss. 4. Cookery, German. 5. Cookery, Austrian. I. Iaia, Sarah Kelly, 1943–
Festive baking in Austria, Germany, and Switzerland. II. Title.
TX763.I25   1988
641.8′65′0943—dc19   87-37388
                                                                                        CIP

ISBN 0-385-19731-4

Copyright © 1988 by Sarah Kelly Iaia

DESIGNED BY BONNI LEON

All Rights Reserved
Printed in the United States of America
November 1988
First Edition in the United States of America

BG

CONTENTS

ABOUT THE AUTHOR

During seven years of living in Austria, Germany, and Switzerland, Sarah Kelly passionately pursued the art of festive baking with home bakers and professionals in countless *Konditoreien* and village bakeries.

Her interest in this baking tradition dates to childhood memories of German-American Christmas cookies and confections. Ms. Kelly is a graduate of the London Cordon Bleu School of Cookery. Her experience in the world of food ranges from running a cooking school in San Francisco to consulting for the Time/Life Good Cook series to publishing articles for *Connoisseur, Cuisine,* and *Food and Wine*.

She now works for the New York branch of Austria's largest bank, Creditanstalt-Bankverein. She lives in New York City with her husband Antonio Iaia, a designer.

INTRODUCTION

"Why *Lebkuchen*?" asked a good friend during the writing of my book. What could possibly possess me to spend all my time and energy on the seemingly esoteric subject of baking in the German tradition? My passion began with my first· spicy Honey Cake Square, sandwiched with moist fruit and nut filling and glazed with sugar icing . . . followed by slices of buttery *Zopf*, the braided Sunday bread of Switzerland . . . then the melt-in-your-mouth sponge/ meringue layers of *Kardinalschnitten*, filled with coffee cream. Encounters with strudels and *Salzburger Nockerl* and vanilla crescents and stollens compelled me to find out their origins and how they were made.

Although my firsthand exposure to this baking tradition came later, my interest began in childhood. The baking tradition in my family came from my mother's side, whose roots are

German. Christmas baking was a family affair, with my father and me shelling nuts while my sister and mother baked cookies and caramelized confections. It was only natural that when I finally went to Austria, Germany, and, later, Switzerland to work, my attention was drawn to the varied assortment of breads and pastries.

Living there gave me the opportunity to sample these delicacies. Baking there was not so simple. In German-language cookbooks, instructions are generally minimal since, until recently, most home bakers knew the basic techniques. To Americans, however, many of the doughs and techniques are unfamiliar.

But the many baking friends I made—home bakers as well as professionals—slowly enlightened me, giving rare insiders' tips on how to achieve excellent results. Once I had achieved some proficiency, 4 A.M. rendezvous with bakers were meetings of ecstasy, as I watched yeast doughs transformed into braids and buns, cakes layered, pastries twisted, and chocolate churned. After several years I set out to document what I had learned. Old and new German-language cookbooks provided background on quantities, techniques, history, and regional variations. However, it is the many cakes and pastries I ate and the practical experience of watching professionals and baking with friends that gave me an up-to-date perspective on the subject and the necessary technical skills to write this book.

With my outsider's account of what I've eaten, baked, and loved, where these items are found and how they can be reproduced, I hope to communicate my own joy and good fortune and inspire in others some of my excitement for festive baking and its traditions.

CONTENT AND ORGANIZATION

These recipes explore the vast and artistic array of seasonal and specialty baked goods—cookies, cakes, pastries, breads, and unusual desserts—which appear in Austria, Germany, and Switzerland to mark various holidays throughout the year. Since many of these specialties traveled with immigrants to the New World, laying the groundwork for some of our own baking traditions, you'll find here many American favorites and their origins.

I have selected only recipes that I feel qualify as festive baking, either because they have a historical association with certain holidays or events, or because they fall outside the realm of everyday baking, as they require unusual equipment, effort, or skill. The recipes reflect contemporary taste, ingredients, and equipment.

I have assumed that you have not had an opportunity to see or sample many or all of these items, so I have briefly described each in the recipe introductions; included are history, personal notes, degree of difficulty, preparation time, and storing capabilities so you can decide, without reading through the recipe, whether or not it is something that will appeal to you and can be made with the time and equipment available.

To provide continuity in technique, the chapters have been organized according to dough type. In as many cases as possible, I have given a basic dough recipe that, with additions, will yield a variety of specialties. This way, you can make up one dough (even a double recipe) and produce two or three different items—an especially useful time-saver for Christmas baking.

Because baking is one of the most demanding and unforgiving culinary disciplines, the recipes allow for variations in ingredients, climate, altitude, and equipment. The reference chapters at the end on Gift Ideas and Entertaining will give you practical suggestions on how to use these recipes for American holidays and special occasions. Mail Order Sources will help you find special ingredients or equipment.

OLD WORLD BAKING TRADITION

Of all the culinary traditions, baking best synthesizes the history, religion, artistry, superstitions, and fantasies of a people. The baked goods in this book reflect the evolution and migration of recipes from these countries sharing a common language, the symbolic custom of baking to communicate joy and good fortune, and the strong force of tradition.

Long ago, bread, the basic food of the diet, became the symbol of both life and fruitful harvests or fertility in pagan and Christian ceremonies. As the variety and refinement of flours increased and breadmaking skills improved, symbolic baking increased in importance. Artistic breads for special occasions started to appear and became especially important in the German baking tradition.

Decorative breadmaking was possible because, Northern Germany expected, the area was a wheat-growing region. Unlike the coarse rye flours used for daily loaves, wheat is the only grain that can produce a bread both soft and light enough to model. Most people lived in villages, and baking was generally done in communal ovens or by professional bakers as fuel was limited. Proud of his art, the baker developed designs that differentiated breads for special occasions from the daily loaves, shaping, plaiting, and twisting wheat dough into different forms.

The sweet cakes that first appeared in the Middle Ages and marked special occasions were also made with wheat flour and expanded the scope of symbolic baking. Although sugar was scarce until the seventeenth century, honey was readily available. When mixed with flour and spices, it sweetened one of the earliest fancy cookies—*Lebkuchen*, which were printed with elaborately carved molds or cut in heart shapes and colorfully decorated. Besides *Lebkuchen*, other sweet cakes and cookies were devised. Since most of these were for special occasions and were given as tokens, the shapes were often of pagan origin or were symbolic of a mythical or historical event.

Today in the German-speaking countries hundreds of different cookies, cakes, pastries, and breads were baked for special occasions—for the most part based on traditional recipes. However, there are numerous contemporary influences on the quantity and mix of baked goods, including communications, taste, new ingredients, economics, modern equipment, and lifestyle.

Because of improved communications, a common language (with regional variations), and the proliferation of cookbooks, many of the baked goods that were local specialties are now found in the best Konditorei and household repertoires throughout the region. The influence of other countries is also apparent both in ingredients and imports of baked goods, though foreign cakes and pastries are generally not consumed on important holidays.

Although women, both as bakers and discriminating customers, keep baking standards high, they are also increasingly joining the work force, reducing the time they have for all the household arts, including baking. In Germany especially, it is apparent that traditional home-baking skills are beginning to disappear with the younger generation. While Swiss and Austrian women now also pursue careers, they appear more conditioned to uphold basic household traditions. In both countries, one still observes high baking standards in the home.

Festive Baking Tradition in America

Little did I realize as a child that, every Christmas, the candied peel I chopped, the butter I creamed, and the spices I measured were all part of a baking tradition not invented by my grandmother. Like many of our Christmas customs in America—the decorated tree, evergreen wreaths, Santa Claus—holiday baking owes much to the traditions brought into this country long ago by German-speaking immigrants. Some came for economic opportunity. Others, coming from Moravia, Bohemia, Silesia, Alsace, and Switzerland, established communities in Pennsylvania, South Carolina, Kansas, and other states where they could live and work together with those of their own beliefs without fear of persecution or discrimination. Their traditions of folk art, crafts, social mores, and superstitions lived on in their homes and left their mark on America as a whole—most of all on our culinary tradition.

While today we think of many of our favorite baked goods as American, it might be surprising to find out how many were actually adopted from the German-speaking settlers: jelly doughnuts, vanilla crescents, and gingerbread; icebox, piped, and cut-out butter cookies; marzipan and fruit bread; apple crisp, cheesecake, and coffee cake, to name a few.

I hope that, through this book, you will become acquainted with some new delicious treats that will become part of your *own* baking tradition.

The list below constitutes the major holiday dates and occasions for which special cakes, cookies, breads, or pastries are baked. Besides religious holidays (both Catholic and Protestant, depending on the region), a few secular holidays are observed with specialty baking.

JANUARY 6

Twelfth Night (*Dreikönigsabend*) is celebrated in many German-speaking regions with *Dreikönigskuchen*, generally a round wreath made of rich yeast dough with a single almond or trinket baked inside.

MARDI GRAS AND SHROVE TUESDAY

(*Fasching* or, in Switzerland, *Fastnacht*, and *Rosendienstag*). Several cities are famous for their *Fasching* celebrations, most notably Munich, Mainz, Cologne, and Basel. However, *Fasching*—the period following Advent and preceding Lent—is observed throughout the German-speaking countries with costume balls, parades, satirical skits, and special food, most notably a variety of deep-fried pastries that are bought from street vendors or made at home. On Shrove Tuesday, in most regions, it is traditional to eat jelly doughnuts like *Berliner Pfannkuchen.*

FEBRUARY 14

St. Valentine's Day. Breaded hearts are made of yeast dough (follow the directions for *Osterkranz,* shaping the braid in a heart rather than a wreath), or large cookies are made of *Lebkuchen* (see *Lebkuchenherzen*). This is an observance of recent origin with special baked goods produced more in bakeries than in homes.

EASTER

(*Oster*). While not celebrated to the extent that it is in the neighboring Eastern European countries, Easter is generally observed by commercial and home bakers with special yeast breads—braided wreaths, Easter-egg nests, fish, doves, among others. (See *Oster-Hefegebäck.*)

MOTHER'S DAY

(*Muttertag*), of recent origin. Bakers in many parts bake heart-shaped cakes, often small, for the children to present to their mothers.

NOVEMBER 2

All Soul's Day (*Allerseelen*). In earlier times, the *Zopf* (braided bread) was traditionally baked on November 2 in Germany, although nowadays braided loaves are baked throughout the year, generally for Sunday.

NOVEMBER 11

Feast of St. Martin (*St. Martinstag*) celebrated in some of the Protestant areas. In the Würzburg area, bakers produce a small *Martinsweck* (a rich yeast bun with two "ears" on either side and a braid across the top).

CHRISTMAS MARKET

(*Weihnachtsmarkt*). A Christmas fair—generally from the first part of December until the twenty-third of the month—is held in the marketplace of many German-speaking cities. The most famous is held in Nürnberg. Frankfurt, Munich, Rothenburg ob der Tauber, Vienna, and Strassburg are only a few of the other cities which observe this custom. In Nürnberg, market stalls feature the famous *Nürnberg Elisenlebkuchen* as well as decorated Lebkuchen hearts (*Lebkuchenherzen*) and figures made of prunes (*Zwetschgenmännlein*). In Strassburg, *Lebkuchen* pigs (*Lebkuchen Glücksschweinchen*), symbolizing good luck are sold by vendors who write a name on each pig when it is bought. Fruit breads, too, are generally a feature of the markets, *Hutzelbrot* and *Früchtebrot*. Other sweets that are a standard item at these fairs include caramelized almonds (*Gebranntemandeln*), nougatine (*Türkischerhonig*), and chocolate-dipped marshmallow confections (*Negerküsse*).

DECEMBER 6

St. Nikolaus Day. In most German-speaking areas, the children receive their gifts on this day rather than at Christmas as is customary in the English-speaking world. Something made of marzipan is traditional, (see Chapter III) as well as either Lebkuchen or rich yeast dough treats: Santa Claus figures (*Weihnachtsmänner*) or the Swiss figures called *Grittibänzen*, (called *Stutenkerl* in Westphalia) which wear neckties and carry pipes in their mouths. The introduction to Marzipan carries additional historic notes on St. Nikolaus.

DECEMBER 24 AND 25

Christmas Eve and Christmas (*Heiliger Abend* and *Weihnachten*). Christmas Eve is traditionally a family celebration, with the Christmas tree lit for the first time and a festive dinner eaten thereafter. The many Christmas cookies (*Weihnachtsgebäck*) that have been baked, received as gifts, and possibly purchased are finally fully displayed for consumption. Some of the most famous of these are gingerbread (*Lebkuchen*), printed anise cookies (*Springerle*), and cinnamon stars (*Zimtsterne*). With few exceptions, however, most of the cookies given in this book would be considered appropriate for Christmas baking. Those cookies in the *Lebkuchen* chapter are generally baked only at Christmas time. Large tangled snowballs (*Rothenburger Schneeballen*) are an interesting deep-fried pastry made for Christmas. Rich breads are also baked for the Christmas holidays (*Weihnachts-Hefegebäck*). In addition to those mentioned as part of the Christmas market and St. Nikolaus Day selection, there is also one of the most famous fruit-nut filled loaves—

Dresdner Christstollen, as well as numerous different braided loaves. In Austria, house-wives also bake and exchange their finest tortes (see Chapter 6 on cakes and pastries) as well as breads and cookies.

DECEMBER 31 AND JANUARY 1

New Year's Eve and New Year's Day (*Silvester* and *Neujahrstag*). Various yeast breads and deep-fried pastries are prepared for the celebration on New Year's Eve, an occasion which is generally celebrated with the family. Yeast specialties include Bacon Bread (*Speckkuchen*), New Year's Good-Luck Pigs (*Neujahrs-Glücksschweinchen*), and Braided Yeast Pretzel (*Geflochtene Neujahrs-Brezeln*). Many of the items in Chapter 4 on Basic Deep-Fried Pastry Dough would be traditionally consumed on New Year's, the selection varying in different regions. Jelly doughnuts (*Berliner Pfannkuchen*), which are tradition-ally eaten on Shrove Tuesday, are also eaten on New Year's Eve in many places.

FIRST COMMUNION, CONFIRMATION, WEDDING, BIRTHDAY

For any of these occasions, there is usually a special cake, either homemade or purchased from the best-known local bakers. See Chapter 6 on cakes and pastries, for a selection.

LOCAL VILLAGE FAIRS, TRADE FAIRS, CHURCH FAIRS

(*Volksfeste, Messen*, and *Kirchweihen*). For these regional fairs, local bakers and itinerant vendors normally prepare deep-fried pastries, among them Apple Fritters (*Apfelküchel*), Mardi Gras Pastries (*Eieröhrli*), Slip-knot crisps (*Schlupfküchlein*). See Chapter 4 on deep-fried pastries.

SUNDAYS

Because Sunday is the baker's day off, the housewife often bakes a special Sunday bread herself. Two traditional favorites are the Braided Loaf (*Zopf*) and Alsatian Coffee Cake (*Kugelhopf*). In addition, the coffee hour on Sunday is a special focal point for which either the housewife bakes a special cake or pastry herself to be consumed at home or the family has an outing (an *Ausflug*) which terminates at a charming country inn or well-known café with a pause for *Kaffee* and *Kuchen*.

STANDARD AND SPECIAL BAKING EQUIPMENT

Most of the recipes in this book can be made with standard baking equipment, a general list of which is given below (knives and cooking pots excluded). A number of recipes, however, call for special equipment. In case you are buying new equipment, I have, whenever possible, given my preferences for various models or materials and reasons for this preference.

Standard Baking Equipment

APPLIANCES

BLENDER—especially useful for grinding nuts very fine; see Baking Tips.

ELECTRIC MIXER—hand or counter model. I have always used a hand mixer which I like because it can be moved around in corners and can be used for beating mixtures over heat (as is the case with a few of the meringue recipes and with all of the whisked egg recipes unless a hand whisk is used).

FOOD PROCESSOR—good for sifting powdered sugar—just pour it in and turn on the machine; puréeing both thick and thin mixtures; softening butter that has just come out of the refrigerator; and grinding quantities of nuts and bread crumbs. (If the nuts must be very finely ground for marzipan, however, a blender must be used.) I don't recommend using the food processor for pastry doughs and many cookie doughs. A food processor spins so quickly, even when using a quick Stop/Start technique, that the batter is blended completely into the flour. Pastries and delicate cookies, in order to be light, require that small, even bits of butter remain in the dough. When baked the butter melts, leaving tiny air pockets throughout. Dough made in a food processor creates a greasier end product, which is appropriate when an oilier texture is desired such as that found in chocolate-chip or certain icebox cookies.

BAKING SHEETS—at least two or three if baking cookies. Black steel baking sheets sold in some cookware shops are good for pastry but are not suitable for most of the delicate and sugar-rich baked goods in this book. The black metal conducts the heat more rapidly than light-colored or nonstick baking sheets and has a tendency to burn the bottoms of many of these cookies and cakes before they are baked through. Any other baking sheets are always suitable.

CAKE TINS—8-inch and 9-inch. Springform pans—the kind with sides that can be removed by releasing a clamp—are especially versatile. They are deeper than most, and thus can be used in all cake recipes. When the sides are removed, the base makes a handy stencil for cutting out or marking circles and is useful for putting under cakes that are being decorated. The cake can then be moved easily to a platter, either by lifting it with a large pancake turner or by sliding it carefully onto the platter.

CHEESE GRATER—for grating chocolate and lemon rind, and for flaking the butter in pastry and cookie doughs using my method.

COOKIE CUTTERS—an assortment in decorative shapes. A useful investment is a nest of fluted or plain round cutters in various sizes. Small aspic cutters are suggested in several recipes, but a thimble or small bottle cap can be substituted.

DREDGERS—not essential but especially useful for one who bakes often. Have three—one filled with flour, one with powdered sugar, and the third with granulated sugar. Label them so you don't mix them. I also keep a fourth, filled with cocoa powder. The most important one is the one filled with flour, which can be used to dust your pastry board and rolling pin sparingly when you are rolling out pastry or cookie dough.

FLOUR SIFTER—used for sifting flour and powdered sugar though I prefer the method using a wire sieve which is faster.

KITCHEN SCALES

LEMON SQUEEZER—if not handy, squeeze lemon juice through a closed hand into a bowl. The juice will pass through and your hand will strain out the seeds.

MEASURING CUPS

MEASURING SPOONS

MIXING BOWLS—various sizes, including one medium-sized crockery or glass bowl for making whisked sponge cakes and whisked-egg cookies, and one large bowl—crockery or plastic, not aluminum—for beating a large number of egg whites.

PAPER AND LINERS

ALUMINUM FOIL—especially useful for wrapping food to be frozen.

BUTCHER PAPER (UNWAXED)—can be substituted for parchment paper. It can be found at most butcher shops.

CARDBOARD—for cutting out paper stencils.

NONSTICK BAKING PAPER—available in gourmet shops, is especially recommended for soft whisked-egg cookies and for delicate egg-white cookies—meringues, macaroons, etc.—though it is not an essential item if you follow instructions in the recipes for lining baking sheets. It can be wiped off and reused.

PARCHMENT PAPER—my preference for lining cake tins and baking sheets. It is heavier and thus more durable than wax paper and is fairly resistant to sticking. Unlike aluminum foil, which insulates food from heat and alters baking times, parchment paper allows both heat and any steam to pass through its pores. Parchment paper is available in hardware stores that sell cookware and in gourmet shops. Unwaxed butcher paper can be substituted.

WAX PAPER—especially useful when sifting dry ingredients.

PASTRY BAG—ideally one medium-sized (holds 2 cups) and one large (holds 4 cups). I prefer pastry bags that are made of thin, flexible plastic over those made of heavy plasticized cotton. They are easier to wash, dry more quickly, and don't absorb flavors. PASTRY BAG TIPS—those which are attached on the outside, over the end of the pastry bag are especially useful if you need to change decorative tips in the middle of piping— you need not remove the piping mixture, a rather messy chore. See Baking Tips for how to fill a pastry bag.

PASTRY BOARD—marble, synthetic, or wood. A marble slab makes an especially suitable pastry board for butter-rich pastry and butter cookie doughs because of its constant cool temperature and glassy surface. Almost as good are the new synthetic white boards now on the market, which have the added advantage of being light, relatively nonstick, and dishwasher safe. A wooden pastry board should be reserved for pastry only; if used as a general chopping board, it will take on food flavors that are passed on to the pastry.

PASTRY BRUSHES—several; one always kept dry for brushing flour from pastry or cookie dough.

PASTRY WHEELS—zigzag and plain, for decorative pastry work—cutting out free-form flowers and leaves, for instance—or for cutting out printed cookies.

PIE PANS—can be substituted in some recipes calling for tart tins if they are shallow enough (1 inch).

PLASTIC WRAP—which goes under the manufacturer's names of Handy, Reynolds, or Saran Wrap, is especially good for wrapping cookie and pastry dough because it sticks directly to the surface of the dough, ensuring that there will be no spots on the pastry round that dry out when the dough is refrigerated, something that often happens when wax paper or aluminum foil is used. Dry spots on the surface of the dough discolor and leave hard bits scattered over the surface of rolled-out pastry. Wax paper or aluminum foil can be substituted if you take care to wrap it closely and tightly around the dough.

ROLLING PIN—I prefer a long, cylindrical rolling pin for general use (mine is approximately 1¾ inches in diameter), the same diameter throughout. The style without handles gives much better control for pastry making, though one with handles is fine for cookie doughs. The French style of rolling pin with tapered ends is useful for rolling out very firm doughs because it gives added leverage. However, one that is the same diameter throughout will ultimately roll the dough out more evenly.

RULER—for measuring cookies, especially.

SCISSORS—for cutting stencils.

SPATULAS

LARGE METAL SPATULA—for spreading icings and removing cookies from baking sheets. If you have two that match, they will be especially good for cutting butter into flour as described in the directions for making butter pastry and butter cookie doughs.

PASTRY SCRAPER—thin metal rectangle with wooden handle, now also made in tough plastic. Used to scrape sticking dough from a pastry board, for which a metal spatula can also be used. It is also used to work chocolate and icing mixtures on a marble slab or clean countertop.

RUBBER SPATULA—to scrape out dough, batters, egg whites, and icings from mixing bowls.

SMALL METAL SPATULA—not essential but useful for removing small cookies from baking sheets and doing touch-up work on icing and decorations.

SPOONS

LARGE METAL SPOON—better than a rubber spatula for folding in beaten egg white or flour, since the sharp edge of the spoon cuts more efficiently through the mixture.

SLOTTED SPOON—required for deep fried pastries.

WOODEN SPOONS—two or three at least. One with a hole in it is useful, though not essential, for stirring thick batters and thin bread doughs as covered in the chapter on batters and deep-fried pastries.

STORAGE CONTAINERS—airtight tins with lids are good for storing those cookies that should be stored at room temperature. For refrigerator storage, plastic containers with lids can be used.

TART TINS—10-inch or 11-inch, preferably tin (which conducts heat better than ceramic) with a fluted edge and removable bottom. When removing the sides from such a form, place the baked tart on top of a large tin can. Carefully release the outside rim from the pastry. It will fall down on the counter, leaving the pastry exposed.

THERMOMETERS

CANDY/DEEP-FRY THERMOMETER—for certain meringues, nut brittle, and deep-fried pastries (if an electric deep fryer is not used).

OVEN THERMOMETER—especially useful for proving oven temperature is accurate.

WIRE SIEVES—small and large, for sifting flour and powdered sugar and for straining. Sifting is recommended in the recipes not only to eliminate lumps but also to aerate the flour or powdered sugar, which lightens it.

WIRE WHISKS—small and large, for beating egg mixtures. In many cases an electric or rotary beater can be substituted.

SPECIAL BAKING EQUIPMENT

IRONS

SNOWBALL IRON (*Schneeballeisen*)—a hinged, perforated ball with long handles used to deep-fry snowball pastries (*Rothenburger Schneeballen*). A substitute method is given in the recipe, since this is an item not easily obtainable even in Germany.

WAFER IRON (*Waffeleisen*), decoratively imprinted or embossed—used for thin, sweet, and savory crisp wafers made of batter or pastry. They are available in both long-handled hinged models, for use on a burner, or in electric models, less frequently exported. A waffle iron cannot be substituted because the grooves of the grid are too deep. Rcipes in this book using such an iron include *Eiserkuchen*, *Wasserbretzeli*, and *Kümmelbretzeli*.

MOLDS

Savarin Mold—plain tube pan called for in *Frankfurter Kranz*.

Small Decorative Tin Molds, generally used for candies or special cookies such as *Basler Brunsli*.

Stollen Form—hinged iron mold with a traditional stollen shape. Such forms are used by professional bakers to give their loaves of stollen uniform shape and to keep the stollen from browning. Home bakers, however, rarely use such forms. The recipe for *Dresdner Christstollen* gives a technique for baking without a form.

Wooden or Ceramic Molds, decoratively carved or imprinted, and carved wooden rolling pins—required for many of the traditional cookies in this book, including *Springerle*, some *Lebkuchen, Berner Haselnussleckerli, Frankfurter Brenten, Züri Leckerli, Alte Züri-Tirggel*, and *Spekulatius*. See individual recipes for notes on using traditional molds where possible. While old molds are increasingly difficult to find in the German-speaking countries, since they are collector's items often hung on the kitchen wall, contemporary molds are being produced and are exported. They are usually available only in large, well-stocked specialty cookware shops and from gourmet mail-order companies.

PANS

Bundt Pan—the trade name for a tube pan with a vertical decorative fluted design.

Kugelhopf (Gugelhupf) Pan—deep tube pan: made of ceramic or metal with decorative flutes that generally twist around the outside of the pan, used to bake Kugelhopf. A plain savarin mold or Bundt pan can be substituted.

Rehrücken Pan—metal baking tin shaped in a half cylinder with parallel ridges on either side, usually about 1 foot long. It is used to bake a special Austrian cake that is meant to resemble a roast rack of venison.

Rolling Pin with Decorative Carved Patterns—substitutes for carved or imprinted molds.

INGREDIENTS AND THEIR PREPARATION

Bread Crumbs

- To make homemade bread crumbs, you can remove the crusts if you don't want to go through the final step below of pressing the processed crumbs through a wire sieve. Otherwise use the following method: Break the bread into small (½ inch or smaller) pieces. If the bread is fresh, spread it out in a single layer on a large baking sheet and dry it out in a preheated 325-degree oven for approximately 20 minutes, or until the bread is dry throughout but not yet colored. Do not allow the bread to brown. Using the cutting blade on a food processor, start the machine before adding up to 2 cups of bread through the feeder tube. Turn the machine on and off several times to process the crumbs evenly. When done, remove the crumbs and continue with the remaining dried bread until finished. If you have not removed the crusts from the bread, some of the crumbs will be slightly coarser than others. You should therefore pass the crumbs through a wire sieve into another bowl, pressing them with the back of a wooden spoon to break the large bits into finer crumbs. Store in an airtight container until needed.

Butter

- I always use sweet, unsalted butter which is generally made of higher-quality cream than salted butter and imparts a much richer, fresher flavor to all baked goods.
- In recipes that call for softened butter, you can accelerate the process if yours is stone cold by cutting it in pieces and spinning it for several minutes in a food processor. You will have to turn the food processor on and off several times and scrape down the sides, but you'll have soft butter in no time.

Chocolate

- All but one recipe calls for semi-sweet chocolate. Make sure to buy good-quality chocolate. One very good brand that is available in most gourmet shops and many supermarkets is Lindt Excellence.

- It is best not to attempt melting chocolate over direct heat. The bottom of the chocolate pieces will scorch when the fat in the chocolate is not allowed to melt completely. This is best accomplished using a double boiler, over 2 inches of water that is kept at a simmer. However, I prefer to place a shallow heatproof soup plate or bowl over a pan filled with several inches of simmering water. Because the plate or bowl is shallow, it is particularly easy to scrape out every bit of chocolate with a rubber spatula; and if you just need the chocolate for glazing or dipping, you can keep it in the shallow container.
- Avoid melting chocolate near an uncovered pan of simmering or boiling water or in a dish that does not overlap the top of the pan of simmering water, as a drop or two of water in the chocolate will cause it to "seize"—become dry and grainy. If this should happen, add a teaspoon or so of vegetable oil to the chocolate, stirring until smooth. Chocolate can be melted with a large quantity of liquid (in several recipes it is melted together with an equal weight of cream), but minuscule amounts of liquid should be avoided.

CREAM

- The cream used in all these recipes is heavy or whipping cream. Half-and-half is not rich enough for the majority of these recipes, most of which require that the cream be whipped.
- Cream can be whipped with a large wire whisk, a rotary beater, or an electric mixer. For best results, chill the blades and the mixing bowl in the freezer for about 15 minutes and make sure the cream is well chilled before beginning. I prefer to use a large whisk because I find I can beat more air into the cream, making it lighter, and can see and feel the consistency of the cream as I beat, stopping when it's fluffiest but before it has curdled. A rotary beater gives control also, but doesn't beat the same amount of air into the cream. Electric mixers are quick and work well but you must watch the cream very carefully at the end to avoid curdling. Some people beat the cream until quite thick with an electric beater, then finish it at the end with a whisk. A few electric mixers come with very thin beaters just meant for beating cream and these work especially well, beating the cream a little less rapidly so the cream thickens gradually.
- If the weather or the kitchen is extremely hot, you might want to put the chilled mixing bowl in another bowl filled with ice. However, I've only found this necessary under extreme conditions.
- Whipped cream that is being served with cakes or tarts is usually not sweetened in the German-speaking countries. It can be either lightly whipped, so it falls in cloudlike dollops (which I prefer), or whipped stiff.

- I usually avoid whipping cream at the last minute for dinner parties by whipping it 2 to 3 hours ahead, fairly stiff, and refrigerating it, covered. Just before serving, I take my whisk and whip it again. It thickens in a few seconds.
- If you wish to sweeten or flavor it, you can add 1 to 2 teaspoons powdered sugar and 1 teaspoon of vanilla extract per cup before you begin beating.

Eggs

- Eggs used in these recipes are large eggs (approximately 2 ounces each). If you have larger or smaller eggs and wish to substitute them in a recipe, multiply the number of eggs required in the recipe by 2, which will give you the number of ounces required— for example, 4 eggs would mean that the recipe calls for 8 ounces of eggs. Then use a kitchen scales and weight out the correct number of eggs.
- To bring refrigerated eggs to room temperature quickly, place them in a bowl, cover them with hot tap water for 2 minutes, and drain off the water.
- Lightly beaten egg is often used to glaze baked goods. The white alone gives a clear, shiny glaze; a whole egg produces a medium brown glaze; and the yolk, usually beaten with a tablespoon of cream, produces a rich brown glaze. Bread that is glazed is usually glazed twice: once after it has been shaped but before it has gone through the proving stage, and then again just before it is baked.

Egg Whites

- Although eggs are easier to separate when they are cold, the whites beat to greater volume when they are at room temperature.
- Because most of the egg whites in this book are eventually beaten together with sugar to produce a stiff meringue, I recommend using an electric beater because beating with a whisk or rotary hand beater is too tiring. When beating egg whites, make sure the mixing bowl and rubber scraper are perfectly clean with no trace of fat, and completely dry. A speck of water or fat in the bowl will prevent the egg whites from thickening properly.
- If a speck of yolk should fall into your whites when you are separating your eggs, the easiest way to remove it is by scooping it out with a half eggshell, to which it will adhere naturally. The least bit of fat from the yolk will also keep the whites from thickening properly. You can also take the precaution of separating your whites into a small bowl

one at a time, then pouring each one into the larger mixing bowl. This way you don't run the risk of ruining an entire bowl of egg whites by breaking a complete yolk in the bowl just at the end.

- Whenever you're beating egg whites, don't stop half way through for a phone conversation. Use stiffly beaten egg whites immediately once they are beaten. They will deflate if you let them rest and then go back and beat them a second time.

- Unbeaten egg whites keep very well in the refrigerator. I usually keep a small covered container just for that purpose, labeling it when the first white went in. I keep them for a month in the refrigerator, if I know I will need them in the near future. Otherwise I freeze them 2 at a time in small freezer bags. When thawed and back at room temperature, they can be beaten as if they were fresh.

FLOUR

- With a few exceptions, the flour used in all but the yeast recipes is all-purpose flour. I prefer unbleached flour such as Hecker's, which more closely resembles the flour used in Central Europe, but bleached flour can also be used.

- For yeast breads and strudel dough, however, bread flour—hard wheat flour—is generally called for because of its high gluten content. Gluten, a protein, becomes elastic when worked and activated by moisture, which helps the bread expand as carbon dioxide is liberated from the yeast. It also helps the bread keep its shape in baking.

- While whole wheat and rye flours are used a great deal in Germany and Switzerland for everyday baking, white flour, which was a luxury in the past, is generally preferred for special baking.

LEAVENING AGENTS

Besides stiffly beaten egg white and alcohol, which causes leavening when heated, the other standard leavening agents include:

BAKING POWDER AND BAKING SODA

- Even in many contemporary German-language cookbooks, one or both of these powders have replaced the leavening agents used in years past. To neutralize an acidic factor such as honey or spice, baking soda is combined with baking powder in certain recipes (mainly in Lebkuchen), with the main leavening action left to the baking powder.

TRADITIONAL LEAVENING AGENTS IN GERMAN-LANGUAGE COOKBOOKS

I include a brief description of these ingredients for the interest of those who read German cookbooks.

- *BACKPULVER* (baking powder)—made up of baking soda, an acidic substance such as cream of tartar, and starch.
- *HIRSCHHORNSALZ* (powdered ammonium carbonate, formerly made of powdered deer horn). Used only in thin, flat baked goods (traditionally in Lebkuchen), it imparts a very crisp texture. However, it must be heated to an inner temperature of 60 degrees C. for the strong-flavored ammonia gas to be released. It is generally sold in glass tubes and must be kept tightly sealed.
- *NATRON* (bicarbonate of soda). It works the same way as Pottasche. If not used with something acidic, it has a bad odor.
- *POTTASCHE* (today, a powdered chemical preparation of potassium carbonate). When heated, it releases carbon dioxide and remains odorless. It is generally first dissolved in liquid before being used, at which point the dough should be used right away. After baking, it has the property of absorbing moisture, helping to keep baked goods moist (see *Pfeffernüsse*). It is generally sold in glass tubes and must be kept tightly sealed.

YEAST

Yeast, which comes in both fresh cakes and dried granular forms, is a living organism activated by warmth (as low as 50 degrees F.) but killed by heat any higher then 140 degrees F. Cold, on the other hand, simply retards its growth without killing the organism, so that unbaked bread dough can be frozen, and when brought back to room temperature, the yeast will reactivate. Sugar, which is added to yeast to activate it, serves as its food. However, too large an amount will inhibit its growth. For this reason, only a small amount of sugar is first combined with the yeast in the two Basic Sweet Yeast Dough recipes, with the remainder added after the yeast has had a chance to develop in the "sponge."

Salt also has a retarding effect and when placed in direct contact with the yeast will kill it. Because of this, salt is often added after the initial "sponge" stage.

Fresh yeast, which is called for in most of these recipes, should be light in color and should crumble easily. When old it will shrivel at the edges and turn brown, and should be thrown out. Fresh yeast is usually creamed with a small amount of sugar, which turns it into a liquid. Any additional liquid in the recipe should feel warm to the hand (75 to 80 degrees F.).

Dry yeast is activated by being mixed with a small amount of sugar and water that feels hot to the hand (90 to 110 degrees F.), or heated according to the manufacturer's directions. Once it has been combined with the sugar and water, if it doesn't rise in 10 minutes the yeast is bad and a new packet should be used.

To substitute dry yeast for fresh yeast, use 1 tablespoon of dry yeast for 1 ounce of fresh yeast, and use some of the liquid given in the recipe to dilute it, warming it as described above.

When yeast is activated, it produces alcohol and carbon dioxide—the gas that causes the dough to rise. Punching and kneading help to distribute the gas through the dough and give it a finer, more even texture. If yeast is allowed to overexpand, it may use up its energy and have little power left to make the bread rise during baking. On the other hand, if the dough isn't left to mature fully, the loaves will be small and dense. In general, bread that has risen slowly has a more even texture and balanced flavor.

I prefer fresh yeast, because I have always found that my bread has risen higher, even when I've forgotten loaves that were proving and would, under normal circumstances, have collapsed in the oven, the yeast having spent itself.

LEMONS

- Many of the recipes call for grated lemon rind. To grate, use the finest blades of a grater, being careful to grate only the yellow rind and not the white fleshy part below. A pastry brush is useful for removing clinging bits of rind from the grater.

NUTS

- Many of the recipes call for various kinds of ground nuts. Once they have been shelled and blanched or skinned (if called for), they can be ground in a blender, food processor, or nut grinder. To grind nuts in a blender, have the machine running at high speed before dropping up to ½ cup of nuts into the machine at one time through the hole at the top. They will grind very fine in a matter of seconds. When they are completely ground, they will be stuck to the sides of the container. Empty the container completely before grinding more nuts. For recipes such as marzipan, which require that the almonds be ground as fine as dust, a blender is the only normal household appliance that will grind them fine enough. With a food processor, place up to 1 cup of nuts in the container of the machine. Turn the machine on and off repeatedly until the nuts are chopped or ground to the desired consistency. For most of the recipes other than marzipan, unless specifically stated, a food processor can be used for grinding the nuts. Nut grinders come in different models, though generally speaking the nuts are simply put through a slot at the top and a handle is turned to grind them. Regardless of what method you use, grinding nuts freshly makes a big difference in the flavor of the cookie, cake, or tart, and is worth the trouble if you have the time (even though almonds, in particular, can be bought already ground).

ALMONDS

- To blanch almonds (to remove their skins), place them in a bowl and cover them with boiling water. After 2 or 3 minutes, their skins should slip off easily. Test one. If successful, pour off the water and slip off the skins of the other almonds.
- To split almonds, first blanch them and slip off all the skins. While they are still soft, insert the point of a small sharp knife along the side of each, then carefully cut through. This will produce 2 perfect almond shapes with a flat side where they were cut. Work quickly. Once the almonds are dry again, they will generally break in pieces when you try to split them. For decorating, unless otherwise stated, place them on a cookie or cake rounded side up.
- To grind almonds that have just been blanched, first dry them on paper towels. (They must be completely dried out.) Then either leave them in a dry place (not, ideally, a steamy kitchen) for several hours or, to accelerate their drying, place them in one layer on a baking sheet in a 250-degree F. oven for 15 to 20 minutes, being careful not to let them brown. Grind as described under "Nuts."
- When chopping almonds or any other rounded nut like hazelnuts by hand, the nuts can be chopped more easily if you sprinkle your board first with a little granulated sugar to keep them from slipping.

HAZELNUTS

- To remove the skins from hazelnuts, place them in one layer on a baking sheet in the middle of a preheated 425-degree F. oven for about 5 to 7 minutes, watching them closely. The hazelnuts are ready when they have begun to give off an aroma and the skins are darkened, shriveled, and beginning to flake off. Remove the baking sheet from the oven. When the hazelnuts are cool enough to handle (although you can begin while they are still warm), place them in a large wire sieve, about ½ cup at a time, and roll them back and forth, pressing them in well with your hand as you roll them. The mesh of the wire should help grate the loose skins from the nuts. If the skins do not come off easily, return the nuts to the oven for several minutes longer and test again. When one batch is finished (any small clinging bits of skin you can remove with your fingers), place the skinned hazelnuts in a bowl and proceed with the rest.

  NOTE When hazelnuts are moderately fresh, the skins are much tighter. Such hazelnuts generally take slightly longer in the oven than the kind one normally gets. When the skins are so tight it is often not possible to remove every bit. However, when the nuts are fresh the skin is more nutlike than dry and flaky, so it will not hurt if a little skin remains on such hazelnuts that are to be ground. When speaking of moderately fresh hazelnuts, I am not referring to the green cob nuts still in their shells. These nuts are too green and cannot be used.

OIL FOR DEEP-FRYING

- My preference is corn oil, which imparts a distinct, delicate corn flavor and richer color than other oils to deep-fried pastries. However, safflower or other vegetable oil (other than olive oil) can be substituted.
- Make certain you have sufficient oil for your deep fryer so that when the basket is submerged the pastries will be covered by oil. For most deep fryers, 2 1½-quart bottles of oil—that is 12 cups—should provide more than sufficient quantity.
- So that oil can be used again for deep-frying (not any other purpose), it can be filtered. To filter, allow the oil to cool to room temperature. Place a double thickness of cheese-cloth or a Handy Wipe, doubled, in a funnel placed over the original oil bottle. Slowly pour the oil into the funnel, allowing that quantity to filter into the bottle before pouring more. Replace the lid on the bottle and label it "deep-frying oil" so it is not mistakenly used for another purpose.

SALT

- Although many people today try to limit the salt in their diets, the amount of salt called for in these recipes is proportionately minuscule. If it is eliminated from butter cookies and pastries, the end product tastes flat. In the case of bread dough, it is required in the chemical process to halt the action of yeast.

SPICES

- For Christmas baking in particular, standard spices called for in this book include:

allspice	mace
anis (ground and whole)	nutmeg
cardamom	poppy seeds
cinnamon	sandalwood, powdered (used in Swiss bak-
cloves	ing for its musky flavor and red color)
coriander	vanilla bean (vanilla extract can be
ginger	substituted)

SWEETENERS
HONEY

- The oldest sweetener for cookies and cakes, honey is a traditional ingredient in Lebkuchen and is especially good for baking that is done in advance, since it keeps very well.
- For best results, buy pure honey. If a recipe calls for warming it, don't allow it to boil as this makes cookies especially hard and brittle.

MOLASSES

- The traditional sweetener for the North German version of *Lebkuchen—Braune Kuchen—* molasses gives these cookies their distinctive dark brown color.

SUGAR

- Most of the recipes in this book call for superfine sugar because it is more refined than granulated sugar and takes far less beating time to break down, giving superior results for baked goods. In older German recipes, it is common to find directions for beating the sugar and eggs for 30 to 40 minutes. With the very refined sugars we have today, such lengthy beating is no longer necessary.
- Powdered sugar, which is used for icing and dusting cakes and cookies, should always be sifted before using (see notes on *Sifting*).
- Decorating sugar, often available in supermarkets before holidays, can be procured from a bakery supply shop or specialty shop. It is only suggested in several recipes, with granulated sugar as a substitute. As it has much coarser grain than granulated sugar, it makes an attractive finish on certain cookies and breads.

BAKING TIPS

General Rules

• Read the recipe through first and have all ingredients premeasured, utensils ready, and baking sheets or tins prepared as directed.
• Preheat the oven approximately 10 minutes before you will be ready to bake.
• When baking something for the first time and always when baking cookies, watch closely so as not to overbake. Rely on the description for doneness given in reach recipe, since baking times are approximate, varying somewhat with different ovens, baking equipment, and density of baked goods.
• Allow all baked goods to cool to room temperature, on a rack unless otherwise directed, before storing in tins, refrigerating, or freezing.

Rolling Out Pastry and Butter Cookie Doughs

Cookie dough that is rolled out and cut out in small shapes is more manageable than pastry that is rolled out in a round and transferred to a cake or tart tin. Even if the cookie dough sticks to the board (which, ideally, it shouldn't), small cookies can easily be loosened from the board with a thin metal spatula. A large round of pastry, on the other hand, will generally tear if it has stuck to the board and you try to move it.

While you need not be such a perfectionist with your cookie dough, it offers you a good chance to practice rolling-out technique, which will aid you immeasurably when you come to roll out pastry.

As I mentioned in the equipment section, I prefer a long, cylindrical rolling pin (mine is approximately 1¾ inches in diameter), the same diameter throughout, without handles. It gives much better control for pastry making, although for cookie making you will have no trouble using a model with handles. The "quick, short turns" that I refer to below would not apply if using a rolling pin with handles, which rolls in one continuous movement.

- Make sure the dough has chilled long enough to firm it before rolling it out.
- When rolling out, flour only the pastry board and rolling pin, never the dough itself. This prevents adding excess flour to the dough, which would make it dry and tough.
- Before rolling a round of dough that has just come from the refrigerator, hit the round forcefully with the side of your rolling pin in 2 or 3 places to help flatten it out. Do so repeatedly if the dough has been refrigerated for a long period and is extremely hard. Make several gentle rolls forward. Then use your hands to force the ragged edges which will have appeared back into a smooth round. In the early stages of rolling out, when the dough is still fairly thick, continue this process.
- Always roll in quick short turns away from you in the beginning. Lift the pastry after each roll and give it a quarter turn. This will ensure that it rolls out evenly and doesn't stick to the board. Reflour the board or rolling pin as needed. A flour dredger is ideal for this purpose because it dusts only a small amount of flour on board or rolling pin and sifts it at the same time.
- Work as quickly as possible so the dough doesn't get too warm and eventually greasy.
- If the dough should stick to the board, lift it up immediately, scrape away the sticky dough with a metal spatula or pastry scraper made for that purpose, and reflour the board lightly, working as quickly as possible. The same treatment works for a sticky rolling pin.
- Try to roll your dough out as evenly as possible. For cookies this will ensure that all your cookies are the same thickness (which is more pleasing aesthetically) and that they all bake for the same amount of time. For pastry rounds, it means you won't have an overcooked or undercooked spot on one side of the pastry.

Lining Tart Tins

- To transfer a round of dough to a tart tin, use the following method with a rolling pin without handles (the pastry twirls right off a rotating rolling pin): Place your rolling pin in the middle of the pastry. Fold one half of the round over the pin and carry the dough to the tin draped over the rolling pin. Lay the pastry round bottom side up (the side that was facing the board originally) in the tin. Brush off any excess flour with a dry pastry brush. This will help keep the pastry as light and flaky as possible.
- For lining a tin your pastry round should be, ideally, about 4 inches larger than the tin; for a pie pan, it will need to be slightly larger to account for the deeper sides. Ease the pastry gently into the corners of the tin and smooth out the bottom. Flouring the back of your index finger, press the pastry well into the corners, at the same time pulling extra pastry down into the side areas so that the sides are slightly thicker than the base. Go around a second time, pressing the pastry well against the side of the tin.

Baking Pastry and Butter Cookie Dough

• Refer to individual recipes for specific instructions. In general, however, tarts and pies made of a rich short crust (in this book, Mürbeteig) are generally baked either just above center or in the center of an oven heated to 375 degrees F. Butter cookies are generally baked on buttered, floured baking sheets in the middle of a slightly cooler oven, generally about 350 degrees F. unless otherwise directed. For thick, shaped cookies such as pretzels and "S's," I find they tend to spread slightly less in baking if they are baked on unbuttered baking sheets. However, this is the exception. Butter is used on baking sheets rather than shortening or oil because both of the latter impart their own distinct flavor to butter cookies which is not in harmony with the butter in the dough. To butter the baking sheets, scoop up a tablespoon of soft butter with a small piece of paper towel and spread evenly over the surface. To flour them, using a flour dredger, sieve, or sifter, lightly dust the surface evenly with flour. Turn over the baking sheet on its side and rap it several times on the counter over the sink to shake off the excess.

Preparing Cake Pans, Molds, and Baking Sheets

• For plain round cake pans and baking sheets with rims that are being lined for sheet cakes, grease the bottom and sides of the pan generously with softened butter. Put the soft butter on a crumpled piece of paper towel and rub it around the tin. Then place the tin or baking sheet on top of a piece of parchment or butcher paper. Using a pencil, trace around the bottom of the cake tin or baking sheet onto the paper. For springform tins, remove the bottom of the tin to get the most accurate measure. In all but the latter case, cut the paper liner out a fraction of an inch inside your tracing, to make up for the fact that it will be inside the tin and you were tracing on the outside, which adds about ⅜ of an inch. Place the lining in the bottom of the tin, smoothing it to the edges. For best appearance, it is important to have the paper liner exactly the right size so that when the cake is unmolded, the edges, too, unmold straight and even. If the paper is slightly short, some of the edge will be left in the pan. If it is too large, the edge will be slightly rounded but generally uneven. For cakes that are to be heavily iced, this is not an important point. However, since often one simply dusts a cake with powdered sugar, a well-executed cake is especially appreciated. After the pan or baking sheet has been lined, butter the piece of paper well with soft butter. Then dust the entire tin or baking sheet with flour. For this purpose, a flour dredger is especially useful (see equipment section). Cake tins and square or rectangular baking tins with high sides should be rotated to spread the flour evenly. Turn them over and tap out the excess flour. To line a baking sheet with a very low rim, see the directions given in the recipe for *Maronioberschnitten*, which tells how to extend the height of a baking sheet with paper.

- Tube tins such as *Kugelhopf*, savarin, *Rehrücken*, or Bundt tins are best coated with butter if they are first placed in the freezer for 15 minutes or the refrigerator for 20 minutes. While the tins are chilling, melt and cool about 4 tablespoons of butter. Using a pastry brush, coat the chilled tins generously with melted butter, getting well into the crevices with your pastry brush. Chill again. Coat a second time with butter. Some recipes will call for first sugaring the tins and then flouring them. In other instances, where you won't want an extra coating of flour, I instruct you to chill the tin again until it is needed, which will firm the butter coating.

PREPARING BAKING SHEETS FOR COOKIES

Different methods are used for *Lebkuchen* and butter cookies, merginues, other egg-white cookies, and soft whisked-egg cookies. Consult specific recipes for procedure.

PASTRY BAGS

For other notes on pastry bags and tips, see Equipment, **Pastry Bag** and **Pastry Bag Tips**. To fill a pastry bag, first fit it with the tip specified in the recipe. Some tips must be placed inside the bag. Others are fitted on the outside of the bag, screwed onto a mount which is placed inside the bag. With most bags, you must cut the tip of the bag with scissors so that the tip can protrude. If the hole is cut too large, pressure on the bag will force the entire tip (as well as the filling) out of the bag. So be conservative when you are cutting.

- To fill a pastry bag once it has been fitted with a tip, twist the end with the tip several times to prevent any filling flowing out while you are filling the bag. Turn down a 3 to 4-inch collar all around the bag. Place your left hand under the collar, holding the bag with the palm of your hand and your thumb wrapped around the side underneath the collar. Using a rubber spatula, scoop up the mixture that is to be placed in the bag and scrape it off into the bag by pushing the rubber spatula against the thumb that is supporting the bag from the outside. Continue until the bag is filled not quite to the collar. Don't fill the bag too full or the filling will squeeze out the top when you are using it. Pull the collar up and twist the top securely to hold in the filling. Hold the bag at the top with your right hand which is also grasping the twisted top. If you are holding it correctly, you should be able to use the bag with one hand so that the other hand is free to help guide the tip. Applying pressure by pressing your right hand against the bag, always keeping the top twist tight with your thumb and index finger, pipe the mixture as described in the recipe.

- For piping the thick fingers, rounds, or ovals called for in several meringue recipes, hold the bag upright to produce the best shape.
- If you've never worked with a pastry bag, a good way to gain experience is to make up a batch of boxed mashed potatoes. Then practice different shapes and try different tips.
- It is useful to have 2 or 3 different-sized bags. A larger bag is specially helpful when you must pipe a large mass in a spiral, as in the case of *Preiselbeerenschaumtorte*, where a heated meringue mixture must be piped, ideally in an uninterrupted spiral, over the top of the cake.

FOLDING-IN TECHNIQUE

Some recipes call for folding in the final ingredients—stiffly beaten egg whites or, for whisked-egg or creamed mixtures, flour and sometimes melted butter.

- For folding, I prefer a large metal spoon—the really large kind that often comes in sets with a few other matching kitchen tools. The sharp edge of the spoon is especially efficient at cutting through the mixture while its rounded edge fits the sides of the bowl to pull up any unfolded mixture lurking at the bottom. If you don't have a large metal spoon, you can substitute a rubber spatula.
- To fold, cut the spoon or rubber spatula straight through the final ingredient on the top (stiffly beaten egg whites, flour, or melted butter) to the bottom of the bowl. Lift up as much mixture as you can from the bottom, bring it up to the surface, and turn the spoon or spatula completely over so the mixture falls off on top. This is known as cutting and folding. Spin the bowl a quarter turn and repeat. Continuing rotating the bowl in quarter turns, cutting and folding just until the mixture is mixed in. Flour is mixed in when you no longer see any clumps or pockets as you turn the mixture up and over. Egg whites are mixed in when you no longer see any large clumps or distinct streaks of white. At this point, it is important to stop folding. The cutting and folding process is meant to preserve as much air as possible in the whisked eggs or beaten egg whites. You must therefore be careful not to beat or stir the mixture when the recipe calls for folding, and not to overfold.

Sifting Flour, Powdered Sugar, and Other Dry Ingredients

While there are large cups with a spring action made especially for this purpose, the easiest way to sift dry ingredients is using a wire sieve. Holding the sieve, about half full, over your mixing bowl, simply tap the side of the sieve with the side of your hand and the dry ingredients pass through easily. In a recipe with spices, salt, and baking powder, I usually suggest that you sift them together with the flour to mix them well and break up any clumps.

For powdered sugar that has been on the shelf for some time and has many clumps, I find a food processor excellent for reducing the sugar back to a powder. Simply measure out the amount you need, put it in the food processor, and turn the machine off and on several times until the sugar is smooth.

Storing

- Different types of cookies that are to be stored at room temperature (*Lebkuchen*, whisked-egg cookies, and meringues, among others) should be stored separately so the flavors don't mix. Separate each layer with a piece of wax paper or aluminum foil so they won't roll around in the container. Ideally, store them in an airtight tin with lid. Lebkuchen and whisked-egg cookies that get too hard after prolonged storage can be softened in two ways: Either place a slice of apple or potato in the container for two days, which will produce some moisture, or leave the tin open in a steamy kitchen for several hours. In general, this category of cookies has especially good keeping properties, in many cases up to three months or more.
- Most butter cookies can be stored in a jar or tin with lid at room temperature for at least a week. They will keep longer, but they begin to lose their fresh butter taste. They will keep fresher in the refrigerator, ten days or longer, and can be stored there in any container with a tight-fitting lid. For longer storage, however, it is best to freeze them. If they are flat, simply stack them neatly and package them tightly in aluminum foil. For more delicate, decorated cookies, it is necessary to put a piece of foil or greaseproof wax paper between layers before wrapping.
- Breads in general freeze extremely well. I always bake the shape first, allow it to cool completely, then wrap it tightly in several thicknesses of aluminum foil before freezing. It can be frozen for up to three months, unless otherwise directed in the recipe.
- Deep-fried pastries have a very short life and are best eaten shortly after they are made.
- Most cakes and tarts have fairly good keeping properties and can be frozen successfully, though it is important to consult each recipe for specific instructions. For cakes that are heavily decorated with butter cream, I find it is usually easiest to freeze them for several hours first, so the butter cream is quite firm, before covering them with a loose wrapping.

1

LEBKUCHEN

Gingerbread has long been a favorite in America, brought here by both our British and Germanic ancestors. However, what we know as gingerbread today is far different from the first spice cakes and cookies of Central Europe. Called *Lebkuchen* and sweetened with honey, these cakes and cookies first appeared in the Middle Ages. Sugar was scarce until the seventeenth century, but honey was readily available, generally from monasteries, which kept bees to provide candle wax. In Germany, where they are first recorded in correspondence dated 1320, *Lebkuchen* were originally made in monasteries; eventually special guilds were formed for the bakers. The *Lebküchner* or *Lebzelter* (Austrian), as the guild bakers were called, were given special privileges, practicing their highly respected craft in many cities, from Vienna and Basel to Leipzig and Aachen. Eventually, however, Nürnberg became the most prominent producer, because it was a distribution center for oriental spices and the center of Bavarian honey production.

The earliest recorded German recipe for *Lebkuchen*, from the sixteenth century, now in the Germanisches Nationalmuseum in Nürnberg, calls for honey, sugar, cinnamon, nutmeg, ginger, pepper, and flour. None of the eggs, butter, or leavening agents one generally finds in recipes today was used; nor were chopped nuts or minced candied peel a part of the mix. This recipe, like most, has been refined and enriched over time. Today there are many variations under many names: *Lebkuchenzelten* (simple *Lebkuchen*), *Honigkuchen* (honey cookies, which can be spiced or not), *Pfefferkuchen* (heavily spiced gingerbread), *Leckerli* (Swiss gingerbread with mixed candied peel and nuts), to name a few. All of these contain honey and are made according to a standard formula: the honey is heated with the sugar (if called for) and butter or lard (if called for), before being mixed with the dry ingredients and then the eggs. The one exception is *Nürnberger Elisenlebkuchen*, perhaps the most famous *Lebkuchen*, which has been included in this chapter but is actually made according to the whisked-egg method (see p. 123).

From the seventeenth century on, *Lebkuchen* were made in both a simple form—plain flat cookies, sold in bundles or wrapped in colored paper—and in more elaborate forms— generally printed with molds made of carved wood, or occasionally of ceramic or metal. The special cookies were sold at fairs, carnivals, and markets and given to celebrate birthdays, marriages, and saints' days or to show special affection. The embossed pictures depicted an appropriate scene: a biblical or historic subject, decorative hearts, lords and ladies, stags and hounds. In time, *Lebkuchen* developed aesthetically to reflect both the artistic styles of the time, classic or romantic, and the Germanic love of folklore. In addition to using molds to imprint patterns, bakers during the Romantic period decorated their *Lebkuchen* with colorful pictures, or drew on them hearts and flowers, names and sayings, in colored sugar icing. This tradition is still alive, and large decorated *Lebkuchen* hearts are an expected offering at regional fairs (see *Oktoberfest Lebkuchen-Herzen*) and Christmas markets.

Because of the versatility of the dough, many shapes, fillings, and uses are possible. In this book, *Lebkuchen* is turned into hearts and pigs and candleholders; joined together to make a gingerbread house (*Hexenhäuschen*); sandwiched with fruit and nuts (*Honigkuchenwürfel*); and filled with marzipan (*Biberli*). Best of all, it can be imprinted in traditional wooden molds with a symbolic motif (see *Gedrückter Lebkuchen* and *Alte Züri-Tirggel*).

While most of the recipes in this chapter require no special equipment, I have given directions for mold *Lebkuchen* because the effect is so beautiful and the technique is rarely discussed in modern cookbooks. Both wooden and ceramic molds are now sold in specialty cookware shops and can be used for many different recipes.

Because honey keeps exceptionally well, *Lebkuchen* can be baked well in advance and stored in an airtight tin at room temperature for up to three months or more. Commercial and home bakers use this to special advantage at Christmas time, baking their cookies and small cakes in October. For the best flavor, *Lebkuchen* should be stored for at least two weeks before they are eaten, as the spices ripen with time. If *Lebkuchen* become too hard once they are stored, which often happens, they can be softened by leaving the tin open in a steamy kitchen or by placing a slice of raw apple or potato in the closed tin for a few days.

BASIC LEBKUCHEN DOUGH
LEBKUCHENTEIG

3⅓ cups all-purpose
  flour
1 teaspoon baking
  soda
1 teaspoon baking
  powder
1 tablespoon
  cinnamon
1 teaspoon ground
  cardamom
½ teaspoon ground
  cloves
½ teaspoon pow-
  dered anise
½ teaspoon nutmeg
½ teaspoon ginger
½ cup plus 2
  tablespoons honey
1 cup superfine
  sugar
½ cup (1 stick)
  unsalted butter
1 large egg, lightly
  beaten

It is important to heat the fat, sugar, and honey sufficiently to allow the sugar to dissolve, but not let the mixture come to a boil as a certain amount of evaporation will occur, making the gingerbread brittle. Because different brands of honey have different degrees of concentration and because humidity varies, the amount of flour required will also vary slightly. When all the ingredients have been kneaded together and the dough is still warm, it will be soft and look somewhat moist and sticky, but will not stick to your hands. Once the dough cools and has rested for a time, it becomes quite firm.

For the best flavor, make any cookies or cakes using this dough several weeks or even months before they are needed.

Sift the flour onto one sheet of wax paper and the other dry ingredients onto another. Heat the honey, sugar, and butter together over low heat, stirring all the time until the butter has melted and the sugar has dissolved. Do not allow the mixture to boil. Remove the pan from the heat. Stir in the sifted spices. Gradually beat in the sifted flour, adding as much as is needed to make the dough, when stirred, pull away from the sides of the pan. You will need most of the amount given. Allow the dough to cool for 5 minutes. If the pan is still very hot, remove the warm dough to a bowl. Beat in the lightly beaten egg and then knead the dough with your hands first in the pan or bowl, then briefly on a flat surface. If the dough is too sticky to handle, knead in a little more flour until it no longer sticks to your hands.

If not using immediately, wrap the warm dough in plastic wrap and leave at room temperature until required.

VARIATION

In some of the plainer recipes, additional texture and flavor can be imparted by adding, for the quantity of basic dough given above:

⅔ cup mixed candied fruit, finely chopped
1 cup blanched almonds, finely ground

Add the mixed fruit and/or ground almonds to the Basic Lebkuchen *Dough just before adding the flour to the mixture of honey, sugar, and butter.*

VERZIERTER LEBKUCHEN

DECORATED LEBKUCHEN

Makes about 35 3-inch cookies

Basic *Lebkuchen* Dough, after it has rested overnight, can be rolled out ⅛-inch thick and cut out with decorative cutters before being baked. However, traditionally it is rolled out slightly thicker—¼ inch— and cut out in simple 3-inch stars, hearts, or rectangles, which are decorated with split almonds in the corners and a halved candied cherry in the center. If you don't have a large cookie cutter, you can make a stencil from a piece of cardboard and use it as a pattern, cutting out hearts or stars around it with a knife. For puffier cookies, the dough can be rolled out, cut and baked as soon as the dough is made, while it is still warm. They can be left unglazed or brushed with a lightly beaten egg before they are baked.

BAKING AND STORING

Bake one sheet at a time in the middle of a **preheated 350-degree F. oven** until lightly colored and puffed, approximately 15 minutes. Loosen with a metal spatula and leave on the baking sheet for 2 minutes to firm slightly. Remove to wire racks to finish cooling. When cool, these cookies can be stored in an airtight tin for three months or longer.

VARIATION

Lebkuchen *shapes can be used for Christmas tree decorations if a small hole is pierced in each with a skewer before baking. When they come out of the oven, enlarge the holes with the skewer, since they have a tendency to close up during baking. A narrow length of red ribbon or string can be threaded through them once they have cooled.*

GEDRÜCKTER LEBKUCHEN

Printed Lebkuchen

Makes about 25 to 30 4-inch cookies

From the Middle Ages on, *Lebkuchen* were traditionally printed with decorative wooden molds, though *Lebkuchen* made with molds, are less frequently seen today. Any decorative mold can be used to make *Lebkuchen* as described below. One traditional type that is still made is the *Berner Honiglebkuchen* from Bern, Switzerland. A small bear (the symbol of Bern) is embossed in the center, and they are cut into rectangles. Once they have cooled, the bear only is brushed with a glaze to make it shine.

PRINTING

For printed *Lebkuchen*, use the Basic *Lebkuchen* Dough. While it is still soft and warm, break off a piece of dough and flatten it with your hands into a round or oval almost as large as your mold. Place a damp cloth under the mold to prevent it from slipping. Brush the mold lightly with oil and place the flattened piece of dough on it. Roll your rolling pin (ideally one without handles) back and forth over the mold, pressing the soft dough into the carved indentations in its surface. Carefully pull the piece of dough away, place it on a lightly buttered and floured baking sheet, and trim the edges with a sharp knife.

BAKING

Lebkuchen can be baked right away, making them puffier. Or they can be left to dry out overnight, uncovered, at room temperature, which will help set the pattern. The next day, bake them in the middle of a **preheated 350-degree F. oven** until they color—approximately 15 minutes, though the time varies with the size of the cookies. Remove small cookies to a wire rack to cool. Larger cookies should be loosened with a metal spatula and allowed to cool for several minutes on the baking sheet to firm up before being removed to wire racks.

LEBKUCHEN GLÜCKSSCHWEINCHEN

LEBKUCHEN *GOOD-LUCK PIGS*

Makes about 20 6-inch pigs

In German-speaking countries the pig motif is used on cookies, marzipan sweets, wooden tree ornaments, and greeting cards to symbolize good luck. While no longer a part of Germany, the city of Strassburg in French Alsace reverts to German tradition at its annual Christmas market (*Weihnachtsmarkt*) where *Lebkuchen* pigs, 7 inches long, are lined up by the score, awaiting customers whose names will be piped on them in white icing. Small and large pig cutters are available in specialty cookware shops. However, a simple pig stencil can also be cut from cardboard. Pigs etched with names make amusing decorations or place cards on the Christmas dinner table. If a small hole is pierced in the pigs before they are baked, they can be hung on the Christmas tree with a thin piece of red ribbon. They can also be decorated before baking with split blanched almonds and halved candied cherries.

Make up one recipe of Basic *Lebkuchen* Dough, with or without the addition of finely chopped candied fruit and ground almonds. While the dough is still warm, roll it out ¼ inch thick on a lightly floured board. Using a special cutter or a 5 to 8-inch stencil and a sharp knife, cut out the pigs. If they are not to be iced after baking, decorate them with split blanched almonds at either end and a halved candied cherry in the center. If they are to be hung, make a hole in the top center with a skewer. Place on buttered and floured baking sheets, leaving 1 inch between them. Allow to rest for 1 hour at room temperature.

Preheat the oven to 350 degrees F. Bake, one sheet at a time, in the middle of the oven until lightly colored—approximately 12 to 15 minutes. Loosen them carefully with a metal spatula and leave for 2 minutes on the baking sheet to help firm them. Remove to a wire rack to finish cooling. If they have a hole at the top which has closed in baking, reopen it using a skewer while they are still hot.

If they are to be decorated with icing, use the recipe for royal icing under *Oktoberfest Lebkuchen-Herzen*. Place the icing in a piping bag fitted with a fine writing tip. Pipe a line around the edge of the pig to frame it. Pipe a face. In the center, pipe a name or a decorative design of hearts and/or flowers. Allow to dry completely, approximately 30 minutes, before storing.

OKTOBERFEST LEBKUCHEN-HERZEN
OKTOBERFEST LEBKUCHEN *HEARTS*

Lebkuchen hearts are traditionally seen all over Germany, both at Christmas markets and at regional fairs such as the Oktoberfest in Munich. In earlier times they were shaped in decorative wooden molds. Today they are generally iced with chocolate and decorated with hearts, flowers, and nostalgic sayings in sugar icing. They hang from satin ribbons in fair booths to be bought by a friend or lover and hung around one's neck.

Whether intricately or simply decorated, *Lebkuchen* hearts make charming presents for Christmas, birthdays, Mother's Day, or Valentine's Day.

ONE DAY IN ADVANCE

Make up Basic *Lebkuchen* Dough.

THE NEXT DAY
BEFORE BAKING

Butter and flour baking sheets. **Preheat the oven to 350 degrees F.** Fold a piece of heavy paper in half and cut out a heart 7 to 10 inches high to be used as a pattern. Set aside.

ROLLING AND CUTTING OUT

Divide the dough in two and roll out while still warm in rectangles ¼-inch thick. Place the pattern on the rolled-out

MAKES APPROXIMATELY SIX 9-TO-10-INCH HEARTS

1 recipe Basic Lebkuchen *Dough, increasing both the baking soda and baking powder to 1½ teaspoons*
CHOCOLATE ICING
4½ ounces semi-sweet chocolate, broken in pieces
1 teaspoon vegetable oil
7 tablespoons water
3 cups powdered sugar, sifted
ROYAL ICING
2 egg whites
2½ cups powdered sugar, sifted
Water as needed
Food coloring (optional)
EQUIPMENT
Pastry bag with fine writing tip
Paper stencil
Narrow satin ribbon for hanging

dough and cut out the hearts with a knife, rekneading the scraps and rolling them out once more. Use a skewer to make two holes, ½ inch apart, in the top middle of each where the heart comes to a bow. Lay the hearts at least 1½ inches apart on buttered and floured baking sheets.

BAKING

Bake them one sheet at a time in the middle of the oven until they are lightly colored and puffed, approximately 15 to 20 minutes. Loosen them from the baking sheet with a metal spatula and allow them to cool and firm on the sheet for several minutes before removing them to wire racks to finish cooling. If the holes at the top have closed up during baking, enlarge with a skewer while the hearts are still warm.

PREPARING THE CHOCOLATE ICING

While the hearts are baking, make the chocolate icing. Melt the broken chocolate pieces with the vegetable oil in the top of a double boiler, or rest a heatproof soup plate or shallow bowl over a smaller saucepan filled with 2 inches of simmering water. Stir the chocolate occasionally until it has melted. Remove from the heat and allow to cool.

Put 7 tablespoons of water into a large mixing bowl. Gradually beat in the sifted powdered sugar, using an electric mixer or a wooden spoon, beating at high speed for at least 7 to 8 minutes until the sugar has completely dissolved. Add the melted chocolate and beat for another minute or two, scraping down the sides of the bowl so that the chocolate gets thoroughly blended. Add enough extra water, one teaspoon at a time, or additional sugar to make an icing that will pour or brush easily but still be thick enough to leave a smooth, opaque coating. When not using the icing, keep a piece of aluminum foil pressed against the surface so it doesn't dry out.

ICING

When the hearts are cooked and cooling on wire racks but are still warm, brush them evenly with the chocolate icing using a pastry brush. Allow the chocolate icing to dry completely (10 to 30 minutes depending on humidity and kitchen temperature).

PREPARING THE ROYAL ICING

While they are drying, make the Royal Icing. Using an electric mixer, beat the egg whites at high speed until they are frothy and beginning to thicken. Gradually beat in the sifted powdered sugar. Beat for at least 8 minutes to dissolve the sugar, adding additional water or sugar as needed to make a thick icing which will hold its shape when piped.

DECORATING

Fit a piping bag with a fine writing tip. If desired, you can divide the icing and color each part differently to make multicolored hearts and flowers. Pipe a scalloped border around the edge of the heart. In the center, you can pipe a name, hearts and flowers, or a saying such as *Du allein* (only you) or *Ich liebe Dich* (I love you). Once they are decorated, allow the hearts to dry completely. Lace a thin, long strand of satin ribbon through the two holes at the top of each heart and tie the ends in a knot. Traditionally, the ribbon is long enough so the heart can be hung around someone's neck.

GEFÜLLTE LEBKUCHEN HERZEN

MARZIPAN-FILLED LEBKUCHEN HEARTS

*MAKES APPROXI-
MATELY 24
3-INCH SAND-
WICHED HEARTS*

1 recipe Basic
  Lebkuchen *Dough*
*1-pound block
  marzipan*
ROYAL ICING
2 egg whites
*2½ cups powdered
  sugar, sifted*
Water as needed
EQUIPMENT
*3-inch (or larger)
  heart cookie
  cutter*
*Slightly smaller heart
  cookie cutter*
*Pastry bag with fine
  writing tip*

ONE DAY IN ADVANCE

Make up Basic *Lebkuchen* Dough and allow to rest, well wrapped, overnight at room temperature.

THE NEXT DAY
ROLLING AND CUTTING OUT

Preheat the oven to 350 degrees F. Butter and flour baking sheets. Divide the dough in two. Roll out ¼ inch thick. Using the larger heart cookie cutter, cut out an even number of hearts, rekneading the scraps and rolling them out again. Dust a board lightly with powdered sugar. Roll out the marzipan on the board in a thin sheet. Using the smaller heart cutter, cut out half as many hearts as there are *Lebkuchen* hearts. Place a marzipan heart on half of the *Lebkuchen* hearts. Moisten the edges of the *Lebkuchen* hearts with water. Place a *Lebkuchen* heart on top and press the edges well together to seal them. Place on a buttered and floured baking sheet. Bake, one sheet at a time, in the middle of a preheated oven for 15 to 20 minutes or until they co'or. Remove from the baking sheet and allow to cool on wire racks.

PREPARING THE ICING

To make the Royal Icing, beat the egg whites until frothy and beginning to thicken. Gradually add the sifted powdered sugar. Beat at least eight minutes to dissolve the sugar, adding additional water or sugar as needed to make a thick icing which will hold its shape when piped.

DECORATING

Fit a pastry bag with a fine writing tip. Pipe a fine grillwork, if desired, first piping parallel diagonal lines every ¼ inch in one direction, then crossing them with an equal number of parallel lines from the other direction. Alternatively, pipe a plain line around the edge of each heart, piping hearts and flowers or names or initials in the center. Allow the icing to set completely before storing the hearts.

LEBKUCHEN STERNE MIT KERZEN

LEBKUCHEN STAR CANDLE HOLDERS

*MAKES 7 TO 8
   CANDLE
   HOLDERS*

*1 recipe Basic
   Lebkuchen Dough
Split blanched
   almonds
   (see Almonds)
1 egg, lightly beaten
ICING
1 egg white
1⅓ cups powdered
   sugar, sifted
EQUIPMENT
Heavy paper for
   stencils
Small round aspic
   cutter, thimble,
   or small bottle lid
Small (½-inch diam-
   eter) red, white,
   or green candles*

Lebkuchen moves from the cookie tin to the mantel-piece in the form of candle holders. Made from a pyramid of three stars, the candle holders are charmingly decorated with split blanched almonds. The icing serves as cement, so make sure it is thick enough to hold the stars securely, adding additional sugar to thicken it if necessary. Use a minimum amount of icing—just in the center of the stars, so that when they are assembled it doesn't show. These make unusual gifts for Christmas and are a good project for children.

MAKING THE STENCILS

Using heavy paper folded in half, cut out three 6-pointed stars—4, 3, and 2 inches across. Set the paper stencils aside.

CUTTING OUT AND DECORATING

Make the *Lebkuchen* dough and divide it in two. Roll each half out ⅜ inch thick while still warm. Using a sharp knife, cut out one of each size star for every candle holder, rekneading the scraps and rolling them out again. Use a small round aspic cutter (or thimble or small bottle lid) to cut out a small circle from the center of the two smaller stars. Place a split blanched almond on each point of the two larger-sized stars, the almonds pointing away from the center. Brush all the stars with lightly beaten egg. Allow to rest for 1 hour, uncovered, at room temperature.

BAKING THE DOUGH

One hour later **preheat the oven to 350 degrees F.** Bake one sheet at a time on buttered and floured baking sheets in the middle of the oven until lightly colored and puffed, approximately 15 to 20 minutes.

PREPARING THE ICING

While the stars are baking, make the icing. Beat the egg white with an electric mixer until frothy and starting to thicken. Gradually beat in the sifted powdered sugar, beating for at least 8 minutes to dissolve the sugar. If necessary, add a bit more sugar, a tablespoon at a time, to make the mixture thick enough to be used as "cement." Keep a piece of aluminum foil pressed on the surface of the icing when not using it.

COOLING BAKED *LEBKUCHEN*

When the stars are done, loosen them with a metal spatula, leaving them on the baking sheet for several minutes to help firm them before moving them to a wire rack to cool. If the holes have closed up too much, enlarge them with a small knife or skewer while the stars are still hot.

ASSEMBLING AND FINISHING

Using a small spoon or pastry brush, place a 1-inch circle of icing in the middle of the largest star and a rim of icing around the hole of the second-largest star. Stack the stars on top of one another with the points staggered, ending with the smallest star. Press the stars together well, applying more icing if necessary to make them stick, but not so much that it shows.

Allow them to dry for at least 30 minutes. Put a small candle— red, white, or green, the size of the hole—in each holder.

Alte Züri-Tirggel
Old-fashioned Zurich Printed Wafers

*MAKES ABOUT 50
2-INCH WAFERS*

*1¼ cups honey
1 tablespoon ginger
1 tablespoon
cinnamon
¼ teaspoon ground
cloves
¼ teaspoon nutmeg
3⅔ cups sifted flour,
or as needed
FOR THE MOLDS
Vegetable oil
EQUIPMENT
Carved wooden molds
of any size,
preferably shallow*

At Christmas time in the famous Zurich pastry shop Sprüngli, and in all the gourmet food shops scattered to the right and left of the glittery Bahnhofstrasse, Zurich's main shopping street, thin round flat *Tirggel*—spicy honey cookies delicately embossed with scenes or designs— are fancifully displayed in pyramids of graduating sizes.

Tirggel differs from most other *Lebkuchen* in that they are paper-thin and light in color, with only the embossed pattern being allowed to brown.

This recipe produces a very brittle *Lebkuchen* that takes a pattern better than the Basic *Lebkuchen* Dough recipe. However, most people nowadays are used to a certain amount of butter or shortening in their *Lebkuchen* and will prefer the Basic *Lebkuchen* Dough recipe for flavor. For patterned Christmas-tree ornaments or wall hangings, however, the following dough produces the most beautiful results. Make a small hole in each cookie with a skewer before baking so that they can be hung. They can be stored in airtight tins at room temperature for 3 months or more.

PREPARING THE DOUGH

Butter and flour baking sheets. Heat the honey with the spices, stirring constantly over a medium low heat, until the honey is very hot to the touch but not boiling. Remove the pan from the heat. Gradually beat in the sifted flour while the mixture is still hot, adding as much as is needed to make the dough pull away from the sides of the pan when stirred. The amount will vary slightly according to the concentration of the honey used and the humidity. When the dough is well blended and still warm, but cool enough to handle, knead it for 1 to 2 minutes on a lightly floured board.

Preheat oven to 475 degrees F.

MOLDING

The method traditionally used is to roll out a small piece of dough on an oiled carved mold. Because the dough is soft, it sinks into the crevices of the mold, picking up all the details of the carving. This method is suitable if your molds are shallow. For deeply carved molds, however, it is best to roll out the dough very thin and then, using a plain pastry wheel or knife, cut out a piece of dough the right size and press it into the oiled mold. Traditional *Tirggel* molds are round, but you can use any shape or size mold to print the *Tirggel* dough. According to the type of mold you are using roll out small pieces of the dough directly onto the mold, which should first be brushed with oil, or roll out the dough ⅛ inch thick and cut out pieces the size of your molds, pressing the pieces into the oiled molds and then removing them.

BAKING

Depending on the molds you are using, you may have to vary the oven temperature. For shallow relief a very hot oven will be best; for higher relief you might have to lower the temperature slightly. Place the cookies on lightly buttered and floured baking sheets. Bake the *Tirggel* on the top rack in the oven—this is important since only the pattern is supposed to brown. This will ensure that *Tirggel* with a high relief are cooked clear through. (Watch them closely). Allow to cool on the baking sheet for 2 minutes, then remove to a rack to cool completely. Store in airtight tins at room temperature.

HONIGKUCHEN VOM BLECH
DECORATED LEBKUCHEN SHEET CAKE

*MAKE 20 LARGE
RECTANGLES*

*1 recipe Basic
Lebkuchen Dough,
with added finely
chopped candied
fruit and ground
almonds
1 egg, lightly beaten*
DECORATION
*Split blanched
almonds
(see Almonds)
Halved candied
cherries*
EQUIPMENT
*Rimless baking sheet
or baking sheet
turned upside
down; minimum
size 13 × 13
inches (or make
the cake to fit
your baking
sheet, using 2
smaller sheets
if necessary)*

Making *Lebkuchen* in a sheet cake is especially simple. The warm dough made according to the basic recipe is rolled out directly on a rimless baking sheet, marked off in rectangles, and decorated before baking. The sheet is baked, and the large cookies/cakes are cut out when done. This method produces an especially thick cookie or cake, the type often seen at Christmas fairs in Germany, and is quicker to make than the other methods.

ROLLING OUT AND DECORATING

Make up Basic *Lebkuchen* Dough. Butter and flour one 13 × 13-inch rimless baking sheet or use the underside of one with rim. While the dough is still warm, roll it out on the prepared baking sheet in a rectangle 12 × 12½ inches, leaving a small amount of space on your baking sheet to allow for expansion. Brush the dough with lightly beaten egg. Using a sharp knife, mark off rectangles 2½ × 3 inches. You can cut clear through the dough. It will cook together when baked, but can be easily separated when done. Place a halved cherry in the center of each rectangle and a split almond in each corner.

BAKING AND STORING

Preheat oven to 350 degrees F.
Bake in the preheated oven until golden, approximately 25 to 35 minutes. When done, remove from the oven and cut through the marked rectangles while the cake is still warm. Trim off any rough outer edges. Allow the cake to cool on the baking sheet before removing the individual cakes. Store in an airtight tin at room temperature.

HONIGKUCHENWÜRFEL
HONEY CAKE SQUARES

This iced sheet cake cut into bite-sized squares is made with two layers of *Lebkuchen* sandwiched with a fruity apricot/raisin/almond filling which keeps it moist. A favorite Christmas treat of mine for many years, this recipe came from a friend in Frankfurt. I once forgot a tin which I had purposely put out of my own reach high on a cupboard shelf. When I discovered it eight months later, the little cakes were better than ever—proof that they can be made long in advance and will keep well.

ROLLING OUT

Butter and flour the baking sheet and side aside. Make up the Basic *Lebkuchen* Dough and while it is still warm, divide the dough in two. Roll out one piece directly onto the buttered and floured rimless baking sheet, making a rectangle approximately 13 × 8½ inches. There should be at least a 1-inch rim left free on the baking sheet to allow for expansion. Roll out the second piece the same size as the first on a piece of wax paper or parchment. Set aside.

PREPARING THE FILLING AND ASSEMBLING

Preheat the oven to 350 degrees F. Make the filling. Mix all the ingredients for the filling together in a bowl, adding additional lemon juice if the mixture is too thick to spread. Distribute the filling evenly over the dough on the baking sheet, leaving a ½-inch rim around the edges. Reverse the other half

MAKES ABOUT 55

1 recipe Basic
  Lebkuchen *Dough,*
  p. 40
FILLING
1½ cups coarsely
  chopped
  unblanched
  almonds
1 cup raisins
1¾ cups apricot jam
3 tablespoons lemon
  juice
½ cup firmly packed
  diced mixed
  candied orange
  and lemon peel
ICING
3 tablespoons lemon
  juice
1½ cups powdered
  sugar, sifted
EQUIPMENT
*Rimless baking
  sheet 15 × 11
  inches; or invert a
  baking sheet
  with sides and use
  the underside.*

of the dough quickly on top of the filling, peeling off the paper. Press the edges together well and trim evenly. Bake until golden—approximately 25 to 30 minutes.

PREPARING THE ICING, FINISHING, AND STORING

While the cake is baking, make the icing. Put the lemon juice in a large mixing bowl. Gradually beat in the sifted powdered sugar, beating for at least 8 minutes to dissolve the sugar completely. Add enough extra lemon juice or water or additional sugar to make thin icing of pouring consistency. While the cake is still warm, pour the icing over it, using a pastry brush to cover it evenly. Allow to set overnight at room temperature. The following day, trim the outer edges. Cut the cake in 1¼-inch squares. For the best flavor, store in an airtight tin for several weeks before eating.

BIBERLI

MARZIPAN LEBKUCHEN ROUNDS

These sweet rounds of *Lebkuchen* are filled with marzipan which, when baked in a hot oven, bubbles up and browns to a shiny mahogany. While these cookies are found elsewhere in the German-speaking world, they originate in Switzerland, where they are always diminutive, making them look particularly refined and enticing. Because of the high oven temperature, use aluminum, nonstick, or light-colored steel baking sheets—not black steel, which conducts the heat too rapidly and tends to overcook the bottoms.

MAKES ABOUT 25 TO 30

½ recipe Basic Lebkuchen Dough, p. 40
9-ounce block marzipan
1 whole egg, lightly beaten

THE DAY BEFORE

Make up the Basic *Lebkuchen* Dough and allow to rest, well wrapped, overnight at room temperature.

THE FOLLOWING DAY
ROLLING OUT AND ASSEMBLING

Preheat the oven to 400 degrees F. Butter and flour two baking sheets. Roll out the dough on a lightly floured board in a long, narrow rectangle approximately 5½ to 6 inches wide and ⅜ inch thick. Trim the edges evenly and cut the rectangle in half lengthwise. You should have two strips approximately 2½ inches wide. Roll the marzipan back and forth into a long log ¾ inch in diameter and twice the length of the *Lebkuchen* strips. Cut the log in two. Lay a marzipan log down the center of each *Lebkuchen* strip. Wrap the dough around the marzipan, allowing ¼ inch overlap. If the overlap is greater, trim off the excess. Moisten the edge of the log with water and press the seam together to seal. Cut each roll in ½-inch slices. Using a small metal palette knife or table knife, plump the slices back into a neat circular shape and pat the surface of each to flatten. Brush the top of each round with lightly beaten egg. Place on a buttered and floured baking sheet.

BAKING AND STORING

Bake one sheet at a time in the upper third of the oven until the marzipan is mahogany-colored and bubbling out of the center—approximately 10 minutes. Watch carefully since they burn easily. Remove to a wire rack to cool. Store in an airtight tin for two or three months.

BRAUNSCHWEIGER PFEFFERNÜSSE

BRUNSWICK SPICE NUTS

Pfeffernüsse, one of the older traditional German Christmas cookies from several regions, come in almost as many variations as *Lebkuchen*. Two things, however, they all have in common: a large amount of spice and a small and very thick shape. Brought to this country by early German-speaking settlers, they are a common feature at holiday time in the market stalls of the Pennsylvania Dutch. *Pfeffer*, or pepper, refers not to pepper itself (though it is called for in some recipes), but to the *Pfefferländer* (pepper countries), the name given in earlier times to the areas of the Orient from which spices came.

The majority of *Pfeffernüsse*, like *Lebkuchen*, are made with honey, using the warming method to heat the honey, sugar, and fat, if any is called for. However, a handful of *Pfeffernuss* recipes are based on the whisked-egg method; they are sweetened with sugar and are particularly moist inside.

Pottasche, today a chemical preparation of potassium carbonate, is the leavening agent found in older recipes for *Pfeffernüsse*. After baking, it absorbs moisture, helping to keep the cookies soft. Since most *Pfeffernuss* recipes have no fat, the cookies tend to become hard when stored for any length of time. Baking powder, which is used in the recipe that follows, is substituted more and more in modern German cookbooks because it makes a lighter cookie. It is also more readily available and keeps better.

MAKES ABOUT 60

1¾ cups plus 2 tablespoons all-purpose flour, plus extra flour as needed
2 tablespoons cinnamon
¾ teaspoon ground cloves
1 teaspoon baking powder
½ cup plus 2 tablespoons honey
1 cup water
ICING
4 tablespoons water or lemon juice
2 cups powdered sugar, sifted

The following recipe is a version from Brunswick, East Germany, which requires that the dough be prepared the day before baking.

THE DAY BEFORE
PREPARING THE DOUGH

Sift the dry ingredients together onto a piece of wax paper and set aside. Heat the honey almost to the boiling point, but do not let it boil. Add 1 cup water. While the mixture is still warm, add the sifted dry ingredients and as much extra flour as is necessary to keep the dough from being sticky. The dough will be soft but will firm up once it cools. Wrap the dough in plastic wrap and leave overnight at room temperature.

THE NEXT DAY
BAKING

Preheat the oven to 400 degrees F. Butter and flour baking sheets. Cut the dough into four pieces. Roll each piece of dough back and forth on a board with your hands to make an even roll approximately ¾ inch in diameter. Slice off rounds ½ inch thick. Place them on a buttered and floured baking sheet, leaving 1 inch between them to allow for expansion. To level the tops, run your rolling pin lightly over the cookies on the baking sheet.

Bake one sheet at a time in the middle of the oven until the cookies are firm to the touch and light brown, approximately 10 to 12 minutes.

PREPARING THE ICING

While they are baking, make the icing in a deep bowl. Beat the sifted powdered sugar into the water or lemon juice, adding additional sugar or liquid to make a thin icing. Beat with an electric mixer on high speed for 8 minutes to dissolve the sugar.

ICING AND STORING

When the cookies are done, remove them from the baking sheet and brush off any flour that might have stuck to them from the baking sheet. While they are still warm, place a few at a time in the bowl of icing. Using a wooden spoon, turn them around in the icing to coat well. Remove with a slotted spoon to a wire rack so the excess icing can drip off and the cookies can dry. Place a piece of aluminum foil directly on the icing in the bowl when not in use. Continue icing the remaining batches in the same fashion, making more icing if necessary. If the icing dries out too much, place the bowl of icing in a pan of water that has just boiled. Beat the icing until it is smooth, if necessary adding a teaspoon of water to thin it. Allow cookies to dry completely before storing in an airtight tin for up to two months.

LEBKUCHEN HEXENHÄUSCHEN
GINGERBREAD HOUSE

The gingerbread house—a traditional Christmas project for patient German mothers and professional bakers—is familiar to us from the fairy tale of Hansel and Gretel. The German name *Hexenhäuschen* literally means "witch's house," referring to the fantastic gingerbread house where the children were locked up by the wicked witch. If you have seen some of the whimsical baked creations in shop windows and homes, you can easily understand why the children were lured inside. Part of the allure of these houses—in addition to the heavenly aroma of spice from the *Lebkuchen* and the enticing bits of sweets and cookies decorating the roof and walls—is the imagination that the baker puts into making them. With all the illustrations that have appeared in magazines and cookbooks, it is rare to find anyone who would want to copy someone else's model from a photograph. Each house seems to have its own character and coaxes its maker into the world of fantasy.

So long as you have a large enough selection of different-shaped and -colored sweets, some extra cookies, and lots of royal icing and patience, you will end up with a house that can't help but charm.

Gingerbread houses can be small, medium, or large—it is simply a matter of personal preference. For my taste, the smaller houses are the most appealing since the sweets and cookies that decorate them seem oversized, emphasizing the fantastic nature of the creation. The proportions for the house given in the diagram will produce a relatively small house approximately 9 inches long (measuring the overhanging roof, which expands slightly in baking) and 7 inches wide (the roof measurement from eave to eave).

While some books suggest baking the dough in large sheets, then cutting out the shapes once the dough is baked, I prefer the method given below which requires the pieces be cut out carefully first, using cardboard models, then baked. The roof generally loses a perfect edge; the windows close up a bit; the doors expands, or the base loses its tidy edge. The dough somehow comes to life to create a house with a preordained spirit. It isn't tempting fate, however, because the pieces always fit. And should a roof piece that perhaps was rolled out thicker in one spot than another expand disproportionately when baked, or should the doorway close up too much, you can simply cut off the extra bit or widen the doorway by cutting it with a sharp knife while the baked dough is still warm. Even if you discover a problem once the dough has cooled, you can warm it again for several minutes in the oven and it will cut neatly without breaking. Otherwise, I let the house develop as it wants. Using this system, you will want extra interior supports. Any join that isn't perfect is cemented with lots of icing, then reinforced with several supports. They don't show, so it doesn't matter how many you use, but they do ensure that the walls stand up straight and solid with more than enough strength to support the heavy roof.

You can do as little or as much decorative piping on the walls as you like. I use a fine writing tip to etch subtle scrolls, scallops, or whatever takes my fancy. I recently piped a flower garden at the back of the house, then later "planted" two candy sticks arching in opposite directions, using icing to cement them against the wall.

Since the houses are intended as fantasies, they take well to asymmetrical decorating. You needn't worry about matching a heart shape on one side with a mate on the other. Feel free to be spontaneous.

For decoration, assemble an assortment of sweets and cookies. The sweets I find that work especially well are Dots in assorted colors; jelly rings; flat red-and-white peppermint drops; small candy sticks; M & M's; ribbon candy; and mixed hard candies, especially the variety that has a small decoration in the center or contrasting border. For cookies, I bake extra *Lebkuchen* dough into large and very small rounds—some fluted, some with the centers cut out—and hearts, stars, and pretzels. I ice them with melted chocolate diluted with a few drops of vegetable oil. Any other Christmas cookies or small cakes you have baked can be used as well. The Bählsen brand of *Pfeffernüsse*, available in specialty food stores at Christmas time, make wonderful roof tiles.

Those of you who aren't purists and who don't feel like making gingerbread can use a packaged gingerbread mix, following the directions for cookie dough rather than cake mixture (you won't need the milk called for in the cake instructions). Using this quick method, three boxes is sufficient for the house plan below.

The house will keep for years, stored in several plastic trash bags in a cool dry room.

You will need at least one other person to help when you are assembling the house, at least 3½ hours, and a great deal of patience. But, once completed, the house will give everyone such pleasure, producing a marvelous aroma wherever it is displayed. And, something to keep reminding yourself, it won't have to be made again next year—unless, that is, in the process you become addicted to building gingerbread houses.

DOUGH FOR *LEBKUCHEN*
HEXENHÄUSCHEN

This is simply a larger quantity of Basic *Lebkuchen* Dough with a slightly larger proportion of baking powder and baking soda. It is sufficient to make the gingerbread house and base in the diagram.

PREPARING THE DOUGH

Sift the flour onto one sheet of wax paper and the other dry ingredients onto another. Heat the honey, sugar, and butter together over a low heat, stirring all the time until the butter has melted and the sugar dissolved. Do not allow the mixture to boil. Remove the pan from the heat. Stir in the sifted spices. Gradually beat in the sifted flour, adding as much as is needed to make the dough, when stirred, pulled away from the sides of the pan. You will need most of the amount given. Allow the dough to cool for 5 minutes. If the pan is still very hot, remove the warm dough to a bowl. Beat in the lightly beaten egg and then knead the dough with your hands first in the pan or bowl, then briefly on a flat surface. If the dough is too sticky to handle, knead in a little more flour until it no longer sticks to your hands.

If not using immediately, wrap the warm dough in plastic wrap and leave at room temperature while making the stencils.

MAKING THE STENCILS AND CUTTING OUT

Using a ruler, make cardboard stencils for the structural elements of the house; dimensions are given in the diagram.

Divide the dough in three even portions. Roll out two rectangles with a cutting space measuring 9 × 13 inches and one measuring 10 × 13 inches. If you don't have enough baking sheets, roll out one portion at a time. Cut out the various elements for the house shown in the diagram, using your cardboard stencils. The windows cut out of the side walls can be cut

5⅔ cups all-purpose flour
2 teaspoons baking powder
2 teaspoons baking soda
1½ teaspoons cinnamon
2 teaspoons cardamom
¾ teaspoon ground cloves
¾ teaspoon powdered aniseed
¾ teaspoon nutmeg
¾ teaspoon ginger
1 cup honey
¾ cup plus 1 tablespoon sugar
¾ cup (1½ sticks) unsalted butter
1 large egg, lightly beaten
ROYAL ICING
6 large egg whites
7½ cups powdered sugar, sifted, plus up to ½ cup additional sugar
DECORATIONS
Assorted colorful candies and cookies
EQUIPMENT
Large tray, 12 × 16 inches
Piece of heavy cardboard or baking sheet on which to place the house
Pastry bag with plain writing tip

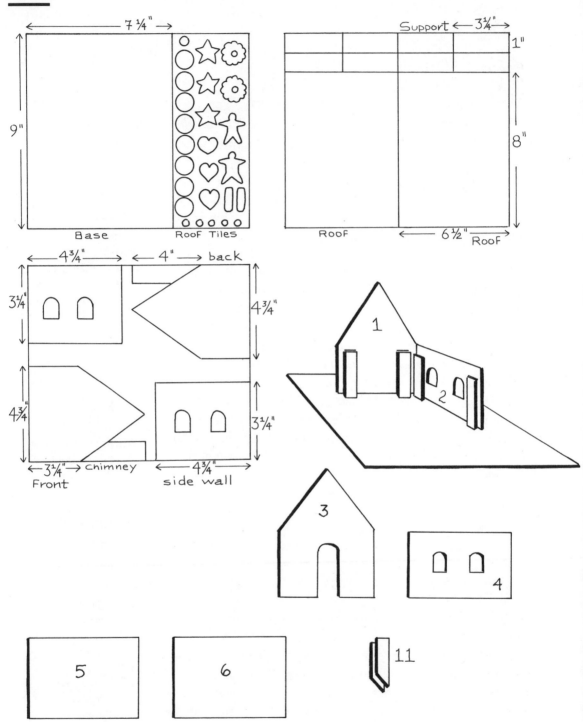

7 ¼ "

9"

Base

Roof Tiles

Support ← 3¼" →

1"

8"

Roof

← 6½" →

Roof

4¾"

← 4" → back

3¼"

4¾"

4¾"

3¼"

← 3¼" → chimney

Front

← 4¾" →

side wall

1

2

3

4

5

6

11

in half lengthwise and the halves used as shutters. Likewise, save the door which you cut out from the front of the house. It can be baked and propped open with icing later on. Cut out at least 8 inner support posts. From the remaining dough, cut out various shapes for roof tiles and decorations. If desired, you can cut out a witch or two gingerbread figures or a tree to place in front of the house. Place the pieces 1½ inches apart on buttered, floured baking sheets. Leave uncovered at room temperature for 1 hour.

BAKING

Preheat the oven to 350 degrees F. Bake the precut pieces, one sheet at a time, in the middle of the oven until golden—approximately 15 to 20 minutes. When done, remove the baking sheet from the oven and loosen the pieces carefully with a metal spatula, leaving them to cool on the baking sheet. If you feel the need to enlarge a doorway or straighten a wall, cut the dough with a sharp knife while it is still warm.

PREPARING THE ICING

When all of the pieces have been baked, make the sugar icing and assemble the decorations. In a large mixing bowl, beat the egg whites with an electric mixer on high speed until frothy and slightly thickened. Beat the powdered sugar into the egg whites, ½ cup at a time, beating well between each addition. When all the sugar has been added, beat the icing for another 5 minutes. To test the consistency of the icing, dip a wooden spoon into it. The icing should be thick enough to form an icicle that will not drop off the spoon. If necessary, add more sugar until the mixture is thick enough. Cover the icing completely with aluminum foil whenever it is not being used. Scoop a large cupful of icing into a piping bag fitted with a plain writing tip. Decorate the shutters, door, doorways, windows, and front and back of the house. Allow the icing to dry completely before proceeding.

ICING, ASSEMBLING, AND DECORATING

Place the base on an attractive tray or piece of heavy cardboard so the house can be moved with ease. Assemble the structural elements on the base in the order given in the diagram, beginning with the back of the house. To assemble, pipe a generous amount of icing on the bottom and side of the back of the house and place it several inches from the edge of the base, centering it. Pipe icing on the bottom and sides of one side piece and join the two pieces of the base. To help support the walls and reinforce the seam where they join, lavishly ice one or two support posts and place them inside the house near the corner seams. Hold each section for at least 5 minutes to allow it to dry before proceeding. When all the wall pieces are standing and well supported from the inside, allow the house to rest for 15 minutes before you decorate it. Meanwhile pipe a large amount of icing on one chimney piece and sandwich the two pieces together, allowing some of the icing to protrude. If you like, you can pipe icicles to drip off the top. Ice some of your cookie decorations with the white icing. For chocolate icing, you can simply add a bit of melted chocolate or cocoa powder to a small amount of the white icing, diluting it with a teaspoon or more of water so it will spread.

After 15 minutes, decorate the sides and front of the house with sweets and cookies. To apply them, first press a large blob of icing where you want to place the sweet, then press it into the middle of the icing. it should stick easily. However, heavier pieces have a tendency to slip at first so you might have to hold them for a minute. Place the shutters on either side of the windows. Allow the decorations to dry for 10 minutes.

JOINING AND DECORATING ROOF PIECES

To roof the house, pipe a generous amount of icing on all the exposed top edges of the house walls and the top edge of each roof piece. Have someone else hold one roof piece standing opposite you on the other side of the house. Join your two roof pieces, making sure they are lined up so the overhang in the front and back are approximately the same and the roof pieces are touching the house walls. Pipe more icing into any cracks where the roof pieces don't quite touch and additional icing down the seam at the top. Hold the roof carefully for about 10 minutes or place props underneath it to free your hands.

Ideally, wait 30 minutes before decorating the roof to make sure it is well secure. You can leave the props in place while decorating. Using a metal spatula, spread the roof pieces generously with icing. In the front and back, you can drip bits of icing over the edges to resemble icicles. Place the chimney piece on the roof. Press cookies into the icing for roof tiles—they can be big and small. You can further decorate some of the cookies with small sweets or run a row of hard candy down the top seam where the roof pieces join, to simulate tiles.

FINISHING

In the front of the house, you can ice and decorate the door and prop it open. A tree or figures can be made to stand on the base in the front of the house.

Some people ice the base, then sprinkle it with sugar to look like snow. However, I usually leave the base gingerbread color. Once it is decorated, allow the house to dry overnight before moving it.

BASLER LECKERLI
BASEL SPICE COOKIES

MAKES ABOUT 70

1 1/4 cups honey
1 2/3 cups sugar
1 1/2 tablespoons cinnamon
1/4 teaspoon ground cloves
1/2 teaspoon nutmeg
1 cup plus 3 tablespoons mixed candied orange and lemon peel
1 cup plus 3 tablespoons coarsely chopped unblanched almonds
Grated rind of 1 lemon
1/3 cup kirsch (or if unavailable, substitute light rum)
4 cups plus 3 tablespoons all-purpose flour, sifted
3/4 teaspoon baking soda
3/4 teaspoon baking powder
ICING
1 1/4 cups powdered sugar, sifted
1/2 cup water

CONTINUED ON
FACING PAGE

The word *lecker*, which in high German means "delicious," becomes a noun in Switzerland where it is applied to a wide variety of finger-length and rectangular cookies that are baked for holidays. While many cities, including Bern and Zurich, have their own versions—each quite different and not necessarily spicy—the honey and spice version from Basel is certainly the most famous. In fact, one bakery in Basel produces nothing but *Leckerli*, which are shipped all over the world in charming tin drum containers symbolizing the Basel *Fastnacht*, a three-day pre-Lenten celebration when the haunting music of pipes and drums played by costumed Baselers fills the air. Though this bakery now lies in the center of the town, most Baselers know the narrow, stepped passage—the *Imbergässlein*—in the hilly periphery of the old city to be the original home of the city's early *Lebkuchen* bakers. The *Imbergässlein* got its name from the many spices, including ginger (*Ingwer*), used by the guild bakers. *Basler Leckerli* are made with a high proportion of honey and sugar, enriched with mixed fruit and nuts, iced and cut into short, thick, narrow rectangles that become crunchy once they cool.

PREPARING THE DOUGH

In a heavy-bottomed saucepan, heat the honey, sugar, cinnamon, cloves and nutmeg over a low flame, stirring until the sugar has dissolved. Do not allow the mixture to boil. Stir in the candied peel, chopped almonds, lemon rind, and kirsch. Sift the flour, soda, and baking powder together and add to the other ingredients while the mixture is still warm. Beat well to form a cohesive dough. If the dough is too sticky to handle (because of the concentration of the honey), add just enough flour to keep it from sticking. When it reaches the proper consistency, it will be very soft but can be handled.

ROLLING OUT AND BAKING

Preheat the oven to 350 degrees F. Butter and flour two rimless baking sheets (or use the underside of two sheets with rims). While still warm, divide the dough in two and roll out rectangles approximately 10 × 12 inches on each of the prepared baking sheets. Bake one sheet at a time in the middle of the oven until golden brown—approximately 30 minutes.

PREPARING THE ICING

When both cakes have been baked, prepare the icing. Heat the powdered sugar with ½ cup water in a saucepan, stirring until the mixture comes to a boil. Allow the syrup to boil until it spins a thread (when a candy thermometer registers 230 degrees F.) Place the saucepan in a pan of cold water to stop the cooking. Pour half of the sugar syrup over each cake while the cake is still warm.

ICING

Rewarm the cake that was baked first for 3 minutes in a **375 degree F.** oven. Spread the icing with a metal spatula or pastry brush to cover the cakes evenly but thinly. Allow the icing to set completely, ideally overnight, as it will cut more neatly the following day. If the icing becomes too thick, add 2 teaspoons of water and reheat it briefly.

THE FOLLOWING DAY: CUTTING AND STORING

Using a long, sharp knife, trim off the crusty outer edges. Cut the *Leckerli* into narrow bars, ⅞ inch wide and 2 inches long. For the best flavor, store for several weeks in an airtight tin at room temperature. *Leckerli* keep for three to four months and improve with age.

*EQUIPMENT
2 rimless baking
  sheets, or turn
  baking sheets with
  rims upside down
  and use the
  undersides*

NÜRNBERGER ELISENLEBKUCHEN

NUREMBERG LEBKUCHEN

2 large eggs
1⅔ cups superfine
  sugar
¼ teaspoon ground
  cloves
1 teaspoon cinnamon
½ teaspoon baking
  powder
Grated rind of 1
  lemon
⅓ cup mixed candied
  lemon and
  orange peel, (citron)
  finely minced
2 to 2⅓ cups
  unblanched
  almonds, finely
  ground
ICING
3½ cups powdered
  sugar, sifted
6 tablespoons water
EQUIPMENT lem/juice
Oblaten or edible rice
  paper

nutmeg
Rhum aroma
Bittermandel (2)
lemon

One of the most unglamorous *Lebkuchen* cookies, as well as one of the most delicious and famous, the *Elisenlebkuchen* from Nuremberg, defies the original definition of *Lebkuchen*. It is not made with honey. The best *Elisenlebkuchen*, furthermore, are not made with flour. In fact, to be called *Elisenlebkuchen* the cookies must, by law, contain no more than one tenth their weight in flour, with a third to half their weight made up of ground nuts (almonds or a mixture of almonds and hazelnuts). With the exception of spices, *Elisenlebkuchen* have little in common with the original model, and they are made by a completely different technique based on whisked egg and sugar. They are, however, the *Lebkuchen* most exported and are a major industry of Bavaria.

Traditionally mounded on *Oblaten* (rounds or rectangles of edible rice paper), the nut-rich dough is sometimes decorated before being baked with blanched almonds, and afterward is usually glazed with sugar icing or chocolate. The mixture must be thick enough not to spread too much, and at the same time loose enough to produce a cookie with a moist interior. *Elisenlebkuchen* are sold in many specialty foods shops around Christmas time. If you wish to try your hand at baking them at home, find a cookware shop or professional bakery supplies shop that carries *Oblaten* or edible rice paper. *Elisenlebkuchen* can be made in rounds as small as 3 inches across to as large as 6 inches. Decorate larger *Elisenlebkuchen* with a blanched almond in the center and several others placed near the edge. Those decorated with almonds can be left plain or iced in sugar icing. Chocolate icing will not show off the almonds so should be used on plain cookies. Cookies iced in white will look somewhat transparent at first. By the next day, however, they will have turned a rippled opaque white, their traditional appearance.

The amount of ground almonds used varies somewhat depending on how finely ground and how oily or dry they are. A blender is recommended for grinding the nuts.

4 TO 24 HOURS BEFORE BAKING
PREPARING THE DOUGH

Choose a heatproof crockery or glass mixing bowl that will fit into a saucepan with its base resting well above the bottom of the pan. Bring 2 inches of water to a boil in the saucepan and remove from the heat. Set the bowl in the pan, put the eggs and sugar in the bowl and, with a hand-held electric mixer, beat rapidly at high speed until the mixture is thick and mousselike— about 4 minutes. To test the consistency, use the beater to lift a little of the mixture and trail a letter M over the mixture in the bowl. If the shape of the letter holds for 3 seconds, the mixture is sufficiently beaten. If the shape dissolves, beat longer, then test again.

Remove the bowl from the pan of water and continue to beat for a further 3 minutes. Add the cloves, cinnamon, baking powder and grated lemon rind and fold several times. Then add the finely minced mixed peels and 2 cups of ground almonds. Blend the mixture well then allow to rest for 5 minutes. In the meantime, place the *Oblaten* or edible rice paper on top of buttered baking sheets.

TESTING THE MIXTURE

Now, test the *Elisenlebkuchen* mixture. Place 2 tablespoons (or more for very large cookies) in a mound on one of the

Oblaten. Wait for 3 minutes. Within that time, it will have spread and flattened just slightly, but should not have flattened completely. If it looks like a flat pancake and has spread as much as 1 inch (or off the *Oblaten*), return the mixture to the bowl. Add some of the remaining ⅓ cup of almonds. Allow the mixture to rest for several minutes and test again. At this point it should hold its shape sufficiently. Add more ground almonds only if the mixture doesn't pass the test.

ASSEMBLING AND DECORATING

Once the mixture has reached the proper consistency, spoon it on to the *Oblaten* or rice paper. They can be medium-sized (2 heaped tablespoons) or large (4 tablespoons). Allow to set for 3 minutes. Dip your index finger in water and smooth the sides and tops of the mounds. If desired, decorate with blanched split almonds for large cookies, following the instructions above. Leave to dry for 4 to 6 hours or overnight.

4 TO 24 HOURS LATER
BAKING

Preheat the oven to 325 degrees F. Bake, one sheet at a time, in the middle of the oven until barely golden and lightly risen—approximately 20 to 25 minutes. Check several times so that the cookies don't dry out. When done, they should be slightly firm to the touch but still moist on the inside. If rice paper is used instead of precut *Oblaten*, tear the excess rice paper away from each cookie, leaving a round the size of the cookie stuck to the bottom. Remove to a wire rack to cool and proceed with the next tray in the same fashion.

ICING AND STORING

To make the icing, place 6 tablespoons of water in a large mixing bowl. Using a hand-held electric mixer at high speed or rotary beater, gradually beat in the sifted powdered sugar, beating for 5 minutes. Place the bowl in a pan filled with water that has just boiled. Beat for another 5 minutes to dissolve the sugar completely. Add enough extra water or additional sugar to make an icing of thin pouring consistency. Using a pastry brush, brush the top of each cookie that is to be iced. Press a piece of aluminum foil over the icing when not using it. For chocolate icing, beat 3 to 4 ounces of melted semi-sweet chocolate into the sugar icing, adding a bit of extra water to thin it. Brush the tops with the chocolate icing and allow them to dry completely before storing them. Store well wrapped in an airtight tin in a cool place for up to three weeks.

BRAUNEKUCHEN

MOLASSES CRISPS

*MAKES ABOUT 50
2-INCH COOKIES*

*HEATED
INGREDIENTS
5 tablespoons un-
salted butter
5 tablespoons lard
¼ cup plus 1
tablespoon
molasses
⅔ cup sugar
DRY INGREDIENTS
1¾ cup plus 2
tablespoons all-
purpose flour
½ cup cornstarch
1 teaspoon cinnamon
¼ teaspoon ground
cloves
⅛ teaspoon nutmeg
⅛ teaspoon
cardamom
½ teaspoon baking
powder
½ teaspoon baking
soda
ADDITIONS
Grated rind of 1
lemon*

CONTINUED ON
FACING PAGE

These thin cut-out cookies from northern Germany—
the *Lebkuchen* of the North—differ from variations farther south in that they are made with molasses rather
than honey, which accounts for their dark color, and with
a high proportion of fat, some of it lard, which adds flavor
and body.

This family recipe comes from a good friend in Schleswig-
Holstein who emphasizes that the dough should be rolled
out as thin as possible for the cookies to become crisp. For
the best flavor, bake them several weeks in advance.

ONE DAY IN ADVANCE
PREPARING THE DOUGH

Warm the butter, lard, molasses, and sugar over low heat,
stirring until the mixture is hot and the sugar and fat have
dissolved. Allow to cool for several minutes. Sift the dry ingredients together onto a piece of wax paper. Add them gradually to
the heated ingredients, beating well with a wooden spoon. Add
the lemon rind, candied peel, and chopped almonds and stir in
well. The dough will be very soft but should not stick when
handled. If it is sticky, add just enough flour to keep it from
sticking. If it is too crumbly, add a teaspoon or more of warm
water. Wrap well in plastic wrap and leave at room temperature
overnight; do not refrigerate.

THE FOLLOWING DAY
CUTTING OUT

The next day, **preheat the oven to 350 degrees F.** Divide the dough into two pieces. Roll out each piece on a lightly floured board until ⅛ inch thick—that is, very thin. Use cutters to cut out decorative shapes, traditionally hearts, stars, pretzels, rounds, and crescents, but any decorative cutter can be used. Place on buttered and floured baking sheets.

BAKING

Bake for about 13 minutes or until the edges have shrunk and the cookies have begun to change color. Because of the high sugar content, they are baked at a moderate temperature so they won't burn. However, they must be watched carefully since they color rapidly once done.

FINISHING AND STORING

Remove to a wire rack to cool. Though icing is not traditional, they can be piped with Royal Icing (see *Hexenhäuschen*) in decorative patterns if desired. Store in an airtight tin at room temperature.

1 tablespoon candied orange and lemon peel, finely chopped
¼ cup finely chopped blanched almonds
EQUIPMENT
Decorative cookie cutters

2

BUTTER COOKIES—BUTTERPLÄTZCHEN

Butter cookies, a mainstay in American baking, hold an equally important place in the German-speaking countries, particularly in Austria, where butter plays an important culinary role. Although many of the familiar Austrian selections, such as (*Vanillekipferl*) Vanilla Crescents and (*Spitzbuben*) the familiar jam-filled rounds with three small holes in the top are also baked in Germany and Switzerland, the butter content is frequently reduced in the recipes used in those countries.

Besides the two cookies mentioned above, other favorites were brought to this country by German-speaking immigrants, beginning in the seventeenth century when religious sects settled in the Pennsylvania Dutch (originally called *Deutsch*—German) country and South Carolina. Later settlers, especially those in the rich farming and dairy lands of the

Midwest, also continued their Old World baking tradition, helping to popularize many of the cookies we bake here today, such as Sand Tarts (*Heidesand*), Butter Thins (*Mailänderli*), Yolk Cookies (*S-Gebäck*), Printed Almond Crisps (*Spekulatius*), Spritz Cookies (*Spritzgebäck*), and Black-and-White Cookies (*Schwarz-Weiss-Gebäck*). As is the custom here, butter cookies are particularly in evidence at Christmas in the German-speaking countries, but are also favored throughout the year as an accompaniment to afternoon coffee or tea.

In this chapter, a variety of techniques are employed since the pliability of rich butter cookie dough makes it especially versatile in the number of ways it can be shaped: molded into rods (*Mandelstifte*), balls (*Gewürznüsse*), crescents (*Vanillekipferl*) and pretzels (*Butterbrezeln*); piped into initials (*Spritzgebäck*); rolled and cut out with plain or decorative cutters (*Mailänderli*); or formed into logs and sliced (*Heidesand*).

One thing butter cookies have in common in all three countries is that they are generally very small—tiny mouthfuls, perfectly executed. With this in mind, I have kept most of the cookies in these recipes small and have attempted to give as many technical hints as possible for producing a perfectly finished cookie. Because these are a visual as well as an edible art form, the finishing is important and well worth the effort.

With all but the piped and spooned cookies, it is important to allow sufficient time for the dough to chill properly before it is shaped or rolled out. Otherwise it will become too greasy to use and the cookies will be hard. Any time the dough becomes too soft, simply refrigerate it for fifteen minutes or a little longer and then proceed. For cookies that have been shaped, I have usually given instructions for refrigerating them before they are baked. This will help prevent excessive spreading. Additionally, I have found that for thicker, shaped cookies, such as crescents and S's, it is better not to butter the baking sheet, as the extra butter encourages spreading. For all the other butter cookies, however, you must butter and flour the baking sheets in advance, rubbing softened butter on a piece of paper towel, spreading it thoroughly over the baking sheet, dusting it well with flour, then shaking off the excess.

The method I use for flaking butter in the basic rubbed-in dough—using a cheese grater instead of a knife—is one I also use for pastry making and have found to be especially fast and easy. When making a rubbed-in dough, however, it is important to observe the instructions for having the butter well chilled so that it will grate easily. If your butter has been left out and is somewhat soft, try putting it in the freezer for ten to fifteen minutes.

Knead together any scraps left over from cutout cookies, wrap them well, and refrigerate for fifteen to thirty minutes before rolling them out again so that they aren't greasy.

For cookies made with dough that has not been glazed, it is traditional to allow them to color only barely around the edge and otherwise remain pale yellow. Because butter cookies color rapidly once they are cooked, it is important to watch them carefully.

While most cookies are removed immediately with a metal spatula to wire racks to cool, if one is particularly thick or delicate, I would suggest loosening it with a metal spatula first but not removing it immediately, so that the cooling process gives it a chance to firm so it will be less likely to break.

For storing at room temperature, I recommend, conservatively, one week's storage for unspiced butter cookies and ten to twelve days for those that are spiced. They can certainly be eaten two weeks after they have been baked, but I find that the delicious butter taste has gone by then. If they are to be stored for a longer period they should be well wrapped and frozen. Thawing time is no more than thirty minutes, and usually much less.

For additional hints on rolling out dough or pastry, see Baking Tips.

FLAKED-BUTTER TECHNIQUE

MASTER RECIPE

SÜSSER MÜRBETEIG
BASIC RUBBED-IN DOUGH

2½ cups all-purpose
  flour
⅛ teaspoon salt
⅔ cup superfine
  sugar
½ cup (2 sticks)
  unsalted butter,
  well chilled
Grated rind of 1
  lemon
2 large egg yolks
1 teaspoon vanilla

Sift the flour and salt together into a large mixing bowl. Add the sugar. Coat the butter with flour from the bowl to make it easier to handle and grate it directly into the flour, using the coarse blades of a cheese grater. As the butter is grated, occasionally mix in the flakes with the flour, using your fingertips, before grating more. Add the grated lemon rind. Using two round-bladed knives, cut the butter into the flour until the texture resembles coarse meal. Shake the bowl, which will cause any larger pieces of butter to rise to the surface. Pick up the mixture with your fingertips and quickly rub any larger bits of butter into the flour, letting it fall back in the bowl. Continue until the butter is well blended but not greasy—40 to 60 seconds.

Mix the egg yolks lightly with a fork and combine with the vanilla. Using the fork, mix the egg into the flour mixture until well distributed. Then, using your hands, work the dough into a ball. Knead the dough lightly on a floured board until it forms a cohesive mass—no more than 1 minute. Pat the dough into a flat round, or a log if so specified in the recipe. Wrap it tightly in plastic wrap and refrigerate for at least 1 hour or overnight before using. Use as directed in the recipe.

NOTE. If the dough has been refrigerated for a long time, and is especially hard, allow it to soften at room temperature for about 10 minutes. Hit it several times with a rolling pin to help soften it, then pull it back into a flat round before rolling it out.

MAILÄNDERLI

MILANESE BUTTER THINS

Though not evident from the name, *Mailänderli* are as Swiss as Lindt chocolate or Emmenthal cheese—at least to the Swiss who bake and consume them with relish. Cut out in thin flowers, stars, hearts, and crescents, this traditional favorite differs from other cut-out butter cookies only in the large amount of sugar used, a factor responsible for their crisp texture.

Makes about 80 thin 2-inch cookies

To make, simply increase the sugar in the Basic Rubbed-In-Dough to 1¼ cups. Roll out very thin, cut out as desired, brush with lightly beaten egg, and bake in an oven **preheated to 350 degrees F.** until lightly colored—approximately 12 minutes.

BUTTERBREZELN
BUTTERY PRETZELS

MAKES ABOUT 70

*1 recipe Basic
Rubbed-in Dough
Powdered sugar, or
one of the icings
that follow*

Of the butter cookies found in Germany and Austria, the pretzel shape, copied from the salt-strewn yeast dough pretzels sold in market stalls and at fairs, makes one of the most charming cookies. The shape itself has a long history. Thought once to have been a symbol of the solar cycle, it was used by early Christians in the Roman Empire to make a Lenten flour/salt/water pretzel, the crossed arms symbolizing Christianity. Called *bracellae*, "little arms," the shape traveled north and became known as *Brezel* (pretzel).

As cookies, pretzels come in many variations: the dough enriched with egg yolks (*Eigelbbrezeln*); with hazelnuts (*Haselnussbrezeln*); or iced with vanilla icing (*Vanillebrezeln*); lemon icing (*Zitronenbrezeln*); rum icing (*Punschbrezeln*); or chocolate (*Schokoladenbrezeln*). They are equally attractive simply dusted with powdered sugar while still warm.

PREPARING THE DOUGH

Prepare the Basic Rubbed-In Dough and roll it into two logs 1½ inches in diameter. Wrap them tightly in plastic wrap and chill for 1 hour or until firm. Butter and flour baking sheets.

SHAPING THE PRETZELS

Cut the logs into ¼-inch slices, cutting only a few at a time. Form each slice into a log shape, then roll it back and forth on a pastry board until it is 6 inches long. The strip should be approximately ¼ inch in diameter. Use the first strip as a measure for the rest so that the pretzels will be uniform in size.

To shape the pretzels, bend the arms around to form an oval, then cross one arm over the other, at the top of the pretzel. Arrange the pretzels about 1 inch apart on unbuttered baking sheets and place them in the freezer for 10 minutes or the refrigerator for 30 minutes. Meanwhile, **preheat the oven to 350 degrees F.**

BAKING

When well chilled, bake one sheet at a time on the middle rack of the oven until the pretzels are pale yellow—approximately 12 to 14 minutes. They should not be allowed to brown. Remove them to a cooling rack. Keep any unbaked pretzels in the refrigerator.

FINISHING

If you are dusting them with powdered sugar, do so while they are still warm, pressing the sugar through a tea strainer or using a dredger. Otherwise, ice with one of the following icings.

VANILLEBREZELN

ICING FOR VANILLA PRETZELS

2⅓ cups powdered sugar, sifted
1½ teaspoons vanilla extract
4 tablespoons water

To make the icing, use a hand-held electric mixer at high speed or rotary beater. Gradually beat the powdered sugar into 4 tablespoons water and the vanilla extract, beating for approximately 5 minutes. Place the bowl in a pan of shallow water that has just boiled and beat for another 3 to 4 minutes, or until the icing is warm and the sugar has completely dissolved. The icing should be thin enough to brush on the pretzels easily using a pastry brush. If it is too thin or too thick, adjust the consistency with a little more sugar or water. Brush each pretzel with the icing, getting into the corners with your brush, and dry on a wire rack before storing. Refrigerate in an airtight tin for up to seven days or freeze for up to three months.

ZITRONENBREZELN

ICING FOR LEMON PRETZELS

2⅓ cups powdered sugar, sifted
Finely grated rind of 1 lemon
4½ tablespoons lemon juice

Make the icing, and ice according to the technique for *Vanillebrezeln*.

SCHOKOLADENBREZELN

ICING FOR CHOCOLATE PRETZELS

2½ *cups powdered sugar, sifted*
4½ *tablespoons water*
3 *ounces semi-sweet chocolate,*
  broken in small pieces
1 *teaspoon vegetable oil*

Make the icing according to the technique for *Vanillebrezeln*, using
4½ tablespoons water. Melt the broken pieces of chocolate with the oil
in the top of a double boiler or in a heatproof soup plate or shallow bowl
placed over a saucepan filled with 2 inches of simmering water. Stir
occasionally until the chocolate has melted. Remove from heat. Stir
the chocolate into the warm icing, adding a few drops more water, if
necessary, to reach a thin coating consistency. Ice and store as above.

PUNSCHBREZELN

ICING FOR RUM PRETZELS

2⅓ *cups   powdered   sugar,*
  sifted
4½ *tablespoons rum*
1 *to 2 drops red food coloring*
  (optional)

Make the icing and ice according to the technique for *Vanillebrezeln*.
If desired, the icing can be tinted with a drop or two of the red food
coloring to give it a pale pink tint.

SCHWARZ-WEISS-GEBÄCK

BLACK-AND-WHITE COOKIES

The use of contrasting-colored doughs to make interesting designs is a favorite technique in German baking. Once you have made your basic butter cookie dough and colored half of it with cocoa powder, you can choose from one or more of the following designs: chessboard, snail, peacock's eye, pig's ear, or marbled rounds, the latter an especially good way to use up scraps of different-colored dough.

The cookies can be stored in an airtight container for up to one week, or frozen for up to three months.

SCHACHBRETT

CHESSBOARD

MAKES ABOUT 35

PREPARING THE DOUGH

Make up the dough following the instruction in the basic recipe, and divide it in half once it is kneaded. Work 2 tablespoons of cocoa powder into one half of the dough, kneading it well until blended evenly. Pat each piece of dough into a flat round. Wrap in plastic wrap and refrigerate for several hours.

The following directions use the brown dough as an outside wrapper, but you can also make these cookies using the reverse colors.

ROLLING AND CUTTING THE DOUGH

After the brown and white doughs have been refrigerated for several hours, remove them from the refrigerator. On a lightly floured board, roll out one third of the chocolate dough in a rectangle ½ inch thick and measuring 2 × 7 inches. It is important to use a ruler to measure so that the chessboard pattern is even. Using a piece of cardboard or a ruler as a guide, cut the rectangle lengthwise into four even strips, each ½ inch wide. If they have stuck to the board, loosen them carefully with a metal spatula and set them aside. Knead any scraps back into the remaining chocolate dough. Roll this dough out on a lightly floured board into a 7-inch square. Make sure the dough is not sticking to the board and can be picked up. Use a metal spatula to loosen it if necessary. Trim the edges neatly, using a piece of cardboard or a ruler as a guide.

Roll out slightly more than one third of the light-colored dough into a rectangle ½ inch thick and measuring 2½ × 7 inches. Cut the rectangle lengthwise as before, this time into five even strips, each ½ inch wide.

ASSEMBLING

Brush the brown square of dough lightly with water, using a pastry brush, to help make the strips adhere. Measure the square, making a mark in the center where it measures 3½ inches. Place a dark strip of dough straight down the center. Brush the sides of the strip lightly with water. Place a light-colored strip on either side. Brush the tops and sides of the strips lightly with water. Continue in the same fashion with two more layers of three strips: the second layer should have a light strip in the center with a dark strip on each side of it; the third should be exactly like the first. Continue brushing the sides and top of the strips lightly with water as new strips are applied. When you have done this you will see a "chessboard" of nine squares at each end.

Pull the two sides of the wrapper up and fold them around the chessboard. Measure the overlap—it will be approximately ¾ inch. So that the overlap is no more than ¼ inch, lay the two sides of the wrapper back on the board and trim off the excess evenly with a sharp knife. Rewrap the chessboard. Brush a little water on the edge where the seam joins and press the dough together well to seal the seam. Smooth out the seam with your finger so it has the same thickness as the rest. Wrap the dough in plastic wrap and chill for 1 hour or until firm.

BAKING

Butter and flour baking sheets. **Preheat the oven to 350 degrees F.** Slice the logs ¼ inch thick and place 1 inch apart on the prepared baking sheets. Bake, one sheet at a time, in the middle of the oven until lightly colored—approximately 12 minutes. Refrigerate any un-baked cookies while the others are baking. Remove to wire racks to cool before storing.

UTILIZING SCRAPS

You will have quite a bit of light-colored dough and a few scraps of chocolate dough left over. You can either roll them out separately for simple cutout cookies, using decorative cutters, or you can partially knead the two colors together to produce a marbled effect, following the instructions for *Marmorkeks* below.

SCHNECKEN

Snails

*MAKES ABOUT 80
2-INCH COOKIES*

PREPARING THE DOUGH

Make up the dough following the instructions in the basic recipe, and divide it in half once it is kneaded. Work 2 tablespoons of cocoa powder into one half of the dough, kneading it well until evenly blended. Pat each piece of dough into a flat round. Wrap in plastic wrap and refrigerate for several hours.

ASSEMBLING

Roll out equal-sized rectangles of light and dark dough, each ⅛ inch thick. Make sure they do not stick to the board; use a metal spatula to loosen them if necessary. Brush the surface of each lightly with water. Lay one on top of the other—whichever color is on the bottom will be the color on the outside edge of the cookie. Trim the edges so they are perfectly even. If you want small cookies, roll the dough from the long side of the rectangle into a log. For larger cookies, begin rolling from one of the short sides of the rectangle until you have a log. At either end you will see a spiral of dark and light dough. Brush the edge with water and press the seam well to seal it. Smooth out the seam with your finger so that it has the same thickness as the rest. Wrap the dough well in plastic wrap and refrigerate for 1 hour or until firm.

BAKING

Butter and flour baking sheets.

Preheat the oven to 350 degrees F. Slice the log ¼ inch thick and place 1 inch apart on the prepared baking sheets. Bake one sheet at a time in the middle of the oven until the Schnecken are lightly colored—approximately 12 minutes. Refrigerate any unbaked cookies while the others are baking. Remove to wire racks to cool before storing.

SCHWEINSÖHRCHEN

PIG'S EARS

*MAKES ABOUT 60
3-INCH COOKIES*

PREPARING THE DOUGH

Make up the dough following the instructions in the basic recipe, and divide it in half once it is kneaded. Work 2 tablespoons of cocoa powder into one half of the dough, kneading it well until blended evenly. Pat each piece of dough into a flat round. Wrap in plastic wrap and refrigerate for several hours.

ASSEMBLING

Roll out equal-sized rectangles of brown and white dough ⅛ inch thick, making sure they do not stick to the board. Brush each with water. Lay one on top of the other. The color of dough underneath will be the color that shows on the outside. Beginning with the short sides of the rectangle, roll both sides of the dough toward the center. You should have two rolls of equal size that meet. Brush the seam where they meet with water and press them together well so they stick. Wrap well in plastic wrap and refrigerate for 1 hour or until firm.

BAKING

Butter and flour baking sheets.

Preheat the oven to 350 degrees F. Slice the log ¼ inch thick and place slices 1 inch apart on the prepared baking sheets. Bake one sheet at a time in the middle of the oven until lightly colored—approximately 12 minutes. Refrigerate any unbaked cookies while the others are baking. Remove to wire racks to cool before storing.

*MAKES ABOUT 80
2-INCH COOKIES*

PFAUENAUGEN

PEACOCK'S EYES

PREPARING THE DOUGH

Making up the dough following the instructions in the basic recipe, and divide it in half once it is kneaded. Work 2 tablespoons of cocoa powder into one half of the dough, kneading it well until blended evenly. Pat each piece of dough into a flat round. Wrap in plastic wrap and refrigerate for several hours.

ASSEMBLING

Using the color that you want to show on the outside edge, roll that color dough out into a narrow rectangle, 5 inches wide and approximately ¼ inch thick. Take the dough of the other color and, using your fists or a rolling pin, beat it into a rectangular or oval shape so that it can be rolled into a log. Using the palms of your hands, roll it back and forth on a lightly floured board to form an even-sized log the same length as the other rectangle of dough. It should be approximately ¾ inch in diameter. (If the rectangle is slightly longer, cut it even with the log and use the scraps of dough for cutout cookies.) Make sure the rectangle does not stick to the board, loosening it with a metal spatula if necessary. Brush lightly with water. Lay the log of dough down the center. Pull the rectangle of dough around it. Where the seam joins, there should be no more than ¼ inch overlap. Once you have wrapped it around the log and measured it, lay the overlapping side back on the board and trim the excess off evenly with a sharp knife. Rewrap the log. Brush a little water on the edge where the seam joins and press the dough together well to seal the seam. Smooth out the seam with your finger so it has the same thickness as the rest. Wrap the dough in plastic wrap and chill for 1 hour or until firm.

BAKING

Butter and flour baking sheets.
Preheat the oven to 350 degrees F. Cut the log ¼ inch thick and place the slices 1 inch apart on the prepared baking sheets. Bake one sheet at a time in the middle of the oven until lightly colored—approximately 12 minutes. Refrigerate any unbaked cookies while the others are baking. Remove to wire racks to cool before storing.

MARMORKEKS

MARBLED ROUNDS

PREPARING THE DOUGH

*MAKES ABOUT 90
1¾-INCH
COOKIES*

Make up the dough following the instructions in the basic recipe, and divide it in half once it is kneaded. Work 2 tablespoons of cocoa powder into one half of the dough, kneading it well until blended evenly. Pat each piece of dough into a flat round. Wrap in plastic wrap and refrigerate for several hours.

ASSEMBLING

This is a good way to use up scraps of different-colored dough. Otherwise, use equal portions of dark- and light-colored dough before they have been refrigerated so they are quite soft. Or, if they have already been refrigerated, leave them at room temperature until they are soft enough to knead. Break each piece of dough into several pieces. Knead all the pieces together, pressing them together with the palm of your hand and folding the dough piece in half. Continue several times until the dough is well streaked. Roll the dough back and forth on a lightly floured board into an even-sized log, approximately 1¼ inches in diameter. Wrap the log in plastic wrap and refrigerate for several hours or until very firm.

BAKING

Butter and flour baking sheets.
Preheat the oven to 350 degrees F. Cut the log ¼ inch thick and place the slices 1 inch apart on the prepared baking sheets. Bake one sheet at a time in the middle of the oven until lightly colored—approximately 12 minutes. Refrigerate any unbaked cookies while the others are baking. Remove to wire racks to cool before storing.

SPITZBUBEN
JAM-FILLED BUTTER COOKIES

MAKES ABOUT 45

*1 recipe Basic
    Rubbed-in Dough
    (p. 82)
FILLING
1¼ cups raspberry
    and/or apricot
    jam
1 teaspoon lemon
    juice (if using
    apricot jam)
TO FINISH
Powdered sugar
EQUIPMENT
2-inch or 3½-inch
    fluted or plain
    round cookie cutter
Small aspic cutter or
    thimble*

These pretty fluted rounds filled with apricot or raspberry jam, found in all German-speaking countries at Christmas time and throughout the year, are characterized by three small holes in the top which reveal the jewel-like filling. There are now round cookie cutters on the market (use for the tops only) which cut out three holes at the same time as cutting out the round. However, as most people won't have this specialized cutter, the holes can be made with small aspic cutters or a thimble. If using aspic cutters, you can make plain round holes or heart- or diamond-shaped holes. The traditional size is approximately 2 inches. A thimble will produce a larger hole, so you can either make one hole in a 2-inch cookie or make three holes in a 3½-inch cookie.

A professional trick to make your cookies look as beautiful as those at the famous Demel's pastry shop in Vienna is to turn the bases upside down when they are removed from the baking sheet and before they are filled. When sandwiched, the fluted edges of top and bottom then meet perfectly.

PREPARING THE DOUGH

Prepare the basic rubbed-in dough as directed in the master recipe. Pat it into flat round, wrap it, and chill it for 1 hour until firm, or overnight. Butter and flour baking sheets and set them aside.

ROLLING AND CUTTING OUT

Roll out the dough ⅛ inch thick on a lightly floured board. Cut out the cookies with a round cutter, preferably fluted. Using a small aspic cutter or thimble, cut out three small holes or one large hole in half of the cookies: these will be the lids. Place the cookies about 1 inch apart on the prepared baking sheets and refrigerate them for 20 minutes or place them in the freezer for 10 minutes. In the meantime, **preheat the oven to 350 degrees F.**

BAKING

Bake the cookies in the center of the oven, one sheet at a time, until barely colored around the edges—approximately 12 minutes. Do not allow them to brown. Transfer them to racks to cool. While still warm, dust the lids with sifted powdered sugar. Turn the cookie bases upside down. Keep any unbaked cookies in the refrigerator while waiting to bake them.

ASSEMBLING AND STORING

You can fill half of them with raspberry jam and the other half with apricot jam.

Stirring constantly, bring the raspberry jam to a boiling point with 1 teaspoon water, but do not allow it to boil or it will lose its bright color. Spread the jam not quite to the edges on each base while it is still warm.

Stirring constantly, bring the apricot jam to a full boil with 1 teaspoon lemon juice, and boil for 30 seconds. Then strain through a sieve, pressing down hard on the apricot pieces. If either jam becomes too thick and cool, reheat briefly with a few drops of water. Spread the jam not quite to the edges on each base. It should not flow out when the lid is placed on top, but there should be enough so that it is forced up slightly through the holes. Line up the fluted edges (if a fluted cutter was used) when placing the lids on top. Allow the jam to cool. Store carefully so the powdered sugar isn't smudged, placing a piece of wax paper or aluminum foil between layers. If necessary, dust smudged cookies with powdered sugar again.

APRIKOSENAUGEN

APRICOT JAM-FILLED BUTTER COOKIES

Almost identical to *Spitzbuben, Aprikosenaugen*, or "apricot eyes"—found in all German-speaking countries—are characterized by a filling of apricot jam which is revealed through one large "eye" (unlike *Spitzbuben*, which have three small holes).

Follow the instructions for *Spitzbuben*, using the apricot filling. For cutters, you will need a 2-inch, preferably fluted cutter, and a 1¼ inch fluted or plain cutter. For the smaller cutter, you can substitute a large metal tip from a piping bag which will cut a hole approximately the right size. Cut large holes out of half the cookies for tops and proceed with the recipe as given.

EIGELBBREZELN
EGG-YOLK PRETZELS

Eigelbbrezeln are a practical solution for the baker who has egg yolks left over after making meringues. Because the dough is very rich and softens quickly, it is best to refrigerate it overnight to allow it to become firm enough for shaping. Additional chilling after the pretzels have been shaped will also improve the finished product.

ONE DAY IN ADVANCE
PREPARING THE DOUGH

Sift the flour and powdered sugar into a large bowl. Add the grated lemon rind. Coat the butter with flour from the bowl to make it easier to handle and grate directly into the flour, using the coarse blades of the grater. As the butter is grated, occasionally mix the flakes in with the flour, using your fingertips, before grating more. Using two round-bladed knives, cut the butter into the flour until the texture resembles coarse meal. Shake the bowl, which will cause the larger pieces of butter to rise to the surface. Pick up the mixture with your fingertips and quickly rub any larger bits of butter into the flour, letting it fall back in the bowl. Continue until the butter is well blended but not greasy—40 to 60 seconds.

Mix the egg yolks lightly with a fork and combine with the vanilla. Using the fork, mix the egg into the flour mixture until well distributed. Then, using your hand, work the dough into a ball. Knead the dough lightly on a floured board until it forms a cohesive mass—no more than 1 minute. Form the dough into

MAKES ABOUT 70

1¾ cups all-purpose flour
1 cup powdered sugar
Grated rind of 1 lemon
12 tablespoons (1½ sticks) unsalted butter, well chilled
5 large egg yolks
1 teaspoon vanilla extract
TO FINISH
Powdered sugar
CHOCOLATE GLAZE (optional)
6 ounces semi-sweet chocolate
2 teaspoons vegetable oil

two logs about 1½ inches in diameter. Wrap tightly in plastic wrap and refrigerate overnight.

THE FOLLOWING DAY
SHAPING

Preheat the oven to 350 degrees F. To shape the pretzels, bend the arms around to form an oval, then cross one arm over the other at the top of the pretzel. Arrange the pretzels about 1 inch apart on unbuttered baking sheets and place them in the freezer for 10 minutes or the refrigerator for 30 minutes.

BAKING

When well chilled, bake one sheet at a time on the middle rack of the oven until pretzels are pale yellow—approximately 12 to 14 minutes. The pretzels should not be allowed to brown. Remove them to a cooling rack. Keep any unbaked pretzels in the refrigerator. Dust with powdered sugar while still warm, or glaze with chocolate as described below.

CHOCOLATE GLAZE (OPTIONAL)

For the chocolate glaze, melt 6 ounces of semi-sweet chocolate, broken in pieces, with 2 teaspoons of vegetable oil in the top of a double boiler or in a heatproof soup plate or shallow bowl placed over a pan filled with 2 inches of simmering water. Stir the chocolate occasionally until melted. Remove the bowl from the saucepan. Using a pastry brush, brush each pretzel evenly with chocolate. If the mixture seems too thick, add a few more drops of vegetable oil. If you feel comfortable doing so, you can also dip each pretzel in the chocolate mixture, holding it carefully with your fingertips. Allow the chocolate-covered pretzels to dry, right side up, on a wire rack before storing.

S-GEBÄCK
S-Shaped Butter Cookies

This favorite German cookie, baked at Christmas time and throughout the year, offers the home baker an opportunity to use up extra egg yolks left over after making meringues. Traditionally, the cookies are coated with beaten egg white and sprinkled with coarse decorating sugar (see Ingredients—Sugar). If you can't get coarse sugar, however, you can simply use granulated sugar.

MAKES ABOUT 40

1 recipe Eigelbbrezeln Dough (p. 97)
TO FINISH:
1 large egg white
Decorating sugar or granulated sugar

One Day in Advance
PREPARING THE DOUGH

Make up the dough as for *Eigelbbrezeln*. Once it has been kneaded, form it into two logs about 2½ inches in diameter. Wrap tightly in plastic wrap and refrigerate overnight.

The Following Day
SHAPING

The next day, **preheat the oven to 350 degrees F.** Working with one log at a time (the other should stay in the refrigerator), cut each into ⅜-inch slices. Form each slice into a log shape and roll it back and forth on a very lightly floured board until you have a roll about ⅜ to ½ inch in diameter and 4 to 5 inches long. Use the first one as a measure for the rest so that they are all the same length. Work with the dough gently but quickly and keep all unused portions in the refrigerator.

Shape the rolls of dough into an S and place on unbuttered baking sheets 1 inch apart. Beat the egg white with a whisk or rotary or electric beater until it is frothy and lightly thickened. Brush the top and a little of the sides with the white, using a pastry brush. Sprinkle each cookie with a little of the decorating or granulated sugar. Brush off any excess sugar from the baking sheet with a dry pastry brush.

BAKING

Bake one sheet at a time in the middle of the oven until the cookies are firm and barely colored—approximately 12 to 15 minutes. Loosen them from the baking sheet immediately, using a metal spatula. Allow to firm for about 2 minutes on the baking sheet, then transfer to wire racks to finish cooling before storing. Keep any unbaked cookies in the refrigerator while waiting to bake them.

SPRITZGEBÄCK
PIPED COOKIES

Soft butter cookie dough piped or forced through a press in decorative shapes produces a tea time and Christmas time favorite in all German-speaking countries. While the letter S seems to be the most popular pattern, you can use any of the shapes suggested in the recipe. If desired, they can be decorated before baking with a tiny sliver of candied cherry, red or green. The decorations should be small to correspond with the delicate appearance of the cookies. However, they need not be decorated at all. An alternative is to dip just the tip of one side of each cookie in a warm chocolate glaze (no more than one third of the cookie), after which they must be dried on a rack before storing.

MAKES ABOUT 60

1 recipe Basic Rubbed-In Dough (p. 82), increasing the large egg yolks from 2 to 3
Red or green candied cherries for decoration (optional)
CHOCOLATE GLAZE
4½ ounces semisweet chocolate
2 teaspoons vegetable oil
EQUIPMENT
Cookie press or large piping bag fitted with large star tip

PREPARING AND TESTING THE DOUGH

Follow the instructions for Basic Rubbed-In Dough. Knead on a lightly floured board until it forms a smooth, soft mass.

Test the consistency of your dough. Place it in a cookie press or large piping bag fitted with a large star tip. If it can be piped easily and hold its shape, use immediately. If it is too firm, leave at room temperature for 10 minutes and test again. If it is too soft, refrigerate for 15 minutes and test again.

PIPING THE DOUGH

Pipe or press the dough onto unbuttered baking sheets, leaving 1 inch between cookies. Traditional designs include S's, wreaths (you can pipe a rosette in the middle), crescents, bars with a rosette at each end, arabesques and, if you like, the initials of your family and friends. At their largest, the cookies should measure no more than 2½ inches since they will spread slightly during baking. If you are decorating with slivers of candied cherries, do so now. Once the dough has been piped out, refrigerate the sheets of cookies for at least 30 minutes before baking. In the meantime, **preheat the oven to 350 degrees F.**

BAKING

Bake in the middle of the oven one sheet at a time until barely colored—approximately 10 to 12 minutes. They should not be allowed to brown. Using a metal spatula, remove immediately to wire racks to cool. Keep any unbaked cookies in the refrigerator while waiting to bake them.

DECORATING

Cookies that have not been decorated with cherries can be dipped in the following chocolate glaze: Break the chocolate in pieces and combine with the oil in a double boiler or in a heatproof soup plate or shallow bowl placed over a saucepan filled with 2 inches of simmering water. Stir occasionally until the chocolate has melted. Remove from the heat. Test the consistency. Dip the tip of one cookie in the chocolate. If the chocolate mixture coats too thickly, add a few more drops of vegetable oil until the consistency is correct, being careful not to add too much. Either dip one third of each cookie in the chocolate or, if it is easier, use a pastry brush to apply the chocolate. Place on wire racks. Allow the chocolate to set completely, leaving the cookies to dry in a cool place (not in the refrigerator) before storing.

CHOCOLATE PIPED COOKIES

To make chocolate piped cookies, sift 3 tablespoons of cocoa powder with the flour into the mixing bowl before adding the butter and other ingredients. Then, at the end, knead the dough well to blend the cocoa color evenly throughout.

MARBLED PIPED COOKIES

Alternatively, once you have made up the dough, you can color half of it, kneading 1½ tablespoons of cocoa powder into the dough. When added at the end, the cocoa powder is more difficult to blend evenly; however, the marbled effect produced is equally attractive.

GIANT PIPED INITIAL

For a gift for a child, you can pipe a giant initial 6 to 7 inches high. To produce a wider trail of dough, use the largest-size star tip you have. Decorate the initial with candied cherries or dust with powdered sugar while it is still hot. Allow large cookies to cool on the baking sheet for 2 to 3 minutes so that they are quite firm before moving them to wire racks to cool.

VANILLEKIPFERL
VANILLA CRESCENTS

MAKES ABOUT 60

2¼ cups all-purpose
  flour
⅛ teaspoon salt
½ cup blanched
  almonds, finely
  ground (see
  Almonds)
⅔ cup less 1 table-
  spoon superfine
  sugar
14 tablespoons (1¾
  sticks) unsalted
  butter
2 large egg yolks
1 teaspoon vanilla
  extract
TO FINISH
⅔ cup powdered
  sugar, sifted
2 tablespoons vanilla
  sugar, if available

One of the most famous Viennese butter cookies made especially at Christmas time, *Vanillekipferl* are distinguished by their familiar crescent shape. While tradition says that Viennese bakers were the first to apply this shape to something edible—baking crescent rolls to celebrate victory over the Turks in 1683—this shape was, in fact, a familiar religious symbol and was used in baking as early as the eighth century at the monastery of St. Gallen in Switzerland, where *panis lunatis* (bread of the moon) was made. Regardless of who baked the first crescent, the shape repeats itself throughout the Viennese baking repertoire.

The dough for the *Vanillekipferl* is traditionally made with ground almonds, lots of butter, and a small amount of sugar, since the cookies are dusted at the end with powdered sugar. While they are generally made with vanilla sugar (which can be made by burying a vanilla pod in 1 pound of sugar in a lidded jar for a week), I have used vanilla extract in the dough recipe since it is more readily available. However, if you have made or can buy vanilla sugar, eliminate the vanilla extract and replace with 1 tablespoon vanilla sugar. You can also mix several tablespoons with the powdered sugar in which the cookies are rolled at the end. Store the cookies in an airtight container in the refrigerator for up to 2 weeks or freeze, well wrapped, for up to 3 months.

PREPARING THE DOUGH

Sift the flour and salt together into a large mixing bowl. Add the ground almonds and sugar. Coat the butter with flour from the bowl to make it easier to handle and grate it directly into the flour, using the coarse side of the grater. As the butter is grated, occasionally mix in the flakes with the flour, using your fingertips, before grating more. Using two round-bladed knives, cut the butter into the flour until the texture resembles coarse meal. With your fingertips, quickly rub any larger bits of butter into the flour, letting it fall back into the bowl. Continue until the butter is well blended but not greasy—40 to 60 seconds.

Mix the egg yolks lightly with a fork and combine with the vanilla. Using the fork, mix the egg and vanilla into the flour mixture until well distributed. Then, using your hand, work the dough together into a cohesive mass—no more than 1 minute. Roll the dough into a smooth log (or two logs, if desired) approximately 1½ inches in diameter. Wrap in plastic wrap and chill for several hours.

SHAPING

Cut the cylinder of dough into slices ⅜ inch thick, cutting a few at a time. Form each slice into a log shape, pressing it together with your fingers, then rolling it back and forth on pastry board, slightly tapering the ends, until it is 3 inches long. Bend gently into a crescent shape. Form the crescents carefully so they are uniform in length and size. Place them at least ¾ inch apart on unbuttered baking sheets. Refrigerate for 30 minutes before baking to help them keep their shape, keeping unbaked cookies in the refrigerator while waiting to bake them.

BAKING AND FINISHING

Preheat the oven to 350 degrees F. Bake the cookies one sheet at a time in the center of the oven until pale yellow, approximately 12 to 14 minutes. Don't allow them to brown. Remove the crescents carefully to a rack to cool. While still warm, roll them in powdered sugar which can be mixed with vanilla sugar, if available. Allow to cool completely before storing.

INGWERPLÄTZCHEN
GINGER COOKIES

MAKES ABOUT 60

2 cups less 2
  tablespoons all-
  purpose flour,
  sifted
⅛ teaspoon salt
1 teaspoon baking
  powder
¾ cup superfine
  sugar
¾ cup (1½ sticks)
  unsalted butter,
  well chilled
1 large egg white,
  lightly beaten
1 teaspoon vanilla
  extract
3 tablespoons finely
  minced stem
  ginger preserved
  in syrup, well
  drained, or can-
  died ginger
⅓ cup unblanched
  almonds, finely
  ground (see
  Almonds)
GLAZE
1 egg yolk
1 tablespoon cream
EQUIPMENT
1½-inch fluted or
  plain round
  cookie cutter

My first job after college was working for a re-
search institute in Munich which had a large staff of
Russian immigrants. Thus I was able to combine two
loves, German and Russian, while earning a salary a hair's
breadth above subsistence level. Nevertheless, I always
found an extra mark each week to treat myself to three
delicious cookies (the purchasing power of my mark) from
my favorite baker in the Theatinerstrasse. My addiction
was *Ingwergebäck*—diminutive buttery mouthfuls filled
with moist chunks of ginger. While I never got the Munich recipe, a friend in Frankfurt provided me with this
recipe which produces an almost identical cookie.

PREPARING THE DOUGH

Sift the flour, salt, and baking powder together into a large
mixing bowl. Add the sugar. Coat the butter with flour from the
bowl to make it easier to handle and grate it directly into the
flour, using the coarse blades of a grater. As the butter is grated,
occasionally mix in the flakes with the flour, using your fingertips, before grating more. Add the lightly beaten egg white,
vanilla, minced ginger, and ground almonds. Mix the ingredients together with your hands and knead gently on a lightly
floured board until well mixed. Pat into a flat round and wrap in
plastic wrap. Refrigerate for at least 2 hours or overnight.

BAKING

Butter and flour baking sheets. **Preheat the oven to 350
degrees F.** If the dough has been chilled overnight and is too

firm, hit it several times with your rolling pin to help soften it, then pull it back into a flat round before rolling. On a lightly floured board, roll out the dough ¼ inch thick and cut out with a fluted or plain cookie cutter. Place the cookies 1 inch apart on buttered and floured baking sheets. With a fork, beat the egg yolk together with the cream and brush each cookie with the glaze. Bake one sheet at a time in the middle of the oven until cookies are golden, 12 to 15 minutes. Keep any unbaked cookies in the refrigerator while waiting to bake them. Remove the cookies with a metal spatula to wire racks and allow to cool completely before storing.

NOTE If the dough becomes soft while you are cutting out the cookies, refrigerate each sheet of cookies for 15 to 20 minutes before baking.

CREAMED BUTTER TECHNIQUE

M A S T E R R E C I P E

RÜHRTEIG

Basic Creamed Butter Dough

1 cup (2 sticks)
  unsalted butter,
  softened
⅔ cup superfine sugar
1 teaspoon vanilla
  extract
1 large egg
2½ cups all-purpose
  flour
¼ teaspoon baking
  powder

Using an electric mixer at medium-high speed, cream the butter, sugar, and vanilla together until light and fluffy. Add the egg and continue beating until the mixture is smooth. Sift the flour and baking powder together into the butter mixture. Fold the butter mixture into the flour first with a spoon and then with your hands, kneading the dough together until the mixture is cohesive and smooth. Form the dough into a flat round (or a log if called for in the recipe). Wrap in plastic wrap and chill for at least 2 hours or overnight. Use as directed.

Basic Cut-Out Butter Cookies

This dough can be rolled out ⅛ inch thick on a lightly floured board and used for any small cookies cut out with decorative cutters (decorate before or after baking as desired). They should be baked one sheet at a time in the middle of a **preheated 350-degree F. oven** for approximately 10 to 12 minutes, or until just colored around the edges. When done, remove to a wire rack with a metal spatula to cool before decorating or storing.

DOMINOSTEINE

DOMINOES

The recipe for these charming dominoes comes from a Frankfurt friend who bakes them at Christmas time. They needn't be reserved just for the holidays, however, and they make an appropriate gift at any time of year. Once glazed with a simple lemon/sugar icing, they are dotted and lined with chocolate.

MAKES ABOUT 65

1 recipe Basic Creamed Butter Dough (p. 108)
GLAZE
2½ cups powdered sugar, sifted
4 tablespoons lemon juice
Water as needed
CHOCOLATE ICING:
3 tablespoons reserved glaze
1 ounce semisweet chocolate
EQUIPMENT
Pastry bag with fine writing tip

ROLLING OUT AND CUTTING THE DOUGH

Prepare the dough according to the instructions in the basic recipe, chilling it for at least 2 to 3 hours. Butter and flour baking sheets. On a lightly floured board, roll out the dough ¼ inch thick. Using a ruler, cut the dough into rectangles measuring 2½ × 1 inch. Remove the rectangles to prepared baking sheets, leaving 1 inch between each, and refrigerate for at least 15 minutes, keeping any unbaked cookies in the refrigerator while waiting to bake them. Meanwhile, **preheat the oven to 350 degrees F.**

BAKING

Before baking, trim any ragged edges neatly with a sharp knife. Bake the cookies one sheet at a time in the middle of the oven until just coloring around the edges—approximately 10 to 12 minutes. Remove with a metal spatula to a wire rack to cool.

PREPARING THE GLAZE AND ICING

When all the cookies have been baked, make the glaze. Using a hand-held electric beater on high speed or a rotary beater, gradually beat the powdered sugar into the lemon juice. Beat for 4 minutes. Place the bowl over a pan of hot water and beat for a further 3 or 4 minutes until the glaze has warmed and is smooth. Adjust the consistency of the glaze with a small amount of water or sugar as needed, so that it will brush easily without being too thick but is not so thin that it is transparent. Brush the surface of each cookie evenly with the glaze using a pastry brush. Leave the cookies on a wire rack until the glaze is completely set.

PREPARING THE CHOCOLATE
ICING AND DECORATING

You should have some glaze left over. Keep it in the pan of hot water while preparing your chocolate. Melt the broken pieces of chocolate in the top of a double boiler or in a heatproof soup plate or shallow bowl placed over 2 inches of simmering water. Beat 2 to 3 tablespoons of the reserved icing into the chocolate. If the mixture is too thick, thin with a few drops of vegetable oil. Place the chocolate mixture in a piping bag fitted with a fine writing tip. When the white icing is completely dry, pipe chocolate dots on the cookies to resemble dominoes. Pipe a line of chocolate across the middle of each. Work quickly so the mixture does not dry out in the piping bag. Allow to dry completely before storing.

MANDELSTIFTE

ALMOND STICKS

These delicious German almond cookies are quick to make and offer a nice contrast to other cut-out and shaped cookies because of their unusual rodlike shape and crumbly appearance—the latter produced by a final coating of egg, ground almonds, and sugar.

PREPARING THE DOUGH

Using the electric mixer on medium-high speed, cream the butter, sugar, lemon rind, vanilla, salt, and nutmeg together until light and fluffy. Add the egg and continue beating until the mixture is smooth. Fold in the ground almonds and sifted flour first with a large spoon and then with your hands, kneading the dough together until the mixture is cohesive and smooth. Form the dough into a flat rectangle. Wrap in plastic wrap and chill for 2 hours or until firm.

SHAPING

Butter and flour baking sheets. **Preheat the oven to 350 degrees F.** Divide the dough into four. Roll each piece back and forth into a roll the diameter of a pencil, approximately ⅜ inch. Cut each roll into 1¾-inch lengths.

COATING

For the coating, mix the ground almonds and powdered sugar together on a piece of wax paper. Beat the eggs lightly with a

MAKES ABOUT 45

½ cup (1 stick)
  unsalted butter,
  softened
⅔ cup superfine sugar
Grated rind of 1
  lemon
1 teaspoon vanilla
  extract
1 pinch of salt
1 pinch of nutmeg
1 large egg, lightly
  beaten
⅔ cup unblanched
  almonds, finely
  ground (see
  Almonds)
1 cup less 2
  tablespoons all-
  purpose flour,
  sifted
COATING
¾ cup unblanched
  almonds, finely
  ground (see
  Almonds)
¾ cup powdered
  sugar, sifted
2 large eggs, lightly
  beaten

fork until they are well mixed. Roll each cookie in egg, then coat completely in the almond and sugar mixture. Place on well buttered and floured baking sheets. Refrigerate for at least 30 minutes before baking.

BAKING AND STORING

Bake one sheet at a time in the middle of the oven until they are lightly colored, approximately 15 minutes. Using a metal spatula, remove to wire racks to cool. Store in an airtight tin at room temperature for up to 1 week, or freezing, well wrapped, for up to 3 months.

HEIDESAND
BUTTERY ICEBOX COOKIES

MAKES ABOUT 70

1 cup (2 sticks)
   unsalted butter
½ cup superfine
   sugar
1 pinch salt
1 teaspoon vanilla
   extract
2 cups all-purpose
   flour
1 teaspoon baking
   powder
TO FINISH
1 egg, lightly beaten
½ cup granulated
   sugar

Heidesand—butter cookies made by cutting thin slices from a chilled log of rich dough—is one of the most familiar names in the German cookie repertoire. While these cookies are always made with butter, sugar, and flour, using the same technique, there are several variations: in some the butter is melted and browned first, giving the cookies a nutlike flavor, while in others it is simply creamed. There are also variations in finishing. I prefer to roll the chilled log in coarse sugar before slicing it, instead of leaving it plain. This gives the cookies an attractive brown edge.

The following recipe, using the brown-butter method, is quick to prepare once the butter has cooled.

PREPARING THE BROWN BUTTER

Warm the butter in a heavy saucepan over low heat, skimming off the froth occasionally, until it turns brown, being careful not to let it burn. Pour it immediately through a tea strainer into a bowl and leave at room temperature until it congeals—approximately 1 hour.

NOTE. You can speed up the process by putting it in the refrigerator and stirring it several times. In this case, however, watch it carefully so it doesn't get hard. It should be very soft.

PREPARING THE DOUGH

Beat the butter together with the sugar, salt, and vanilla, using a wooden spoon. Sift the flour and baking powder together over the butter mixture. Fold it in. Work the dough with your hands until you can bring it into a ball and the consistency is smooth. Place the soft dough on a length of wax paper. Wrap the paper around it and roll it back and forth into a log 1½ inches in diameter. Twist the ends of the paper and refrigerate for at least 3 hours or until the dough is very firm.

BEFORE BAKING

Butter and flour baking sheets. **Preheat the oven to 350 degrees F.** Remove the dough from the paper wrapping and brush the surface, excluding the two ends, with lightly beaten egg. Pour the sugar onto a piece of paper. Roll the log in the sugar until it is evenly coated. Cut the log into rounds ¼ inch thick. Place them 1 inch apart on the prepared baking sheets.

BAKING

Bake one sheet at a time in the middle of the oven until the edges are lightly browned and the surface is firm—approximately 10 minutes. The center of the cookies should remain quite pale. Keep any unbaked cookies in the refrigerator while waiting to bake them. Remove to a wire rack to cool before storing.

SPEKULATIUS

PRINTED ALMOND CRISPS

*MAKES ABOUT 70
COOKIES*

*½ cup plus 1
tablespoon un-
salted butter,
softened*
*⅔ cup superfine
sugar—for vari-
ation, you can
substitute ½
cup plus 1 table-
spoon brown
sugar, firmly
packed*
*Grated rind of 1
lemon*
*1 large egg, lightly
beaten*
*⅓ cup blanched
almonds, ground
(see Almonds)*
1 teaspoon cinnamon
*⅛ teaspoon ground
cloves*
*⅛ teaspoon
cardamom*
*1 teaspoon baking
powder*
*2 cups all-purpose
flour*

CONTINUED ON
FACING PAGE

A Christmas specialty from the Rhineland in Germany, these spicy, crisp cookies printed with decorative
wooden molds representing animals and figures are also a
favorite in Holland, where they are called *Speculaas*.
Speculaas are made into figures as tall as 2 feet to be
given to children on St. Nikolaus Day, December 6. The
German version, given below, is smaller—1½ × 2½
inches—and is decorated with a few flaked almonds before baking. If you have wooden molds—there are some
available specially for *Spekulatius*, though any wooden
molds can be used—you will also need a plain pastry
wheel and a small sharp knife to cut out the figures and
any of the nonprinted areas such as spaces between legs
and arms. If you don't have any decorative molds, you can
still make these delicious cookies, simply cutting them
out with cookie cutters in any shape you choose. As do
many spiced cookies, *Spekulatius* get spicier with age. See
advice on storing in the chapter introduction.

PREPARING THE DOUGH

Cream the softened butter together with the sugar and lemon
rind using a wooden spoon. Gradually beat in the lightly beaten
egg and ground almonds. Sift the spices and baking powder
together with the flour onto the butter mixture, beating them
in. Work the mixture with your fingers, gradually drawing it
into a ball. Knead the dough briefly. Pat into a flat round and
wrap well in plastic wrap. Refrigerate for 2 to 3 hours.

PRINTING THE COOKIES AND
CUTTING OUT

Butter and flour baking sheets. If you are using wooden molds, dust them lightly with flour. Break off and flatten a piece of dough approximately the size of a mold. Lightly flour the surface of the dough and press it into the mold. Place a damp cloth under the mold to keep it from sliding. Using a rolling pin (preferably one without rotating handles), roll the piece of dough back and forth on the mold to press it well into the crevices. Stand the mold on end and rap it firmly on the counter. Carefully release the dough from the mold. Brush off the excess flour. Cut out the shape neatly, removing any nonprinted areas with a small knife and place on prepared baking sheet. Continue with the remaining dough in the same fashion. Reknead the scraps, refrigerate and roll out again.

If you are using cookie cutters, roll out the dough ⅛ inch thick on a lightly floured board. Cut out the dough in the desired shapes.

DECORATING AND BAKING

Sprinkle each cookie with 3 or 4 flaked almonds. Place the cookies on the prepared baking sheets. Refrigerate for at least 30 minutes, keeping each tray in the refrigerator until you are ready to bake it. **Preheat the oven to 375 degrees F.** Bake until golden—10 to 15 minutes, depending on the thickness of the cookies. If the cookies are small, remove them with a metal spatula to a wire rack to cool. If they are large, loosen them immediately with a metal spatula and leave them to firm for several minutes on the baking sheet before removing them to a wire rack to cool.

DECORATION
½ cup flaked almonds
EQUIPMENT
Decorative Spekulatius or other wooden molds, or cookie cutters
Plain pastry wheel and small sharp knife if using wooden molds

GEWÜRZNÜSSE

SPICE BALLS

MAKES ABOUT 40

½ cup (1 stick)
  unsalted butter,
  softened
⅓ cup superfine sugar
1 large egg yolk,
  lightly beaten
1 teaspoon vanilla
1 tablespoon honey
⅓ cup mixed candied
  orange and
  lemon peel, finely
  minced
1¼ cups all-purpose
  flour
½ teaspoon baking
  soda
⅛ teaspoon salt
½ teaspoon
  cinnamon
½ teaspoon
  cardamom
¼ teaspoon ground
  cloves
¼ teaspoon pow-
  dered aniseed
¼ teaspoon nutmeg
TO FINISH
1 egg white, lightly
  beaten with a
  whisk or beater
  until frothy
⅔ cup slivered
  blanched almonds,
  coarsely chopped

This recipe for spicy butter cookie balls comes from Switzerland. They are easy to make and especially enticing with their coating of chopped almonds.

PREPARING THE DOUGH

Butter and flour baking sheets. Using a wooden spoon, cream the softened butter together with the sugar. Add the egg yolk gradually, then the vanilla and honey, and beat briefly to blend evenly. Add the finely minced mixed peels. Sift the flour together with the baking soda, salt, and spices onto the butter mixture. Using your fingertips, mix the minced peels with the loose flour to separate the pieces and prevent them from sticking together. Mix the dry ingredients into the butter. Knead the dough until the mixture is well blended. Form the dough into a flat round. Wrap in plastic wrap and refrigerate for 2 to 3 hours or overnight.

SHAPING AND COATING

When well chilled, break off small pieces of dough and form them into balls 1 inch in diameter. Brush them with lightly beaten egg white and roll them in the coarsely chopped slivered almonds. Place them on buttered and floured baking sheets. Refrigerate for 1 hour, keeping unbaked cookies in the refrigerator until you are ready to bake them.

BAKING AND STORING

Preheat the oven to 350 degrees F. Bake one sheet at a time, in the middle of the oven until golden, approximately 15 to 20 minutes. Cool on a wire rack when done. Store in an airtight tin at room temperature for 10 days or freeze, well wrapped, for up to 3 months.

QUARKGEBÄCK
CURD CHEESE COOKIES

Quark, the versatile low-fat curd cheese used for cheesecakes and herb spreads in Germany and Austria, is similar to ricotta cheese in texture, though somewhat finer, with a flavor somewhere between ricotta and yogurt. When mixed with butter, flour, and sugar, it produces these delicious German cookies—moist in texture and prettily glazed with honey and egg. Because *quark* is rarely available in the United States, I have substituted ricotta in the recipe that follows.

Once baked and cooled, the cookies can be stored in an airtight container in the refrigerator for 1 week or frozen for 3 months or more.

PREPARING THE DOUGH

Sift the flour and salt together into a large mixing bowl. Coat the stick of butter with flour from the bowl to make it easier to handle. Grate the butter directly into the flour, using the coarse blades of a grater. As the butter is grated, mix the flakes in with the flour occasionally, using youir fingertips, before grating more. Using 2 round-bladed knives, cut the butter into the flour until the texture resembles coarse meal. Shake the bowl so any larger pieces of butter will rise to the surface. Pick up the flour/butter mixture in your fingertips and quickly rub any larger bits of butter into the flour, letting it fall back into the bowl. Continue until the butter is well blended but not greasy, 40 to 60 seconds. Using a fork, stir in the ricotta, sugar, lemon rind, and vanilla. Knead the dough gently until the ingredients are well mixed. Refrigerate ½ hour. Knead once more and refrigerate another hour or overnight.

MAKES ABOUT 60 COOKIES

1¾ cup all-purpose flour
¼ teaspoon salt
2 sticks (1 cup) unsalted butter
1 cup ricotta cheese
1¼ cups superfine sugar
Grated rind of 1 lemon
1 teaspoon vanilla extract
GLAZE
1 egg, lightly beaten
2 teaspoons honey
1 teaspoon water
EQUIPMENT
Plain 1½-inch cookie cutter

BEFORE BAKING

Butter and flour baking sheets. **Preheat the oven to 375 degrees F.** On a lightly floured board, roll out the dough ⅜ inch thick. Cut into 1½-inch rounds with a plain cookie cutter. Reknead the scraps, refrigerating them if necessary, before rolling them out again.

Mix the egg, honey, and water together with a fork. Brush the top of each cookie with the glaze. Place the cookies 1 inch apart on the prepared baking sheets. Refrigerate any unbaked cookies until they are baked.

BAKING

Bake one sheet at a time in the middle of a preheated oven until golden, about 15 to 20 minutes.

Remove the sheet from the oven and immediately loosen the bottom of each cookie with a metal spatula. Leave them on the baking sheet for 1 minute to firm before transferring them to wire racks to finish cooling.

FLORENTINER

FLORENTINES

MAKES ABOUT 25

COOKIE
⅔ *cup superfine sugar*
1 *tablespoon un-*
   salted butter
⅓ *cup whipping cream*

CONTINUED ON
FACING PAGE

Found in bakeries in all the German-speaking countries—obviously borrowed from their southern neighbors—these delicious almond and candied fruit crisps are first baked, then coated underneath with chocolate. Many bakeries make both small (1¼-inch) and large (3-to-5-inch) versions, the former being especially suitable for serving with after-dinner coffee. They keep for four to five days if stored in an airtight container in a cool place.

However, it is best not to keep them in the refrigerator as this causes them to lose their crisp texture.

PREPARING THE BATTER

Butter and flour baking sheets. **Preheat the oven to 400 degrees F.** Mix the sugar, butter, cream, and flour together in a saucepan. Stir over a moderate heat until the mixture comes to a boil. Add the remaining cookie ingredients and continue cooking over a low heat until the mixture thickens, approximately 3 minutes. Spoon in small mounds—1 scant tablespoon—onto a buttered and floured baking sheet, leaving plenty of room for the cookies to expand. Use the back of a spoon dipped in hot water to smooth the mixture.

BAKING

Bake in the upper part of the oven until the cookies have caramelized and are golden. Loosen them immediately with a metal spatula. Leave on the baking sheet for several minutes before removing to a wire rack to cool.

PREPARING THE CHOCOLATE GLAZE AND FINISHING

When the cookies are crisp and firm, prepare the glaze. Melt the broken chocolate pieces with the butter in a double boiler or in a heatproof soup plate or shallow bowl placed over a pan filled with 2 inches of simmering water. Stir occasionally. When the chocolate has melted, remove from the pan. Stir in the cocoa powder. The mixture should be thin enough to spread evenly. Adjust with a small amount of vegetable oil if it is too thick, or with cocoa powder if it is too thin. Keep the container of chocolate in a pan of hot water to prevent it from becoming too thick. Turn the cookies upside down. Using a pastry brush, coat the bottoms evenly with the chocolate. When the chocolate is almost cool, use the prongs of a fork to mark wavy or straight lines on the chocolate—the traditional pattern. Allow the chocolate on the cookies to finish setting in a cool place, but not the refrigerator.

*¼ cup all-purpose
  flour, sifted
⅔ cup blanched
  almonds, slivered
⅔ cup mixed candied
  orange and
  lemon peel, finely
  minced*
CHOCOLATE GLAZE
*3½ ounces semi-
  sweet chocolate,
  broken in pieces
1 tablespoon butter
2 teaspoons cocoa
  powder
Vegetable oil, if
  needed*

WHISKED-EGG COOKIES AND CONFECTIONS EIERSCHAUM—UND EIWEISSGEBÄCK

This chapter covers the traditional repertoire of butterless cookies and confections made with eggs and/or flour and ground nuts. Although there are a few exceptions, most of these doughs are made without fat and employ techniques and handling quite different from those found in the *Lebkuchen* and Butter Cookie chapters. In many of the recipes, the dough is shaped or printed and must then dry out overnight, in which case the finished product won't be ready until the following day. While the egg-white cookies and confections in this chapter, such as macaroons and meringues, are well known to Americans, the butterless whole-egg cookies so popular in the German-speaking countries are relatively undiscovered.

WHOLE-EGG COOKIES

In the case of whole-egg doughs, the whisked-egg method (used also for sponge cakes) is generally used. After the eggs and sugar are beaten together over heat to increase their volume and break down the sugar, flour and baking powder are added. The mixture is then pulled together into a ball of dough or left in a batter to make small cakes. Cookies made with this dough are first shaped, or rolled out and printed with decorative molds, then left on baking sheets to dry out overnight. The drying is important. It ensures that the cookies keep their shape when baked, that no fissures develop due to moisture escaping during baking, and that the cookies rise evenly and develop the characteristic *Fuss* (foot) or base, which is darker and grainier than the smooth surface.

Two of the most beautiful cookies from the German tradition are found in this chapter: printed *Springerle* and leaf-shaped *Chräbeli*. The smooth, pristine whiteness of these cookies give them an especially regal character.

Another interesting printed cookie is the Swiss *Wygützli*, which makes lovely Christmas tree decorations. Flavored with nutmeg and cloves, this whole-egg cookie is unusual in that it is colored with red wine and, traditionally, powdered sandalwood—the natural red spice coloring found exclusively in old Swiss recipes, which I have replaced with red food coloring.

Butterless whole-egg cookies have especially good keeping properties and can be stored for at least two or three months in an airtight tin at room temperature. These cookies have a tendency to become quite hard, however, and can be softened in one of two ways: either leave the tin open in a steamy kitchen, or place a slice of raw apple or potato in the closed tin for a few days.

EGG-WHITE COOKIES AND CONFECTIONS

The egg-white cookie recipes are a representative selection of meringues (*Baisers*), macaroons (*Makronen*) and ground nut confections, including marzipan. Generally flourless, they contain a large proportion of sugar, which gives body to the egg whites.

Cinnamon Stars (*Zimtsterne*) and the many forms of marzipan given to children on St. Nikolaus Day, December 6, are part of the traditional Christmas repertoire; other cookies and confections in this group are eaten at Christmas and throughout the year.

Meringues and macaroons, unless coated with chocolate, keep well for two or three months in an airtight tin at room temperature. Baked marzipan, on the other hand, has a tendency to get hard and dry in a short period of time. Store it in an airtight container in the refrigerator to help keep it fresh.

WHISKED-EGG COOKIES

MASTER TECHNIQUE

BASIC WHISKED-EGG TECHNIQUE

For heating the eggs and sugar, use a crockery or glass mixing bowl that will rest on the rim of a saucepan with its base well above the bottom of the pan which has been filled with several inches of simmering water. Neither stainless steel nor plastic mixing bowls are satisfactory for this purpose: stainless steel conducts the heat too rapidly, "cooking" the egg mixture on the sides of the bowl, and gives a slightly gray tinge to the eggs, while plastic does not conduct heat sufficiently to accelerate the thickening process.

Arrange a crockery or glassing mixing bowl over a saucepan of simmering water. Have ready the ingredients for the recipe you have chosen. Once the water is simmering, remove the saucepan from the heat. Put the eggs and sugar in the bowl and, with an electric hand mixer or whisk, beat the mixture at high speed until it is thick and mousselike—about 4 minutes. To test the consistency, use the beater to lift a little of the mixture and trail the shape of the letter M over the mixture in the bowl. If the shape of the letter holds for 3 seconds, the mixture is sufficiently beaten. If the shape dissolves, beat longer, then test again.

Remove the bowl from the pan of water when ready and continue to beat for a further 3 minutes. Continue with the instructions in the recipe.

SPRINGERLE
PRINTED ANISE COOKIES

MAKES ABOUT 38
1¾-INCH
COOKIES

2 large eggs
1⅓ cups superfine
sugar
1 tablespoon light
rum, or as needed
1¾ cups plus 3
tablespoons all-
purpose flour, or
more if needed
1 teaspoon baking
powder
1 tablespoon pow-
dered aniseed
EQUIPMENT
Decorative wooden
molds in any
shape or size, or
decorative wooden
rolling pin

The brittle, eggshell-white, whisked-egg cookie called *Springerle*, which originated in Swabia in the fifteenth century, is traditionally flavored with anise—whole or powdered—and printed with wooden molds as *Lebkuchen* are. In the ancient German duchy of Franconia (Franken), the same cookie or similar versions go by different names: *Würzburger* marzipan from Würzburg (not, as you might expect, made of almond paste); *Reiterle* from Rothenburg ob der Tauber (the same dough, printed with old wooden molds depicting mounted riders or grand ladies, tradition- ally given to children on St. Nikolaus Day, December 6); and *Eierzucker* from Nürnberg, the same dough, flavored with the herbal liqueur arrack and made with traditional molds. In Switzerland, *Springerle* often go by the name of *Anisbroetli.*

There are several theories about the origin of the name *Springerle*: one is that it could mean a small jumping horse, referring to the many molds carved with a horse or mounted rider. However, perhaps the simplest explanation is that the cookies, when baked, do in fact "spring" or rise to double or triple their height, forming the characteristic *Fuss* (foot), or base, which is of a slightly more grainy consistency, and smooth, eggshell-white "heads."

Now a favorite at Christmas time, these cookies were originally baked for other celebrations as well, as attested to by old molds featuring Easter lambs, rabbits, and religious motifs depicting various holidays.

At the beginning of the nineteenth century, it was the fashion to paint every detail of the relief in different colors. Though this is rarely done today, the baker Edmund Prezel, in Rothenburg ob der Tauber, is an exception, stamping his *Springerle* and *Eierzucker* with 200-year-old molds and painting many of the cookies after they are baked.

While few home recipes for *Springerle* or *Eierzucker* contain a commercial leavening agent, those purchased from bakeries all contain a small amount, generally of ammonium bicarbonate (ABC-Trieb). So, baked at home, the cookies barely rise and are never as attractive as their purchased counterparts. Therefore I have followed the baker's example and added a small amount of baking powder to the recipe.

It is important to follow the instructions and allow the cookies to dry out overnight (or even longer if it is extremely humid). This sets the pattern which has been printed. If the cookies are not sufficiently dried, steam will escape through the surface and cause fissures.

It has been my experience that this is not everyone's favorite cookie if they haven't grown up with it. However, few people will deny that this is one of the most aesthetically pleasing cookies in the traditional repertoire. The whisked-egg dough, more than *Lebkuchen* or butter cookie doughs, picks up every detail of the molds that are pressed into it. Provided the cookies are sufficiently dried, they lose none of this detail in baking. The combination of a beautifully ornate picture embossed on a pristine, creamy-white cookie is truly impressive. I have never worried whether or not anyone would want to eat them: they make beautiful presents to hang on the wall or Christmas tree (with a tiny hole pierced in the top before baking).

As for transforming them to suit other tastes, I once presented an eccentric Irish friend in London with an elaborate mounted knight bought from Herr Prezel's shop in Rothenburg. My friend sampled the hard cookie without great pleasure, then whisked it away to the kitchen. A few minutes later, he returned with the now rather soggy knight on a plate—well soaked in sherry, the solution used in the British Isles for revitalizing dried sponge cake. Within minutes, it had disappeared. While this would not be to everyone's taste, the story illustrates that any resourceful recipient of one of these beautiful cookies will no doubt find a way of adapting it to his or her palate.

THE DAY BEFORE
PREPARING THE DOUGH

Whisk the eggs and sugar together in a mixing bowl over steaming water as in the instructions for Basic Whisked-Egg Technique (page 00). Add the rum and beat for a further 30 seconds.

Sift the flour and baking powder together with the powdered aniseed onto the egg mixture and blend well with a spoon. Remove the dough to a lightly floured board and knead it until smooth and cohesive—about 3 minutes. The dough should be quite soft. However, if it is sticky, add a small amount of flour, 1 tablespoon at a time, until the dough can be handled. If it seems too dry and liable to crack when rolled out, knead in an additional teaspoonful of rum until the dough is soft but not sticky. Wrap the dough tightly in plastic wrap and leave at room temperature for 1 hour before using.

ROLLING OUT, PRINTING, AND CUTTING

Butter and flour baking sheets. Roll out the dough ¼ inch thick on a lightly floured board. Dust the wooden molds (or decorative wooden rolling pin) and the dough itself with flour, brushing off the excess. Press the molds or rolling pin firmly into the dough, then lift off carefully. Cut the cookies apart with a sharp knife or a plain pastry wheel.

If the detail on the molds is quite deep, it will be necessary first to cut out an oval or rectangle of dough approximately the same size as the mold. After dusting the mold and dough with flour, press the thin piece of dough well into the mold to pick up all the detail. Tap the mold firmly on the table several times to release the dough. Then use a sharp knife or plain pastry wheel to cut out the shape neatly.

If there is any flour left on the cookies once they have been molded, brush it off with a dry pastry brush. Place the cookies 1 inch apart on the prepared baking sheets. Leave to dry out, uncovered, at room temperature for 15 to 24 hours.

THE FOLLOWING DAY
BAKING AND STORING

Preheat the oven to 300 degrees F. Bake one sheet at a time, in the lower third of the oven, with the handle of a wooden spoon propped inside the oven door to keep it slightly ajar. Bake the cookies until firm, risen, and barely eggshell in color—about 20 to 25 minutes. Do not allow them to color.

Cool completely on a rack before storing. Store in an airtight tin at room temperature for up to three months.

CHRÄBELI

LEAF-SHAPED ANISE COOKIES

A specialty from Baden in Switzerland, traditionally baked at Christmas time, these attractive white cookies flavored with anise are first rolled into short, narrow logs, then cut in three places and curved to produce the characteristic fanned leaf shape. They use the same dough and method as Springerle.

THE DAY BEFORE

MAKES ABOUT 38

PREPARING THE DOUGH

Prepare the *Springerle* dough. Roll it into a log 1½ inches in diameter while it is still warm. Wrap in plastic wrap and allow to rest at room temperature for 1 hour.

SHAPING AND DRYING THE COOKIES

Butter and flour several baking sheets and set them aside. Slice the log into ⅓-inch rounds. Press each round into a log shape, then roll it back and forth on the board until it is 3 inches long and approximately ⅝ inch in diameter. Cut 3 short diagonal gashes on one side of each log, about halfway into the log. Bend the logs in a semicircle so that the "leaves" fan out. (The gashes will be on the outside.) Place them on the prepared baking sheets about 1 inch apart, and allow to dry out, uncovered, at room temperature for 15 to 24 hours.

THE FOLLOWING DAY

BAKING

Preheat the oven to 300 degrees F. Bake one sheet at a time in the lower third of the oven. Insert the handle of a wooden spoon inside the oven door to keep it slightly ajar. If the cookies start to color or crack, lower the oven temperature. They should be a pale eggshell color when done, firm, and well risen with the characteristic *Fuss* (foot), a grainy-textured base. Baking time will be approximately 20 to 30 minutes. Remove to wire racks. When cooled, they can be stored in an airtight tin for up to three months.

WYGÜTZLI
PRINTED RED CHRISTMAS COOKIES

Switzerland (where *Gützli* or *Gützle* means cookies, especially those baked at Christmas) is unique in the German-speaking countries in using an unusual spice, powdered sandalwood. It does have a delicate flavor, but it is favored particularly for the natural red color it imparts to baked goods. Because powdered sandalwood is not readily available, I have substituted red food coloring in this old family recipe. The cookies are further colored by red wine. A hard cookie made like *Springerle*, *Wygützli* also make unusual Christmas decorations, with a hole pierced in the top of each before baking.

For printing, you will need decorative wooden molds or a carved rolling pin. Once printed, the cookies must be dried overnight before baking. After cooling, they can be stored in an airtight container at room temperature for up to three months.

THE DAY BEFORE
PREPARING THE DOUGH

Whisk the eggs and sugar together in a mixing bowl over steaming water as in the instructions for Basic Whisked-Egg Technique (p. 123). Add the warmed red wine, kirsch (or lemon juice), food coloring, and lemon rind and beat for a further 30 seconds, adding more food coloring if necessary to produce a light red mixture. Sift the flour together with the baking powder, nutmeg, cloves, and salt onto waxed paper. Using a large metal spoon, fold the dry ingredients into the egg mixture and knead with your hands until the mixture holds together. Remove the dough to a lightly floured board and knead for another

*MAKES ABOUT 50
1¾-INCH
COOKIES*

2 large eggs
*2 cups superfine
sugar*
*¼ cup dry red wine,
slightly warmed*
*1 tablespoon kirsch
(or substitute
lemon juice)*
*3–4 drops red food
coloring*
*Grated rind of 1
lemon*
*3 cups less 3
tablespoons all-
purpose flour*
*1 teaspoon baking
powder*
¼ teaspoon nutmeg
*¼ teaspoon ground
cloves*
Pinch of salt
EQUIPMENT
*Carved wooden molds
or carved rolling
pin*

minute. The dough should be quite soft but not sticky. If it is, add a small amount of flour, 1 tablespoon at a time, until the dough can be handled. If it seems too dry and liable to crack when rolled out, knead in an additional teaspoonful of kirsch or lemon juice, or as much as is needed, until the dough is soft but not sticky. Wrap the dough tightly in plastic wrap and leave at room temperature for 1 hour before using.

ROLLING OUT, PRINTING, AND CUTTING

Butter and flour baking sheets. Roll out the dough ¼ inch thick on a lightly floured board. Dust the wooden molds or carved wooden rolling pin and the dough itself with the flour, brushing off the excess. Press the molds or rolling pin firmly into the dough, then lift off carefully. Cut the cookies apart with a sharp knife or a plain pastry wheel.

NOTE If the detail on the molds is quite deep, it will be necessary first to cut out an oval or rectangle of dough approximately the same size as the mold. After dusting the mold and dough with flour, press the thin piece of dough well into the mold to pick up all the detail. Tap the mold firmly on the counter several times to release the dough. Then use a sharp knife or plain pastry wheel to cut out the shape neatly.

If there is any flour left on the cookies once they have been printed, brush it off with a dry pastry brush. Place the cookies 1 inch apart on buttered and floured baking sheets. Leave uncovered to dry out, at room temperature for 15 to 24 hours. If using for Christmas ornaments, make a hole with a skewer in the top of each cookie before they are left to dry.

The Following Day
BAKING

Preheat the oven to 300 degrees F. Bake one sheet at a time in the lower third of the oven, with the handle of a wooden spoon propped inside the oven door to keep it slightly ajar. Bake the cookies until firm, risen, and barely colored—about 20 to 25 minutes. Cool the cookies completely on a rack before storing in an airtight tin.

POMERANZENNÜSSE OR POMERANZENBRÖTCHEN

ORANGE NUTS

Many cookie recipes from the traditional German Christmas repertoire call for *Pomeranzenschale*—the rind of Seville oranges (the kind used for marmalade) which was both grated and candied, producing a strong bitter orange flavor. Because candied orange peel, not specifically from Seville oranges, is now readily available throughout the year, contemporary recipes no longer specify Seville oranges. *Pomeranzen*, however, continues to be used in the name of some of these old-fashioned cookies.

THE DAY BEFORE
PREPARING THE DOUGH

Whisk the eggs and sugar together in a mixing bowl over steaming water as in the instructions for Basic Whisked-Egg Technique (p. 123). Add the finely minced candied orange peel and grated lemon rind, mixing them in well to break up any clumps. Sift the flour and baking powder together onto the mixture and blend together well.

Remove the dough to a lightly floured board and knead it until smooth and cohesive—about 3 minutes. The dough should be quite soft. If it is sticky, however, add a small amount of flour, a tablespoon at a time, until the dough can be handled. If you have added too much flour and the dough seems dry and liable to crack when rolled out, knead in a teaspoonful of water (or rum), or as much as is needed, until the dough is soft but not sticky.

MAKES ABOUT 48 COOKIES

3 large eggs, lightly beaten
1⅓ cups superfine sugar
1⅓ cups candied orange peel, finely minced
Grated rind of 1 lemon
2 cups all-purpose flour, plus more as needed
1 teaspoon baking powder

SHAPING THE DOUGH

Butter and flour baking sheets. Form the dough into balls 1 inch in diameter, rolling them under your palm on a pastry board. Arrange them 1 inch apart on the prepared sheets. Leave them uncovered to dry at room temperature for 15 to 24 hours.

THE FOLLOWING DAY
BAKING

Preheat the oven to 300 degrees F. Bake in the middle of the oven until they have risen and colored lightly—approximately 20 to 25 minutes. They should still be moist inside but firm on the outside. Transfer to racks to cool before storing.

PFEFFERNÜSSE

SPICE NUTS

For notes on the origins and storing of *Pfeffernüsse*, see p. 59, *Braunschweiger Pfeffernüsse*, where I follow with a traditional recipe made using the *Lebkuchen* technique. Although both recipes produce a firm, spicy cookie, the whisked-egg method employed in the following recipe produces a lighter cookie than that found in the *Lebkuchen* chapter.

THE DAY BEFORE
PREPARING THE DOUGH

Whisk the eggs and sugar together in a mixing bowl over steaming water as in the instructions for Basic Whisked-Egg Technique (p. 123). Add the rum and beat for a few seconds longer. Sift the spices, baking powder, and flour together onto the egg mixture. Add the ground almonds and finely minced mixed peels. Mix well with a spoon. Remove the dough to a lightly floured board and knead it until smooth and cohesive—about 3 minutes. The dough should be quite soft. If it is sticky, however, add a small amount of flour, 1 tablespoon at a time, until the dough can be handled. If you have added too much flour and the dough seems too dry and liable to crack when rolled out, knead in an additional teaspoonful of rum, or as much as is needed, until the dough is soft but not sticky.

SHAPING THE DOUGH

Form the dough into balls 1 inch in diameter, rolling them under your palm on a pastry board. Arrange them 1 inch apart on buttered and floured baking sheets. Leave them uncovered to dry out for 15 to 24 hours.

MAKES ABOUT 40

2 *large eggs*
1⅓ *cups superfine sugar*
1 *tablespoon rum, or as needed*
1 *tablespoon cinnamon*
¼ *teaspoon ground cloves*
¼ *teaspoon nutmeg*
¼ *teaspoon ginger*
1 *teaspoon baking powder*
1½ *cups plus 2 tablespoons all-purpose flour*
½ *cup unblanched almonds, finely ground (see Almonds)*
1 *tablespoon candied orange and lemon peel, finely minced*
ICING
1½ *cups powdered sugar, sifted*
3 *tablespoons lemon juice*

The Following Day
BAKING

Preheat the oven to 375 degrees F. Bake, one sheet at a time, in the center of the oven until firm and light brown in color—approximately 12 to 14 minutes. During the baking, the balls will burst slightly as moisture escapes from the center, forming cracked patterns on the surface. Transfer them to racks to cool.

PREPARING THE ICING

For the icing, gradually beat the powdered sugar into the lemon juice and beat for 8 to 10 minutes until the sugar has dissolved completely. The icing should be thin enough to brush on with a pastry brush. If it is too thin or too thick, adjust the consistency with more sugar or lemon juice.

FINISHING AND STORING

While the *Pfeffernüsse* are still warm, brush them evenly with the icing. If they have cooled completely, reheat them in the oven for 2 or 3 minutes. Allow the icing to set firmly before storing. Store in an airtight tin at room temperature for up to three months.

ZITRONENPLÄTZCHEN
LEMON SPONGE COOKIES

In this Swiss recipe, a light sponge mixture is spooned in nut-sized mounds that are sprinkled with flaked almonds and baked. An especially delicious accompaniment to any cream or ice cream dessert, these cookies are quick to make and keep well in an airtight tin at room temperature for several months. You will need 1 very large or 2 medium-sized baking sheets. As these cookies are more moist than those in the preceding recipes (more like sponge batter), they should all be baked at once after they are shaped to keep them from deflating. If you have only one oven and the entire batch of cookies won't fit on one rack at the same time, bake one sheet on a higher rack and switch their positions halfway through the baking.

MAKES ABOUT 40

2 large eggs
½ cup superfine sugar
Grated rind of 1 lemon
2 tablespoons lemon juice
1 cup all-purpose flour, sifted
¼ cup flaked almonds, coarsely chopped

PREPARING THE DOUGH

Preheat the oven to 350 degrees F.
Butter and flour 1 very large or 2 medium-sized baking sheets, knocking off the excess flour. Set aside.

Whisk the eggs, sugar, and lemon rind together in a mixing bowl over steaming water as in the instructions for Basic Whisked-Egg Technique (p. 123). Add the lemon juice and beat for another 30 seconds. Add the sifted flour and with a metal spoon carefully fold it in until no pockets of flour remain.

BEFORE BAKING

Scoop a heaping teaspoonful of batter and use a second spoon to ease the batter off in a little mound on the prepared baking sheet. Work as quickly as you can, leaving at least 1½ inches between cookies. When all the cookies are spooned out, tap the baking sheet firmly several times on a counter to flatten the cookies slightly. Sprinkle the top of each with the chopped flaked almonds.

BAKING

Bake them all at one time in the middle of the preheated oven until they are pale yellow and can be loosened easily with a metal spatula from the baking sheet, approximately 13 minutes. Remove from the oven and loosen them all immediately with a spatula, leaving them on the baking sheet for several minutes before removing them to wire racks to cool. When cool, store in an airtight tin at room temperature.

WHISKED-EGG-WHITE COOKIES

MASTER TECHNIQUE

BASIC MERINGUE TECHNIQUE

Snowy plain white meringues—as well as those lightly colored and flavored—are a favorite year-round treat in all German-speaking countries. They are especially popular at Christmas, when they are piped in small wreaths or arabesques and hung on the tree or served with coffee and a selection of other Christmas goodies.

SWISS MERINGUE

Various techniques are used in making meringues. In one method, approximately two thirds of the sugar—preferably superfine sugar, which dissolves quickly—is gradually beaten into egg whites that have been beaten "half stiff," with the remainder of the sugar carefully folded in at the end. This method produces a very light, delicate meringue. In the other, similar method, all the sugar is gradually beaten into the "half stiff" egg whites, producing a slightly stiffer meringue. Both these methods produce what are known as Swiss meringues.

Italian Meringue

Italian meringues, on the other hand, are warmed first before baking. There are two basic techniques for warming: either a hot sugar syrup is beaten into stiffly beaten egg whites (which may or may not have had some of the sugar beaten in), or a stiffly beaten meringue mixture, with all the sugar already added, is beaten in a bowl over a pan of simmering water until warm, then beaten off the heat until cool. This method produces the stiffest meringue, which is especially suitable for dry nut- or fruit-filled meringues that will hold a perfect shape, whether piped or spooned.

Depending on the texture required, both the Swiss and Italian methods are employed in the traditional recipes that follow.

Baking Sheets

For both plain and nut-filled meringues or macaroons, I have found one method of preparing baking sheets or liners to be superior. If you have a large plain wood chopping or pastry board, wrap it twice with aluminum foil. Put a small dab of the meringue mixture in each corner and cover the board with a piece of nonstick baking or parchment paper. Place the board on a baking sheet so it isn't in direct contact with the oven rack. Pipe or spoon your mixture onto the paper and proceed according to recipe directions. By using a board you protect the meringue mixture from bottom heat, which not only keeps the finished product perfectly white but also keeps heat from building up inside, producing cracks in the meringue and/or spreading. If you don't have a suitable board, then simply use parchment or nonstick baking paper on a baking sheet. Buttered aluminum foil can be used for plain and stiff nut-filled meringues. Avoid using black metal baking sheets—they conduct the heat too rapidly through the bottom of the meringues. If you use the lined baking sheet method, as opposed to the lined wooden board, and your meringues stick slightly to the paper when they are done, simply turn the entire sheet of paper, with meringues still attached, upside down on the baking sheet. Moisten the paper with water. Return the meringues to the oven for a few minutes. The paper should peel off easily.

BAKING TIPS

In recipes employing the Swiss technique, the meringues should all be baked at one time once they are shaped, to keep them from deflating and to maintain uniform size. If you do not have enough oven space to bake them all on the same rack, you will have to switch the position of the baking sheets once during baking. This isn't the ideal solution, as the upper baking sheet reflects added heat to the meringues below. However, it's the only solution under the circumstances. I have baked meringues in this way on numerous occasions without difficulty.

To keep them from coloring, meringues should be baked in the bottom third of the oven at a very low heat (225 degrees F.) Their color is meant to be no deeper than eggshell. If you find your oven seems a little too warm—if they are cracking before they are done or coloring—insert the handle of a wooden spoon inside the door to keep it slightly ajar and prevent the heat from building up too much. Alternatively, turn the oven down or off for a period of time. For plain meringues to dry out as much as possible, leave them in the turned-off oven overnight once they have baked. This will keep them dry even with prolonged storage.

Storage

Meringues without chocolate coating keep well for two or three months in an airtight jar or tin at room temperature. They should not be refrigerated or frozen, as this causes them to lose their dry, crisp texture.

In Switzerland, plain meringue is frequently seen piped in 3½-to-4-inch arabesques which, when baked, are placed on their sides in pairs, flat bottoms facing in, and are used to sandwich vanilla ice cream accompanied by a dollop of whipped cream (meringues glacées) or, more simply, to sandwich whipped cream piped in a decorative frill.

The basic recipe that follows can be used for large arabesques, nests (to hold a cream filling or berries and ice cream), wreaths for Christmas-tree ornaments, or any other shape you wish.

MERINGUES
BASIC RECIPE

Preheat the oven to 225 degrees F. Line a large board or baking sheet as described on p. 138. Using an electric mixer, beat the egg whites in a non-aluminum mixing bowl (aluminum will turn them gray) with a pinch of salt. Begin with the mixer on a low speed. When the egg whites are foamy, increase the speed to moderately fast, add the cream of tartar, and beat until the egg whites stand in soft peaks. They should hold their shape but not be dry. Add the sugar by the tablespoonful, beating 20 seconds between each addition, until it is used up. Beat for a further 2 minutes or longer, until the meringue is thick and glossy. Use in one of the following shapes.

MAKES ABOUT 28 SMALL OR 6 TO 8 LARGE MERINGUES

3 large egg whites, at room temperature
Pinch of salt
Pinch of cream of tartar
1 cup superfine sugar

ARABESKEN

MERINGUE ARABESQUES

For large meringue arabesques (to be sandwiched with ice cream or plain whipped cream), use a piping bag fitted with a large star tip. An arabesque is made by piping a closed S-shape figure. Pipe 3½-to-4-inches arabesques on the prepared baking sheet or board, leaving a 1¼-inch space between them. Bake in the lower third of the oven for 1¾ to 2 hours, or until the meringues are completely dry and remove easily from the paper. Turn off the oven, place the meringues back on the baking sheet, and return to oven to dry out overnight. Use immediately or store in an airtight container.

BAISERBAUMBEHANG

MERINGUE CHRISTMAS TREE WREATH ORNAMENTS

Using the basic meringue recipe, 2½-inch wreaths can be made. They can be plain white or colored. For cocoa-colored wreaths, beat 3 to 4 teaspoons of cocoa powder into the meringue mixture just before folding in the final addition of sugar. For pale pink or pale green, beat several drops of red or green food coloring into the meringue before folding in the final addition of sugar.

Pipe the meringues in 2½-inch wreaths on a board or baking sheet lined with parchment or nonstick baking paper (see Equipment) using a piping bag fitted with a medium star tip. If desired, the wreaths can be decorated with a small rosette of meringue and then left plain; or they can be sprinkled with granulated sugar and silver balls; or garnished with a sliver of candied cherry.

Bake for 1 to 1¼ hours, or until the meringues are dry and remove easily from the paper. Turn off the oven, place the meringues back on the baking sheet, and return to oven to dry out overnight. Use a narrow ribbon or a piece of yarn or cord to suspend the wreaths from the tree branches.

If you don't feel like using these for ornaments, they are of course equally nice to eat.

DATTELMAKRONEN

DATE MACAROONS

Chopped dates and ground almonds are combined with a meringue mixture in this German recipe to produce date-shaped cookies glazed with chocolate—a delicious treat with after-dinner coffee or as part of your Christmas baking selection.

PREPARING THE MERINGUE MIXTURE

Preheat the oven to 275 degrees F. Line a large board or baking sheet as described. Using an electric mixer, beat the egg whites in a non-aluminum mixing bowl with a pinch of salt. Begin with the mixer on a low speed. When the egg whites are foamy, increase the speed to medium, add the cream of tartar, and beat until the egg whites stand in soft peaks. They should hold their shape but not be dry. Add the sugar by the tablespoonful, beating 20 seconds between each addition until it is used up. Beat for a further 2 minutes or longer, until the meringue is thick and glossy. Beat in the grated lemon rind and lemon juice for several seconds. Using a large metal spoon, carefully fold in the dates and ground almonds until well mixed.

SHAPING AND BAKING

Spoon the mixture onto the prepared board or baking sheets in 2-inch lengths. Moisten your finger lightly with water and smooth the mixture into a date shape. Bake all of the dates at once in the bottom third of the oven until firm and lightly colored—approximately 1 hour. Remove carefully to a wire rack to cool.

GLAZING

For the chocolate glaze, heat the broken chocolate and vegetable oil in the top of a double boiler or in a heatproof soup plate

MAKES ABOUT 30

2 large egg whites at room temperature
Pinch of salt
½ cup superfine sugar
Pinch of cream of tartar
Grated rind of 1 lemon
Juice of ½ lemon
⅔ cup finely chopped pitted dates
⅓ cup blanched almonds, finely ground
CHOCOLATE GLAZE
3½ ounces semi-sweet chocolate, broken in pieces
1 teaspoon vegetable oil

or shallow bowl over a saucepan filled with 2 inches of simmering water. Stir occasionally until the chocolate is melted. Brush each cooled date completely with chocolate. If the chocolate is too thick, add a few more drops of oil. Allow to set completely before storing in an airtight tin in a cool place for up to ten days.

ZIMTSTERNE

CINNAMON STARS

MAKES ABOUT 35
⅜-INCH-THICK
STARS, 1½
INCHES IN
DIAMETER

2 cups finely ground
  unblanched al-
  monds, plus ½
  cup more as
  needed
1½ tablespoons
  cinnamon
4 large egg whites
4 cups powdered
  sugar, sifted
1 tablespoon kirsch,
  or more as
  needed (lemon
  juice can be
  substituted)

CONTINUED ON
FACING PAGE

White-glazed cinnamon stars appear in all the German-speaking countries at Christmas time. Made from a flourless dough—a combination of ground almonds, sugar, egg white, and cinnamon—they are flavored in Switzerland with kirsch, and in other places often with lemon juice. They vary in size and thickness in different cities.

Household cookbooks always instruct you to cut out the cookies first and then apply the traditional meringue glaze. When they are made in this manner, however, the glaze is rarely even. I finally learned a secret from a Basel baker: first brush the meringue glaze over the entire surface of the rolled-out dough, then cut out the cookies with a star-shaped cutter dipped in hot water to make a clean, even cut.

I am accustomed to thick stars (about ⅜ inch) as they are made in Switzerland. However, the dough can also be rolled out thinner, to approximately ¼ inch, thus increasing your yield of cookies.

Zimtsterne improve with age and can be stored in an airtight tin at room temperature for up to three months.

NOTE Traditionally, a small star cutter is used. If your cutter is more than 1½ inches, cut a small circle out of the center of each star using an aspic cutter or a thimble so that the cookies are not overly moist in the center and fall apart.

*Granulated sugar,
for rolling out*
EQUIPMENT
*1½-inch 5- or
6-point star
cookie cutter*

PREPARING THE DOUGH AND GLAZE

Butter and flour several baking sheets and set them aside.

Combine the 2 cups of ground almonds with the cinnamon in a mixing bowl. Using an electric mixer, beat the egg whites until frothy and slightly thickened. Beat the powdered sugar into egg whites, ½ cup at a time, beating well between each addition. When all the sugar has been added, beat the mixture for a further 5 minutes.

Remove approximately two thirds of the egg-white mixture and blend it together with the ground almonds. Cover the remaining egg-white mixture with a clean, damp cloth. Add the kirsch to the almond mixture and use your hand to blend all the ingredients together to form a cohesive mass. Allow the mixture to rest for 10 minutes. To test the consistency, try rolling out a small piece on a board dusted with granulated sugar (the dough itself can also be sprinkled with a small amount of sugar). If it is too sticky to handle, add more ground almonds, by the tablespoon, until it is manageable. If the dough crumbles or falls apart, add a few extra drops of kirsch or lemon juice and 1 tablespoon of the reserved egg-white glaze.

ROLLING OUT AND GLAZING

When the dough has reached the proper consistency, dust a pastry board lightly with granulated sugar. Shape the dough into a flat round and dust the surface lightly with sugar. Roll the dough out into a rectangle ⅜ inch thick (or slightly thinner, if you prefer). Remove the cloth from the reserved egg-white glaze. Use a metal spatula to smooth an even coating of the glaze over the entire surface of the rectangle, just enough to cover it completely with white. To smooth the surface further, dip the spatula in hot water and run it across the glaze. Make sure you have not used up all the glaze as you will need a small amount to glaze the scraps after they have been rerolled. Cover the remaining glaze again with the damp cloth to keep it from drying out.

CUTTING OUT

Fill a cup with hot water. Dip your star cutter into the hot water each time you cut, leaving as little space between stars as possible. Place the stars on the prepared baking sheets, leaving ¾ inch between each. Knead the scraps together, adding additional ground almonds so that the dough can be rolled out. Roll out, glaze, and cut out as before. Allow to dry at room temperature for 2 hours.

BAKING

Preheat the oven to 275 degrees F. Bake one sheet at a time in the middle of the oven for 20 to 30 minutes, or until the stars are firm and the glaze has dried out. Do not allow them to color. Remove to wire racks to cool completely before storing in an airtight tin.

BASLER BRUNSLI

BASEL BROWNS

A traditional favorite from Basel in Switzerland, *Basler Brunsli*—part cookie, part confection—are as delicious as they are pretty. A flourless dough, composed of ground almonds, chocolate, spices, egg white and sugar, is traditionally pressed into tiny decorative molds to give the *Brunsli* their charming fluted flowerlike shapes. Unmolded and left to dry for several hours, they are barely baked at a low temperature—just long enough to firm the outside and set the design. They should remain quite moist inside, giving them a confectionlike texture. Variations for shaping the dough without the use of molds follow at the end of the recipe.

Brunsli can be stored in an airtight tin at room temperature for up to 3 months.

PREPARING THE DOUGH

Mix the ground almonds, sugar, and cloves together in a bowl. Grate the chocolate on the finest blades of a cheese grater and add to the other dry ingredients. Beat the egg whites lightly and add to the other dry ingredients, along with 2 to 3 tablespoons of kirsch. Knead the mixture well with your hand to form a cohesive mass. If you can roll the dough into balls between the palms of your hand without difficulty, the mixture is the correct consistency. If it is too sticky to handle, add ground almonds by the tablespoon until it is no longer sticky. If it crumbles, add more kirsch. Allow the dough to rest for 30 minutes.

*MAKES ABOUT 35
¾-INCH COOKIES*

1⅓ cups finely ground unblanched almonds, plus more as needed
1¼ cups superfine sugar
½ teaspoon ground cloves
4 ounces unsweetened chocolate
2 egg whites, lightly beaten
2–3 tablespoons kirsch (or substitute rum)
Granulated sugar, for the molds
EQUIPMENT
Small, decorative metal confectionery molds of any shape, approximately 1 to 1½ inches in size; form the dough in balls or roll out (see Variation).

BEFORE BAKING

Line several baking sheets with buttered aluminum foil or unbuttered parchment or nonstick baking paper and set aside.

For molded cookies, pinch off a small piece of dough just large enough to fit into the mold. Press it into the mold. Then tap the mold firmly on a counter to release the cookie. After the first round the mold will be moist, so sprinkle the inside with granulated sugar before you mold each cookie. Place them 1 inch apart on the prepared baking sheets. Allow to dry out at room temperature for up to 2 hours.

BAKING

Preheat the oven to 300 degrees F. Bake one sheet at a time, in the middle of the oven, lowering the temperature to 225 degrees as soon as you place them in the oven. Bake for approximately 15 minutes or a little longer, so that they are firm on the outside but moist inside. Remove to wire racks before storing in an airtight tin.

VARIATION

If you don't have any decorative metal molds, you can use the same dough to make ¾-inch balls or you can roll out the dough ⅜ inch thick on a board dusted with granulated sugar, then cut out with 1-inch cutters. Dust the balls or cutouts with granulated sugar, then continue following instructions in the recipe. For balls, baking time will be approximately 25 minutes; for cutouts, approximately 12 minutes.

BERNER HASELNUSSLECKERLI
BERN HAZELNUT SPICE COOKIES

This favorite recipe is a Christmas specialty from Bern in Switzerland. Traditionally stamped with small decorative wooden molds or a carved wooden rolling pin, these crunchy cookies are made with ground almonds, hazelnuts, and sugar. Because the dough is first allowed to dry out overnight, you will have to schedule finishing the cookies the following day.

Though it's not traditional, if you don't have wooden molds, the cookies can be made using small round or decorative cookie cutters to give them interesting shapes. Stored in airtight tins, they keep well for up to three months.

THE DAY BEFORE
PREPARING THE DOUGH

Combine the ground hazelnuts and almonds with the other ingredients in a mixing bowl. Mix together well. The dough will be very moist and soft but should hold together. Wrap in plastic wrap and leave at room temperature overnight.

THE FOLLOWING DAY
TWO HOURS BEFORE BAKING

Butter and flour baking sheets. Roll out the dough ⅜ inch thick on a board sprinkled lightly with granulated sugar. Dust a decorative wooden mold and the dough lightly with powdered sugar and press it into the dough. Repeat to imprint the pattern across the length of the dough. Brush off the excess sugar.

MAKES ABOUT 45 2-INCH-SQUARE COOKIES

2 cups hazelnuts, roasted, skins removed, and finely ground (see Hazelnuts)
2 cups blanched almonds, finely ground (see Almonds)
2⅔ cups sugar
½ cup mixed candied orange and lemon peel, finely minced
1 teaspoon cinnamon
Grated rind of 1 lemon
2 tablespoons apricot jam
4 egg whites, lightly beaten
EQUIPMENT
Carved wooden molds or, if unavailable, decorative cookie cutters

Separate the cookies with a sharp knife. If using cookie cutters, cut out decorative shapes as desired. Place on the prepared baking sheets. Allow to dry for several hours at room temperature.

BAKING

Preheat the oven to 300 degrees F. Bake one sheet at a time in the middle of the oven for 20 to 30 minutes or until they are golden and semi-firm. They should still seem slightly soft inside but be rigid enough to handle. Loosen the cookies from the baking sheet with a metal spatula as soon as you take them out of the oven. Allow to cool on the baking sheet for several minutes before removing them to a wire rack. When cool, store in airtight tins.

MANDELKÜSSE
ALMOND MERINGUE KISSES

This recipe for snow-white, firm little mouthfuls of almond meringue is made according to the Italian meringue method—the meringue mixture is warmed before it is baked. You can substitute the same amount of finely ground walnuts or shelled, skinned hazelnuts for the almonds, garnishing the meringues with the appropriate nut.

PREPARING THE MERINGUE MIXTURE

Preheat the oven to 225 degrees F. Line a large baking sheet or board as described on p. 138. Set aside.

Use a heatproof crockery or glass bowl that will rest on the rim of a saucepan with its base well above the bottom of the pan. Bring 2 inches of water to the boil in the saucepan, cover the pan, and turn off the heat. Using an electric mixer, beat the egg whites in the bowl with a pinch of salt. Begin with the mixer on a low speed. When the egg whites are foamy, increase the speed to moderately fast, add the cream of tartar, and beat until the egg whites stand in soft peaks. They should hold their shape but not be dry. Add the sugar by the tablespoonful, beating 20 seconds between each addition, until it is used up. Beat for a further 2 minutes or longer, until the meringue is thick and glossy.

Bring the water in the saucepan back to a simmer. Rest the bowl in the saucepan and, using the electric mixer, beat the meringue, scraping down the sides of the bowl frequently, until the mixture is warm—about 5 minutes. Remove the bowl from the pan and continue beating until the meringue and bowl are cool—approximately another 5 minutes.

MAKES ABOUT 36

3 large egg whites, at room temperature
Pinch of salt
Pinch of cream of tartar
1 cup superfine sugar
1 cup plus 1 tablespoon finely ground blanched almonds
1 tablespoon cornstarch
TO FINISH
Split blanched almonds (optional)
Powdered sugar (optional)
EQUIPMENT
Piping bag fitted with plain ¾-inch tip

Mix the ground nuts together with the cornstarch (the cornstarch will help to separate the granules). Using a large metal spoon, fold in the nuts until they are evenly distributed.

PIPING THE MERINGUE

Scoop the mixture into a piping bag fitted with a plain ¾-inch tip. Holding the bag up straight, perpendicular to the prepared baking sheet or board, pipe small ¾-inch rounds, leaving at least ¾ inch between them. When all the meringue mixture has been used up, lightly moisten your finger and smooth the tops and sides (if necessary) of each meringue so it has a perfectly smooth surface. If desired, garnish the top of each with a split blanched almond.

BAKING AND FINISHING

Bake in the lower third of the oven for approximately 1 hour, or until the meringues are completely dry and remove easily from the paper. If desired, dust them with sifted powdered sugar. When cool, store in an airtight tin or jar.

VARIATION

Pipe especially low rounds of meringue and omit the final nut garnish. Save a small amount of the uncooked meringue mixture, covering it with a damp cloth until needed. When the meringues have finished baking, sandwich two together by spreading a small amount of the moist meringue mixture on the bottom of one. Leave on a lined baking sheet in a turned-off oven for several hours to dry out.

FRÜCHTEMAKRONEN

Fruit-Covered Almond Macaroons

In this Viennese recipe, small almond meringues (*Mandelküsse*) are prettily garnished with apricot glaze, topped with rum-soaked fruit, then glazed overall with a thin sugar icing.

MAKES ABOUT 30

1 cup mixed candied fruit, coarsely chopped	1 tablespoon water
3 tablespoons light or dark rum	Candied cherries
1 recipe Mandelküsse omitting the garnish	ICING
¾ cup apricot jam	1½ cups powdered sugar, sifted
	3 tablespoons lemon juice

4 TO 24 HOURS BEFORE
STEEPING THE FRUIT

The day before, or up to 4 hours before baking the macaroons, soak the coarsely chopped candied fruit in the rum. If you warm the rum lightly, without boiling it, it will penetrate the fruit more quickly.

THE FOLLOWING DAY
PREPARING THE MACAROONS

Make and bake the *Mandelküsse* as directed in the preceding recipe, eliminating the split-almond garnish and powdered sugar at the end. When smoothing the little rounds with your fingers, flatten the tops a little so that, after baking, they can be turned upside down and rest fairly flat.

PREPARING THE GLAZE

After the fruit has steeped for at least 4 hours, drain. Boil the apricot jam with 1 tablespoon water, stirring. Strain the hot jam into another saucepan, pressing well against the pulp. Reserve the apricot pulp and add to the rum-soaked fruit.

ASSEMBLING

Turn the macaroons upside down so the flat bottoms are facing up. (Pare a small slice off the bottom if they wobble.) Brush the bottom of each macaroon with the warm jam, reheating it briefly if it becomes too thick. Mix about 2 tablespoons of jam with the drained fruit—enough to bind it. Spoon a small amount of fruit onto each macaroon, dividing it evenly among them. Use a half or a quarter of a red candied cherry (depending on size) to garnish the top of each.

PREPARING THE ICING

For the icing, beat the sifted powdered sugar into 3 tablespoons lemon juice for 8 to 10 minutes until the sugar has dissolved completely to make a smooth icing. The icing should be thin and somewhat transparent. Add an additional teaspoon or more of lemon juice, if necessary, to make a thin icing.

FINISHING

Place the fruit-covered macaroons on a wire rack. Spoon a little icing over each, to cover the fruit. Using a pastry brush, glaze the sides of each to cover. Allow the macaroons to dry completely before storing carefully in an airtight tin. Although they will taste delicious for a longer period, they begin to look a little tired after a week to ten days.

Maronibaisers
Chestnut Meringues

MAKES ABOUT 14

1 cup sugar
½ cup water
4 large egg whites at
    room temperature

CONTINUED ON
FACING PAGE

In both Switzerland and Austria, sweetened chestnut purée is a favorite dessert. Called *Vermicelles* in Switzerland, it is put through a mincer, a small piping bag with a plain tip, or a special multiholed press made just for this purpose, to produce long, tangled strands resembling whole-wheat spaghetti. They are served with a mound of whipped cream. In Austria, the favorite variation—*Kastanienreis* (riced chestnut purée)—is pressed through a coarse wire strainer over a mound of whipped cream. In one of its most luxurious presentations, *Maronibaisers*, small meringue shells are glazed inside with melted chocolate, embellished with a spoonful of morello cherry jam, piped high with whipped cream, and covered all over with riced chestnut purée.

The meringues can be made in advance and stored in an airtight container, while the *Kastanienreis* can be made in advance and frozen. Only the sieving and final assembly with filling and cream need be done on the same day.

For another luxurious Austrian *Kastanienreis* dessert, see *Maronioberschnitten*, made with layered chocolate cake.

PREPARING THE MERINGUE MIXTURE

Preheat the oven to 225 degrees F. Line a large board or several baking sheets as described on p. 138. Set aside.

Place the sugar and ½ cup water in a heavy saucepan and set aside.

To make the meringue, beat the egg whites in a large non-aluminum mixing bowl with an electric mixer on medium high speed until they are half stiff. They should hold their shape but not be dry. Increase the speed and begin adding ¼ cup sugar by the tablespoon, beating for at least 20 seconds between additions. When all the sugar has been added, beat a few minutes longer until the meringue is smooth, thick, and glossy. Immediately heat the sugar and water over a low heat until the sugar has dissolved. Bring to the boil and boil without stirring until the syrup reaches the hard ball stage, 248 degrees on a candy thermometer. While boiling, wash down any sugar crystals from the sides of the pan with a pastry brush dipped in water. Remove the syrup from the heat when it has reached the required temperature and gradually pour it onto the meringue mixture, beating at high speed with an electric mixer. Scrape down the sides of the bowl frequently and continue beating until the meringue is cool.

¼ cup sugar
TO FINISH
3 ounces semi-sweet chocolate, broken in pieces
¾ cup cherry jam (preferably morello or sour cherry) with whole cherries, or substitute raspberry jam
2 cups whipping cream
3 tablespoons powdered sugar, sifted
Halved candied cherries
KASTANIENREIS (RICED CHESTNUT PURÉE)
2 cups sweetened chestnut purée (available in cans at grocery and specialty food stores)
(cont. on pg. 154)
3 tablespoons light or dark rum, or to taste
1 teaspoon vanilla
Powdered sugar to taste (optional)
EQUIPMENT
Large pastry bag with large star tip
Coarse wire strainer for Kastanienreis
Candy thermometer

PIPING

Fit a large piping bag with a large star tip. Pipe the meringue onto the baking sheets in a spiraling motion, beginning in the center, to form a 2½-inch circle. Without stopping the flow of meringue, pipe a second ring of meringue on top of the outside edge to make a tiny nest. Continue until all the meringue has been used, leaving at least ¾ inch between each.

NOTE If the hole in the center has closed up, moisten your thumb with water and rotate it around in the center of the nest to increase the size of the opening.

BAKING

Dust the nests with sifted powdered sugar. Bake in the lower part of the oven for 1½ to 2 hours, or until dry, with the handle of a wooden spoon propped inside the oven door to keep it slightly ajar. This helps keep the oven temperature moderate. If the meringues start to color too rapidly, remove them from the oven and lower the heat. When done, they should be a light eggshell color and should come away easily from the paper. If the bottoms are still slightly moist, turn the meringues upside down and leave them in the oven until they are dry, or simply turn off the oven and leave them upside down for several hours to dry them out completely. Allow to cool to room temperature before continuing with the filling, or store in an airtight container until needed.

FILLING

For the filling, melt the chocolate pieces in the top of a double boiler or in a shallow heatproof soup plate or bowl over a pan filled with 2 inches of simmering water. When chocolate has melted, remove the bowl from the heat. Brush the inside of each meringue with melted chocolate. Allow the chocolate to set while beating the cream. When the cream has begun to hold its shape, add the sifted icing sugar gradually by the tablespoon. Beat until the cream is stiff. Place 1 teaspoon of cream on top of the chocolate, topping it with a spoonful of jam. Place the remaining whipped cream in a piping bag fitted with a plain or star tip. Pipe a high mound of cream on each filled meringue, saving a little for garnish.

PREPARING *KASTANIENREIS*

Using a food processor, mix the chestnut purée together with the rum and vanilla. If desired, add a little powdered sugar to taste and process again until smooth.

Press the mixture, a small amount at a time, through a coarse metal strainer over a piece of waxed paper, using a wooden spoon.

FINISHING

Sprinkle *Kastanienreis* lavishly all over the cream and each meringue. Pipe a small swirl of cream on top. Finish with a halved candied cherry. Chill until needed. *Maronibaisers* are best if served on the day they are filled.

STAMBUL MERINGEN

ISTANBUL MERINGUES

*MAKES 9 LARGE
OR 27 SMALL
MERINGUES*

*3 large egg whites,
at room
temperature*
Pinch of salt
*⅛ teaspoon cream
of tartar*
*1 cup superfine
sugar*
*1 cup walnuts,
coarsely chopped*
CHOCOLATE GLAZE:
*3 ounces semi-sweet
chocolate, bro-
ken in pieces*
1 teaspoon butter
*Few drops of vegeta-
ble oil (optional)*

At Konditorei Frei in Rothenburg ob der Tauber, Germany, large snow-white meringues filled with chopped walnuts and coated underneath with chocolate are a specialty. While proprietor Hans Karl Frei has kept the recipe for his *Stambul Meringen* a secret, I've worked out the following method to produce a similar melt-in-your mouth meringue. As to the name, Frei was unable to elaborate. It derives, no doubt, from the meringue's bold shape which recalls the domes of mosques so dominant on Istanbul's skyline.

THE DAY BEFORE
PREPARING THE MERINGUE MIXTURE

Preheat the oven to 225 degrees F. Line a large board or baking sheet as described on p. 138.

Prepare the meringue mixture using the above quantities following the technique for Meringues—Basic Recipe, p. 141. When the meringue is well beaten, carefully fold in the chopped walnuts with a large spoon.

SHAPING

Using two spoons, place high, round mounds approximately 2 inches in diameter (about 3 heaping tablespoons each) on the prepared board or baking sheet 1½ inches apart. Smooth the mounds to remove any protruding points or edges.

BAKING

Bake on the next-to-lowest shelf of the oven for approximately 2½ hours, checking occasionally to make sure the meringues are not coloring. If they start to color or crack, lower the oven temperature or turn the oven off. When done, the meringues can be removed easily from the baking sheet. At the end of the baking time, turn the meringues on their sides, turn off the oven, and return them to the oven to dry out overnight with the door closed.

THE FOLLOWING DAY
GLAZING

Remove the meringues from the baking sheet. Heat the broken chocolate and butter in a heatproof soup plate or shallow bowl placed over a saucepan filled with 2 inches of simmering water, stirring the chocolate occasionally until it is melted. The chocolate should be of spreading consistency. If it is too thick, add a few drops of vegetable oil. Using a pastry brush, brush the bottoms of the meringues with melted chocolate. Place the meringues upside down on a wire rack to allow the chocolate to dry until almost set. With the prongs of a fork, make a wavy pattern in the soft chocolate on each meringue. Allow the chocolate to dry completely.

STORING

Store the meringues in an airtight container at a cool room temperature (not in the refrigerator, which will cause the meringues to soften). If packing in layers, separate each layer with wax paper or aluminum foil so that the chocolate will not smudge the layer of meringues beneath. If properly stored they will keep two weeks to a month or longer, provided the room temperature remains constant so the chocolate doesn't discolor.

NOTE If smaller meringues are desired, the baking time must be decreased in proportion to the size. Using 1 tablespoon of meringue mixture, the smaller meringues will require approximately 1½ hours of baking before being left overnight to dry out in the turned-off oven.

MASTER RECIPE

MARZIPAN CONFECTIONS

BASIC MARZIPAN

*MAKES ABOUT
1½ POUNDS*

*1⅔ cups blanched
almonds
1½ cups granulated
sugar
½ cup water
2 large egg whites,
lightly beaten
1 teaspoon rose
water
2 tablespoons
powdered sugar,
sifted, or as
needed*

Marzipan—sweet almond paste flavored with rose water—has a special place in German tradition. A favorite sweet in the Middle East, it followed trade routes to the West, appearing first in Italy. From Venice it made its way to German ports such as Lübeck and Königsberg. It was in these cities that marzipan became associated with the Christmas season. Because St. Nikolaus, as the protector of seafarers as well as children, was particularly venerated in these northern ports, it became the custom for children to receive marzipan as a gift from him on his feast day, December 6. It might appear in its simplest form, plain or chocolate-dipped loaves, or in one of many colorful shapes—potatoes, sausages, pigs for good luck, decorative hearts, fruit, flowers, and hedgehogs, to name a few.

Today it is found in all German-speaking countries, either in shapes, or used as a filling in cookies, cakes, and breads such as stollen, or shaped into confections or cookies which are glazed and baked, such as *Königsberger Herzen* (Königsberg hearts), *Züri Leckerli* (Zurich marzipan cookies), or *Frankfurter Bethmännchen* (Marzipan Bethmanns).

While it can be purchased in many grocery shops and most delicatessens, it is best if freshly made, to get the full flavor of freshly ground almonds. However, it is important to grind the almonds to a very fine dust; you will therefore need a good blender (most food processors will not grind the nuts fine enough).

Grind the nuts, in batches, to a very fine powder in a blender at high speed. Some of the mixture may become oily, which is perfectly acceptable. Reserve.

Combine the granulated sugar with ½ cup water in a heavy medium-sized saucepan. Stir constantly over medium heat until the sugar has melted and the syrup begins to boil. At this point, stop stirring and attach a candy thermometer to the side of the saucepan. Boil the syrup until the thermometer registers 240 degrees F. Remove the pan from the heat. Stir in the ground almonds until thoroughly blended. Stir in the egg whites until well mixed.

Return the saucepan to a medium heat. Cook, stirring constantly, until the mixture is smooth and well combined—about 3 minutes. Add the rose water and mix well. Pour the marzipan out onto a work surface that has been lightly dusted with powdered sugar. Let it cool.

When cool enough to handle, knead the marzipan until smooth and pliable. If it is too moist and sticky, knead in powdered sugar, a little at a time. Use extra powdered sugar sparingly; too much will result in a dry marzipan that will crack easily. If it becomes too dry, add a little extra rose water. Wrap the marzipan well in plastic wrap and refrigerate overnight. Use as directed in the recipe.

MARZIPANFIGUREN

MARZIPAN SHAPES

Marzipan can be formed into any shape you can think of, though traditional favorites at Christmas time include small pink pigs (for good luck), fruits (strawberries, apricots, bananas, oranges), vegetables (potatoes, cabbage, leeks), and loaves 3½ inches long, resembling bread.

Use professional paste food colors to color the marzipan, so that you don't dye your hands as well. These are available in professional, bakery supply shops.

MAKING MARZIPAN POTATOES

A simple marzipan shape that requires no special coloring is the potato. Roll small pieces of marzipan in various-sized small balls. Distort their shape slightly so they look like real potatoes. Use the tip of a sharp knife or a skewer to mark a few "eyes" on each. Roll in ground cinnamon or cocoa powder, smudging it away in a few places. For a Christmas gift, the potatoes can be placed in a small bag (you can make one out of coarse cotton) with a drawstring; or they can be placed in a small basket and covered with plastic wrap.

COLORING MARZIPAN

For shapes that need to be colored, pour about 2 tablespoons of water into each of several small cups, depending on how many colors you are using. Dip a fine-tipped brush into the first jar of color and mix the small amount of color that adheres to the brush with the water. Continue in the same way to mix the other colors, using a clean brush for each. Adjust the intensity of the colors—they are subtler if the shades are kept pastel. Let the marzipan shape dry, uncovered, overnight.

COATING LOAVES WITH CHOCOLATE

Plain loaves can be coated with chocolate if desired. For the chocolate glaze, break 3½ ounces (or as much as is needed) of semi-sweet chocolate into pieces. Place it in the top of a double boiler or with 1 teaspoon of vegetable oil in a heatproof soup plate or shallow bowl over a saucepan filled with 2 inches of simmering water. Stir the chocolate occasionally until it is melted. Using a pastry brush, first brush the bottoms of the loaves and leave them in a cool place (not the refrigerator), chocolate side up, to dry. If the chocolate is too thick to coat easily, add a few more drops of vegetable oil. When the bottoms are dry, coat the tops and sides evenly and leave them to dry before storing in an airtight tin in a cool place. If properly stored, the loaves will keep one month or more.

MASTER TECHNIQUE

MARZIPAN BAKING TECHNIQUE

In some of the recipes that follow, marzipan is cut out or shaped and baked. In recipes where the marzipan is baked in an oven 300 degrees F. or lower, as opposed to those where the marzipan is baked in a hot oven or under the grill, the marzipan will stay more moist if you use a large wooden board. Wrap the board twice in aluminum foil to cover it completely. Butter the foil and cover it with a piece of parchment or nonstick baking paper (the butter will help it to stick). Place the board on a baking sheet so that it won't be in direct contact with the hot oven racks. Then place the marzipan on the paper-covered board. If you have more marzipan than will fit on the board at one time, place the rest on another piece of nonstick baking or parchment paper and set aside. When one batch has finished, remove the sheet of paper with the baked marzipan and carefully replace it with the fresh piece of paper holding the unbaked marzipan.

The advantage of the board is that it prevents bottom heat from passing through the marzipan, wood being a poor conductor of heat, and thus allows them to color or dry out on the top without drying out inside.

If you don't have a board, first line your baking sheets with two layers of aluminum foil (since foil is an insulator rather than a conductor of heat). Butter the aluminum foil and cover with a piece of nonstick parchment or baking paper. Then bake as directed.

NOTE Avoid using black steel baking sheets (I'm not referring to the black-coated nonstick baking sheets) because they conduct heat more rapidly than light-colored or nonstick baking sheets.

PISTAZIENKUGELN
PISTACHIO CONFECTIONS

Finely ground pistachios mixed with ground blanched almonds turn this marzipan-type dough a lovely pale green.

TWO DAYS BEFORE
PREPARING THE PISTACHIO PASTE

Follow the recipe for Basic Marizpan, substituting shelled, skinned pistachios for almonds in the quantities given above. Pistachio skins can be removed by covering the pistachios with 2 inches of hot water and leaving them for about 5 minutes. The skins should then slip off easily. Separate those to be used as decoration and split them while moist. Dry the rest out in a 325-degree F. oven on a baking sheet for 5 to 10 minutes (do not let them brown) before grinding in a blender. Proceed as directed in the master recipe. Wrap the marzipan well and refrigerate overnight.

ONE DAY BEFORE
SHAPING AND DRYING

The next day, knead briefly, then break off small pieces and roll them in ¾-inch balls between the palms of your hands. Beat an egg white until frothy. Brush each ball with the egg white, then roll it in sifted powdered sugar. Place on a piece of waxed paper. Garnish each with a half pistachio. Leave, uncovered, at room temperature for at least 24 hours to dry out.

THE FOLLOWING DAY

When completely dry, store in an airtight container in the refrigerator or in a cool place.

MAKES APPROXI-MATELY 55

1 recipe Basic Marzipan (p. 160), substituting 1 cup shelled, skinned pistachios for ¾ cup plus 1 tablespoon of blanched almonds
1 egg white
Powdered sugar
¼ cup shelled, skinned pista-chios, split, for decoration

ZÜRI LECKERLI
ZURICH MARZIPAN COOKIES

While the *Leckerli* from Basel—spicy and honey-based—are the most famous, Zurichers are proud of their own variation made either solely with ground blanched almonds, like marzipan, or with almonds and hazelnuts, mixed with sugar and egg white. Traditionally printed with small rectangular wooden molds, the *Leckerli* are made in four different flavors, each of which has a different tint: white, flavored only with rose water; pale beige, spiced with cinnamon; cocoa, sweetened with chocolate; and rose, scented and colored with powdered sandalwood (red food coloring has been substituted in the recipe that follows).

A visit to Zurich at holiday time should include a stop at the famous bakery Sprüngli, where diminutive four-colored *Leckerli* are exquisitely produced and packaged for gifts or on-the-spot consumption.

If you have the time, make the marzipan yourself. If you are buying the marzipan, make sure it is very fresh, off-white and soft. You can make only one color of marzipan, or divide the marzipan into four and color it as described below. If you are making the marzipan, do so at least one day before the cookies are to be baked so that it can rest overnight. The baking is meant just to firm and finish drying the *Leckerli*, leaving them moist inside. The sugar icing glaze they receive at the end gives them a soft tint.

When finished, store in an airtight container, refrigerated or at room temperature, for two weeks or longer.

WISSI LECKERLI

WHITE ZURICH LECKERLI

*MAKES APPROXIMATELY 45
2 × ½-INCH COOKIES*
*1 recipe Basic Marzipan (p.
160), or 1½ pounds fresh
ready-made marzipan*
GLAZE
½ large egg white
2 cups powdered sugar, sifted
*2–3 tablespoons orange water,
rose water, or if unavailable, plain tap water*

EQUIPMENT
*Small rectangular carved
wooden molds, if available;
or decorative cookie cutters*

THE DAY BEFORE

Make the marzipan as directed in the basic recipe, wrapping
and refrigerating it overnight.

THE FOLLOWING DAY
PRINTING, CUTTING OUT, AND BAKING

Preheat the oven to 300 degrees F. Roll out the prepared marzipan ⅜ inch thick on a board lightly dusted with powdered sugar. Dust
the marzipan and the wooden molds lightly with powdered sugar and
press the molds into the dough. Using a knife or a plain pastry wheel,
separate the cookies, trimming the edges neatly. Prepare a board or
baking sheets as described on p. 138. Bake one batch at a time, in the
upper third of the oven, until the outside crust is firm but the inside
still soft—approximately 15 minutes. Do not allow the marzipan to
color.

PREPARING THE GLAZE

Beat the egg white with a wooden spoon or a whisk until it is frothy
and begins to thicken. Gradually beat in the sifted powdered sugar
alternately with the liquid. Beat for at least 8 minutes to dissolve the
sugar completely. The glaze is meant to be a thin icing of pouring

consistency. If necessary, add a few drops of additional liquid or spoonfuls of sugar to correct the consistency.

FINISHING

When the cookies are done, remove the baking sheet from the oven. Allow them to rest for 1 minute before removing them carefully to a wire rack. While they are still warm, brush them evenly but sparingly with the glaze. Place a damp cloth directly on the surface of the icing to keep it from drying out before using on the next batch being baked. Allow the icing to set before storing the cookies.

VARIATION

Replace half of the ground blanched almonds with skinned ground hazelnuts, grinding them in a blender.

RÖTE LECKERLI

RED ZURICH LECKERLI

Because the traditional flavoring and coloring ingredient—powdered sandalwood—is not readily available, tint the marzipan mixture in the above recipe with several drops of red and a tiny drop of yellow food coloring to produce a pale rose tint. Proceed as for *Wissi Leckerli.*

BRAUNE LECKERLI

BROWN ZURICH LECKERLI

Make the Basic Marzipan mixture, adding 6 ounces of melted semi-sweet chocolate and 1 to 2 tablespoons light or dark rum if needed. To melt the chocolate, break it into pieces and place it in a double boiler or in a shallow heatproof soup plate or bowl over a pan filled with 2 inches of simmering water. Stir occasionally until melted. Knead the cooled chocolate into the prepared marzipan when the marzipan goes through the kneading process before being wrapped and stored. If using prepared marzipan, simply knead the chocolate into the marzipan on a board lightly dusted with powdered sugar. Add just enough extra powdered sugar or rum to make the marzipan malleable. Proceed as for *Wissi Leckerli*.

ZIMMETLECKERLI

CINNAMON ZURICH LECKERLI

Add 1 tablespoon of cinnamon to the marzipan mixture in the master recipe for White *Leckerli* and proceed, making the cookies in the usual way.

KÖNIGSBERGER HERZEN
KÖNIGSBERG HEARTS

*MAKES ABOUT 22
2-INCH HEARTS*

*1 pound marzipan,
purchased or
made according to
the basic recipe
Powdered sugar as
needed
GLAZE
1 egg yolk
1 tablespoon cream
ICING
1 egg white
1½ cups powdered
sugar, sifted
1–2 teaspoons lemon
juice
DECORATION
Candied cherries,
halved
Strips of angelica or
citron
EQUIPMENT
Heart-shaped cookie
cutter 2 to 3
inches high*

These pretty marzipan hearts, framed with a notched rim of browned marzipan and decorated with candied fruit, are sold in delicatessens in many countries in and outside Germany during the Christmas season.

ROLLING OUT, CUTTING, AND ASSEMBLING

If your marzipan is especially moist, knead up to ⅓ cup sifted powdered sugar into the dough to make it firm enough to roll out and cut easily. Test a piece first by rolling it out on a board lightly dusted with sifted powdered sugar. If it is quite sticky, it will need more sugar. Butter baking sheets.

Once the marzipan has been tested, roll the entire mass out ½ inch thick on a board lightly dusted with sifted powdered sugar. Cut out cookies with a heart-shaped cutter. Using the scraps, cut out strips ⅜ inch wide to be used for the rims. Brush the edges of the hearts lightly with water. Using one strip for each side of the heart, joining at the bottom and top points, measure one to establish the correct length. Then trim the other strips you have cut to the correct length, making sure the strips are double the number of hearts that have been cut. Press the rims on well, smoothing the joining seam with your finger. Using the back of a knife, score parallel lines all around the rim for a decorative effect.

GLAZING

For the glaze, mix the egg yolk and cream together with a fork. Using a pastry brush, brush the rim only with the glaze, being careful not to let any of the glaze drip into the center of the heart since it is meant to remain white.

Place hearts on a buttered baking sheet. Only the outside rim of the hearts is meant to brown when they are baked, not the underside, so it is best to use only top heat, browning them under a low broiler. You will need to test one of the finished hearts under the flame before proceeding. If you can regulate your broiler so that the flame is medium rather than high, do so. Otherwise, place in the lowest part of a gas broiler or in the middle of the oven with an electric broiler. Brown until the rim is golden. Remove from the broiler and allow to cool on the baking sheet.

ICING AND DECORATING

Meanwhile, make the icing. Beat the egg white until frothy. Gradually beat in the sifted powdered sugar, beating for 8 to 10 minutes to produce a smooth icing. It should be thin enough to be applied smoothly with a pastry brush, but thick enough to produce an opaque white. If necessary, adjust the consistency with a little lemon juice or additional sugar. Brush the center of each heart with the icing. While the icing is still moist, decorate the hearts. If the hearts are small, quarter the cherries or cut off slivers. Place a piece of cherry at the bottom point of each heart, just inside the rim. Cut two thin slivers, approximately ¾ inch long, of angelica or citron and fan them out from the cherry toward the top of the heart. If desired, place a smaller sliver in the center, extending up from the cherry. Allow the icing to set before storing the hearts in an airtight tin. They will keep moist slightly longer if refrigerated.

FRANKFURTER BETHMÄNNCHEN

MARZIPAN BETHMANNS

MAKES 40

1 pound soft marzi-
pan, bought or
prepared accord-
ing to the recipe
for Basic Marzipan
1 cup powdered
sugar, sifted
Rose water, as
needed
½ cup plus 2
tablespoons whole
blanched almonds,
split (see Almonds)
GLAZE
1 egg, lightly beaten

Named after the famous Frankfurt banking family Bethmann, these charming baked marzipan confections—small triangular shapes elegantly propped by three split almonds—are a specialty of Frankfurt, and are found in all the best bakeries and confectioners' at Christmas. They are quick to prepare, once you have your marzipan, and make an elegant gift for marzipan-loving friends. If making them for a gift, you could mix them with another baked marzipan specialty from Frankfurt—*Frankfurter Brenten* (recipe follows).

THE DAY BEFORE
SHAPING AND DECORATING

Line a board or baking sheets as instructed on p. 138. Set aside.

Break the marzipan into pieces in a mixing bowl. Add most of the sifted powdered sugar and 1 tablespoon of rose water and knead the mixture together well, adding more rose water or sugar as needed, so the marzipan holds together in a firm mass that can be shaped. Divide the mixture into four portions. Roll each into a log ¾ inch in diameter. Cut each log into two even-sized pieces. Using the palm of your hand, roll each piece into a ball on a pastry board dusted with powdered sugar. Press each ball down firmly to flatten the base. If your almonds are not already split, cover them with 2 inches of water that has just boiled and leave them for 3 to 4 minutes. Drain off the water and dry the almonds on paper towels. Using a sharp knife, split the almonds in half lengthwise while they are still soft. Brush each ball lightly with beaten egg. Press three split almonds into the sides so that the points almost meet in the center and the bottoms are at the base. Pressure against the top of the almonds will help create the traditional shape. Brush the almonds with lightly beaten egg. Allow to dry out overnight uncovered.

THE FOLLOWING DAY
BAKING

Preheat the oven to 300 degrees F. Bake one sheet at a time in the upper third of the oven until golden—about 15 minutes. These marzipan cookies should just color, but still be soft in the center. Allow to cool on the board or baking sheet before storing.

FRANKFURTER BRENTEN
FRANKFURT PRINTED BAKED MARZIPAN

*MAKES 30–45,
ACCORDING TO
SIZE*

*1 pound marzipan,
bought or made
according to the
recipe for Basic
Marzipan*
*1 cup plus 2
tablespoons sifted
powdered sugar,
or as needed*
*1 large egg white,
lightly beaten*
*2 tablespoons flour,
sifted*
*Rose water as
needed*
TO FINISH
Granulated sugar

Printed with small decorative wooden molds, marzipan dough is converted into charming, lightly browned cookies dusted with sugar in this traditional Frankfurt specialty. While Brenten are normally very small, 1 × 1¾ inches, you can use small wooden molds or a carved rolling pin—the kind used for *Springerle* and available in specialty cookware shops. In this case, the size of your Brenten will be determined by your molds. If you don't have wooden molds, you can still make the cookies without molding them, cutting them out in the dimensions given above and baking as described in this recipe. Begin this recipe the day before you plan to bake as the cookies must dry out overnight before baking.

Once baked and cooled, they can be stored in an airtight tin for up to one month.

Note If buying prepared marzipan, find some that is relatively soft, indicating freshness. If it is hard, you might need to use an extra egg white to get it to a consistency that can be rolled out and printed, using a food processor with the cutting blade.

THE DAY BEFORE
PRINTING AND DRYING OUT

See the notes under Basic Marzipan, p. 160, on the treatment of baking sheets for baked marzipan. Line a board or baking sheets accordingly and set aside.

Break the marzipan into pieces in a mixing bowl. Add the sifted powdered sugar, lightly beaten egg white, and flour. Knead together, adding a few drops of rose water or small amounts of sugar, as needed, to make a smooth firm mass that can be rolled out. Dust a pastry board lightly with powdered sugar. Roll the marzipan out into a rectangle ⅜ inch thick. Dust the molds (or rolling pin) and the surface of the marzipan with powdered sugar. Press the molds well into the dough, dusting again as needed. Brush excess sugar from the dough with a dry pastry brush. Use a sharp knife or plain pastry wheel to cut out the printed cookies.

Sprinkle each Brenten lightly with granulated sugar. Place ¾ inch apart on the prepared baking sheets. Allow them to dry out for 24 hours.

THE FOLLOWING DAY
BAKING

Preheat the oven to 280 degrees F. Bake one sheet at a time in the upper third of the oven until the cookies are golden—approximately 15 to 20 minutes. Cool on the board or baking sheet for several minutes; transfer to a wire rack to finish cooling.

4

DEEP-FRIED PASTRIES AND GRIDDLE WAFERS— SCHMALZGEBÄCK UND EIERTEIG

A large assortment of pastries are traditionally made during pre-Lenten festivities (*Fasching* or, in Switzerland, *Fastnacht*) and for regional fairs—*Volksfeste, Messen* (trade fairs), *Jahrmärkte* (annual town fairs), and *Kirchweihen* (church festivals). While ambitious home bakers sometimes make these pastries, particularly *Berliner Pfannkuchen* (jelly doughnuts) which are traditionally eaten on Shrove Tuesday, the majority are made by bakers and vendors who travel from fair to fair. Jelly doughnuts and other specialties included in this chapter have made their way to America. In the Pennsylvania Dutch country it is common to find crullers, funnel cakes, and tangle britches, which are just other names for deep-fried *Nudelteig, Berner Strübli* and *Rothenburger Schneeballen*.

Most of these pastries are made from a soft, elastic dough (*Nudelteig*), thin batter (*Eierteig*), or yeast dough (*Hefeteig*) which is shaped or, in the case of batter, used to coat or pour. They are deep-fried in a large or small quantity of hot fat, depending on the pastry. The variety of shapes and resulting textures makes this category of sweets particularly interesting. They range from the amusing *Berner Strübli*—a spiral pastry formed by pouring batter through a funnel in a spiral shape directly into the hot fat—to *Schlupfküchlein* (pastry knots), *Schmalzbrezeln* (yeast-dough pretzels), *Eieröhrli* (paper-thin bubbly pastry rounds), and *Rothenburger Schneeballen* (tangled pastry balls).

DEEP-FRYING

When deep-frying, it is important to keep the temperature of the oil constant, regulating the heat and using a deep-fry thermometer if not using an electric deep fryer; to add additional oil, if necessary, and reheat to the correct temperature before proceeding; and to check a pastry from the first batch to make sure it is cooked clear through, lowering the heat, if necessary, so that the pastry doesn't brown too quickly, or increasing the heat if the pastry has absorbed too much fat and cooked too slowly. I prefer corn oil, which adds flavor to the pastries and produces a warm, golden color. However, safflower or other vegetable oils (with the exception of olive oil) can be used.

GRIDDLE WAFERS

An interesting group of related recipes is for wafers, which are made on a special decoratively embossed wafer griddle. The griddles, which are available in two-handled models to be used on top of a burner as well as electric models, are manufactured in Germany, Switzerland, and Scandinavia and sold in specialty cookware stores.

STORING

Deep-fried pastries, especially, are best eaten shortly after they are made, although some of them, if properly stored according to the instructions in the recipe, will keep for three or four days.

SERVING IDEAS

While many of these pastries are somewhat time-consuming to prepare, they are unusual, festive, and inexpensive to make—a good solution for children's birthday parties or for snack-type sweets for a large group of people.

BATTER PASTRIES

M A S T E R   R E C I P E

BASIC FRITTER BATTER

*¾ cup plus 1
tablespoon all-
purpose flour
1 pinch of salt
⅔ cup beer, at room
temperature
1 egg yolk
1 egg white, stiffly
beaten*

Sift the flour and salt together. Beat the beer together with the egg yolk in a mixing bowl. Gradually beat in the flour to form a thick batter (or mix in a blender or food processor). Allow to rest at room temperature for 1 hour. Just before using, beat the egg white until stiff and fold gently into the batter

APFELKÜCHEL

APPLE FRITTERS

*MAKES 16 TO 20
FRITTERS*

*1 recipe Basic
Fritter Batter,
p. 179*

*1½ pounds large
Golden Delicious
apples*
*Vegetable oil for
deep-drying*
TO FINISH
*½ cup granulated
sugar*
*1 teaspoon ground
cinnamon*
TO SERVE
*Heavy cream, lightly
whipped to form
soft peaks*
EQUIPMENT
*Deep fryer or heavy
pan*
*Deep-fry thermometer
Slotted spoon*

A favorite treat in American homes across the country, apple fritters, or *Apfelküchel*, were introduced here by German emigrants. Today in Germany they are still prepared at home, but are most frequently found at fairs. Because they get soggy after standing for any length of time, they should be prepared just before they are to be served.

PREPARING BATTER AND APPLES

Make the Basic Fritter Batter. Just before frying peel and core apples. Slice through the whole apple to cut rings ½ inch thick. Fold in the final stiffly beaten egg white called for in the batter recipe.

FRYING

Heat at least 3 inches of vegetable oil in a deep fryer or heavy pan until a deep-fry thermometer registers 365 degrees F. Dip each slice of apple in the batter, one at a time, retrieving them with a slotted spoon. Allow them to drain over the bowl for a few seconds before dropping them into the hot fat. Fry a few slices at a time, pressing down in the fat with a slotted spoon so the oil covers them. When golden on the underside, turn and allow them to color on the other side. Remove to paper towels to drain. Sprinkle them on both sides with a mixture of sugar and cinnamon while still warm. Continue until all the batter is used, adding more oil to the pan if necessary, and bringing the oil back to the correct temperature before frying the next batch.

Serve with lightly whipped cream if desired.

SALBEIKÜCHLEIN

DEEP-FRIED SUGARED
SAGE LEAVES

An unusual sweet from Zurich, these batter-dipped sage leaves are deep-fried until crisp, then sprinkled with sugar. Like many things that are deep-fried, they are best if served the same day they are made, perhaps as a novel accompaniment to a glass of white wine or a pretty garnish for a plain fruit dessert.

Make the batter per the master recipe, substituting the ⅔ cup white wine for the ⅔ cup beer used in the recipe. Before adding the beaten egg white, heat at least 3 inches of oil in a deep fryer or heavy-bottomed pan until the deep-fry thermometer reaches **365 degrees F**. Dip each sage leaf in the batter, holding it by the stem so that it is covered completely. Allow to drip over the bowl for a few seconds before dropping into the hot fat. Deep-fry only a few leaves at a time, coating them with batter just before lowering them into the fat. Cook until golden, adjusting the heat to keep a constant temperature. Using a slotted spoon, turn once during frying so the leaves color evenly. Drain the sage leaves and dry on paper towels. While they are still warm, sprinkle generously with sugar.

1 recipe Basic Fritter Batter, p. 179 substituting ⅔ cup white wine, lightly warmed, for ⅔ cup beer used in the recipe
Vegetable oil for deep-frying
30 or more fresh sage leaves with stems, washed and well dried on paper towels
TO FINISH
Granulated sugar
EQUIPMENT
Deep fryer or heavy-bottomed pan
Deep-fry thermometer
Slotted spoon

BERNER STRÜBLI (TRICHTERSCHUEECHLI)

BERN FUNNEL CAKES

MAKES ABOUT 22

3 cups less 2
  tablespoons all-
  purpose flour
¼ teaspoon salt
2 cups whole milk
2 tablespoons un-
  salted butter
3 large eggs, lightly
  beaten
⅓ cup less 2 table-
  spoons superfine
  sugar
Vegetable oil for
  deep frying
TO FINISH
Powdered sugar,
  sifted
EQUIPMENT
Large funnel with
  an opening ⅜
  inch wide
Deep fryer or heavy
  pan
Deep-fry thermometer
Slotted spoon

Strub or *struppig* in Swiss German means rough or unkempt. Formed by pouring batter through a funnel (*Trichter*) in a spiral shape directly into hot fat, *Berner Strübli* emerge from the fat golden brown and indeed quite unruly in form. A similar specialty was brought to America many years ago by the German-speaking immigrants who settled in the Pennsylvania Dutch country. The popularity of funnel cakes has endured, and today they are a regular feature at farmers' markets and country fairs throughout Pennsylvania. The funnel cakes are best eaten shortly after they are made.

PREPARING THE BATTER

Sift the flour and salt together into a large mixing bowl. Heat the milk until warm to the touch, approximately 105 degrees F. Add the butter and stir until it is melted. Make a well in the middle of the flour and pour 1¾ cups of the milk, while still warm, in the well, reserving the remaining milk called for in the recipe. Using a wooden spoon, gradually beat in some of the flour. Add the lightly beaten eggs and sugar and continue drawing in the flour, beating until the batter is smooth.

NOTE The batter can also be made by mixng all the ingredients in a blender or food processor with a large container. The consistency of the batter must be thin enough that it will flow in a steady stream through the funnel. Test the mixture through the funnel and, if necessary, add enough of the remaining milk mixture to bring the batter to a smooth-flowing consistency. Lay out a double thickness of paper towels.

DEEP-FRYING

Heat 3 to 4 inches of vegetable oil in a deep fryer or heavy pan until a deep-fry thermometer registers **365 degrees F.** Holding the funnel well above the fat, pour a ladleful of batter into the funnel. Turn the funnel in increasingly larger circles to form a spiral. Deep-fry only one at a time, moving the spiral in the oil gently once or twice with a slotted spoon so it colors evenly. Remove to paper towels to drain. While still warm, dust with sifted powdered sugar. Continue with the remaining batter until it is used up. If necessary during the cooking process, add more oil to the deep fryer, heating it to the proper temperature before frying the next *Strübli.*

M A S T E R   R E C I P E

EGG-DOUGH PASTRIES

NUDELTEIG

BASIC DEEP-FRIED PASTRY DOUGH

4 large eggs
¼ cup heavy cream
1 pinch salt
1½ tablespoons sugar
2 tablespoons un-
    salted butter,
    melted and cooled
3 cups all-purpose
    flour, sifted

Beat the eggs lightly in a mixing bowl with a fork or small wire whisk. Gradually beat in the cream, salt, sugar, and melted butter. Beat until well blended. Using a wooden spoon, gradually beat in the sifted flour. Knead on a lightly floured board for 3 to 4 minutes. If dough is sticking, add only a small amount of additional flour. This is meant to be a soft dough. Wrap the dough well in plastic wrap and leave at room temperature for 1 hour before using. Use as directed in the recipe.

EIERÖRHLI
MARDI GRAS PASTRIES

In Zurich and Basel, these paper-thin, ruffled rounds dusted with powdered sugar are found at street stands and in pastry shops during *Fastnacht* (Mardi Gras) and *Mustermesse* (a Basel trade fair). Stacked one on top of another, they resemble a milliner's display of broad-brimmed summer hats. The most delicious ones are so thin, they are almost transparent, so the directions for rolling your dough as thin as paper is an important tip from one who has sampled many. Although they require some time to make, they are well worth the trouble. While they will keep three to four days if properly stored, their size and delicate constitution make them somewhat unwieldy for storing in large quantities. These pastries are so pretty and festive, I can imagine them stacked high on a New Year's Eve buffet table or used as an edible centerpiece for a winter's eve dinner or a Halloween party.

MAKES ABOUT 13

*1 recipe Basic
    Deep-Fried Pastry
    Dough, facing page
Flour for dusting
Vegetable oil for
    frying
TO FINISH
Powdered sugar
EQUIPMENT
Heavy-bottomed 7–8-
    inch frying pan,
    about 3 inches
    deep
Deep-fry thermometer
Tongs*

ROLLING OUT

Prepare the dough as described in the basic recipe, allowing it to rest 1 hour. Break off pieces of dough the size of golf balls and roll them out into rounds as thin as possible on a lightly floured board. They should be about 6 or 7 inches in diameter and as thin as paper. Dust them lightly with flour, brushing off any excess with a dry pastry brush. Stack them and cover with a cloth. Lay out several thicknesses of paper towels.

DEEP-FRYING

Choose a heavy-bottomed frying pan just slightly larger than the rounds of dough, at least 3 inches deep. Fill the pan with 1½ to 2 inches of vegetable oil and heat the oil until a deep-fry thermometer registers 365 degrees F. Pick up a round of pastry and with your fist underneath, stretch it carefully to make it even thinner. Fry the rounds one at a time, pressing them under with the tongs or so they are completely covered with oil. When golden on the underside, use tongs to turn them and cook on the other side briefly. They brown fairly quickly, but if they brown too much in 10 seconds, lower the temperature of the oil slightly. Drain on paper towels. While they are still warm, dust generously on both sides with powdered sugar.

SCHLUPFKÜCHLEIN
SLIP-KNOT CRISPS

MAKES ABOUT 40

*1 recipe Basic
  Deep-Fried Pastry
  Dough, p. 184*
*Vegetable oil for
  frying*
TO FINISH
Powdered sugar
EQUIPMENT
*Deep fryer or heavy
  pan*
Slotted spoon
Deep-fry thermometer

In Germany and Switzerland, these amusing slip knots are produced by vendors at fairs throughout the year. When cooled, they can be stored for two to four days in an airtight tin at room temperature. If humidity makes it necessary, they can be crisped in a hot oven (425 degrees) for a few minutes, then dusted again with powdered sugar.

ROLLING OUT AND KNOTTING

Prepare the basic dough as described in the master recipe and
allow it to rest 1 hour. Break off pieces of dough the size of a
golf ball and roll them out as thin as possible on a lightly floured
board in a rectangle that measures 7½ × 5 inches. Cut off the
top and bottom of each rectangle with a diagonal cut so that you
have a parallelogram. There would be a point at the top and
bottom of each strip and the top and bottom should be parallel.
Save all the scraps under a cloth, and when you have used all
the rest of the dough knead the scraps all together well, roll out,
and cut like the others. Make a ¾-inch slit across the center of
each strip. Pick up the bottom point. Fold it up and through the
slit. Pull it out on the other side and press it down slightly
toward the bottom of the pastry. It will look like a flap. When all
the strips have been "slip-knotted," cover them with a cloth. Lay
out several thicknesses of paper towels.

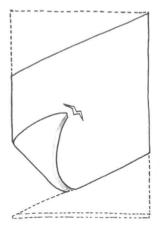

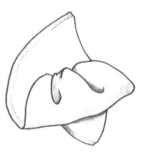

DEEP-FRYING

Fill a deep fryer or heavy pan with 3 to 4 inches of oil and
heat until a deep-fry thermometer registers 365 degrees F. Fry
3 knots at a time, pressing them down with a slotted spoon so
they are completely submerged in the oil. When the undersides
are golden, turn them and cook on the other side briefly. They
brown fairly quickly, but if they brown too much in an 8-second
period, lower the temperature of the oil to 360 degrees. Drain
on paper towels. While still warm, dust generously on both sides
with powdered sugar.

FASTNACHTSKÜCHLEIN
SALTED CARNIVAL CRISPS

MAKES 90 TO 100

2½ tablespoons un-
  salted butter,
  melted and still
  warm
½ teaspoon salt
1⅓ cups warm water
3 cups all-purpose
  flour, sifted
Vegetable oil for
  deep-frying
TO FINISH
Kosher salt or coarse
  sea salt
2–3 tablespoons
  caraway seeds
EQUIPMENT
Deep fryer or heavy-
  bottomed pan
Slotted spoon
Deep-fry thermome-
  ter if deep fryer
  is not automatic

One of many regional variations, these deep-fried carnival crisps from Blätz in Switzerland are sprinkled with salt and caraway seeds instead of sugar. Traditionally eaten during the festivities at *Fastnacht*, the 3-day pre-Lenten carnival celebration that ends on Ash Wednesday, they make a delicious snack or hors de'oeuvre all year round. If made in advance (up to 3 days), they should be stored in an airtight tin. If necessary they can be crisped briefly in a hot oven (425 degrees F.).

PREPARING THE DOUGH

Combine the warm butter, salt, and milk in a mixing bowl and beat well. Gradually beat in the sifted flour. When well mixed, remove to a lightly floured board and knead for 3 to 4 minutes until smooth. If the dough is sticky, add only a small amount of additional flour. Some of the stickiness disappears once the dough is kneaded. The dough should be quite soft. Wrap the dough well and leave at room temperature for 1 hour.

ROLLING AND CUTTING OUT

On a lightly floured board, roll out the dough as thin as possible. Using a pastry wheel, cut out 2-inch squares. Dust them lightly with flour, brush off the excess, stack them, and cover with a cloth. Lay out several thicknesses of paper towels.

DEEP-FRYING

Heat 3 inches of oil in a deep fryer or heavy pan until a deep-fry thermometer registers 365 degrees. Fry the squares a few at a time, pressing them under the oil with a slotted spoon and turning them over when they are brown on the underside. When they are golden, remove to paper towels to drain. If they brown too much in 8 seconds, reduce the temperature of the oil to 360 degrees. While they are still not, sprinkle them with salt and caraway seeds. If not eaten immediately, allow them to cool before storing in a tin with a tight-fitting lid. Crisp in a hot oven **(425 degrees)** if necessary.

ROTHENBURGER SCHNEEBALLEN

ROTHENBURG SNOWBALLS

MAKES ABOUT 18
   PASTRIES

4 large eggs, lightly
   beaten
¾ cup superfine
   sugar
½ cup heavy cream
2 tablespoons
   Zwetschkenwasser
   or slivovitz (plum
   schnapps), or sub-
   stitute kirsch or
   light rum
½ cup (1 stick)
   unsalted butter,
   melted and cooled
4 cups all-purpose
   flour, sifted
FOR DEEP-FRYING
6–8 cups vegetable
   oil
TO FINISH
Powdered sugar
EQUIPMENT
2 3-inch tea strain-
   ers with metal
   handles
Thin wire
Deep fryer or heavy,
   deep pan with
   deep-fry
   thermometer
Chopstick or wooden
   handle

I've eaten these charming sugar-dusted treats in both Vienna and Munich, but I think no other single town or city can claim them as exclusively as Rothenburg ob der Tauber, Germany. In this picturesque medieval town southwest of Nürnberg, pyramids of Schneeballen decorate pastry shop windows throughout the winter months. At Konditorei Frei, the proprietor, Hans Karl Frei, gave me his recipe—a dough rich with eggs and cream and flavored with *Zwetschkenwasser* (plum schnapps)—and several tips. The best *Schneeballen* are made with plenty of eggs and clear schnapps. The latter ingredient not only flavors the dough, but also works with the eggs in the mixture to act as a leavening agent, making for a lighter pastry. When cut in ribbonlike strands that are tangled into a ball and deep-fried in a special iron, the dough is transformed into a large, ruffled snowball approximately 3½ inches in diameter, which is then dusted with powdered sugar to give it its snowy appearance.

MAKING A HINGED FORM

Home bakers in Rothenburg, too, are adept in their preparation, using a special long-handled iron with a slotted hinged ball at the end which is sold in the local hardware stores. Because *Schneeballeisen* (snowball irons) are not readily obtainable, I have improvised a method using two metal-handled mesh tea strainers, 3 inches in diameter. If the strainers have plastic or wooden handles, you must make certain not to lower that part into the deep fat. For this reason, metal-handled strainers are advised. Using a short piece of thin wire, fasten the strainers together looping the wire through the hooks at the top of the strainers. This fastening will serve as the hinge of the device and the handles will be used to open and shut it. The strainers should be attached loosely enough to leave a ½-inch gap when the two halves are closed, allowing for expansion of the snow-balls when they cook. To enable you to keep your hands well out of range of any splattering fat, tie another length of wire through the loops at the ends of the strainer handles, twisting the wire loop once to secure it. A 14-inch length of wire, when doubled through the handles, will give 7 inches of extended handle, allowing for a convenient margin of safety.

USING THE FORM

Dangling the strainer arrangement from the wire extension and wearing a padded oven mitt, you can safely immerse the pastry in the hot fat, keeping your hands well away. To release each snowball, untwist the wire holding the handles and let the snowball fall out onto a paper towel. Take caution that the handles of the strainer have cooled before touching them.

While an electric deep fryer is easier to use since it automatically regulates the temperature of the fat, a deep heavy-bottomed pan used in conjunction with a deep-fry thermometer can be used equally well.

PREPARING THE DOUGH

Beat the eggs and sugar until well combined—1 to 2 minutes. Add the cream, schnapps, and melted butter, beating about 30 seconds until well mixed. Gradually beat in all but ½ cup flour, adding only enough of the remaining flour to prevent the dough from sticking to your hands. Knead well and form into a flat round. Wrap the dough in plastic wrap, and leave at room temperature 2 hours.

FORMING THE SNOWBALLS

In the meantime, prepare the tea strainers as described in the recipe introduction. Break off pieces of dough the size of a large walnut. On a lightly floured board, roll each piece into a rectangle 7 × 5 inches and ⅛ inch thick, rolling out no more than 5 at a time. Cover the pastries and dough not being used with plastic wrap. It won't matter if the rolled-out dough is more oval or slightly imperfect in shape, so long as the dimensions are approximately those given. Turn each rectangle so the long side is facing you. Using a sharp knife or a pastry wheel, cut 8 evenly spaced parallel slashes down the middle of the rectangle, perpendicular to the long side, so that the slashes never cut clear through either side of the rectangle, beginning and ending ½ inch from the edges. The dough when properly cut is still in one piece with the slashes running down the middle.

Thread a chopstick or a thin wooden spoon handle through alternating ribbons of the rectangle. Lift the piece of pastry up with the stick, pulling the alternating ribbons down so they are well separated. Gently remove the pastry from the stick. Tangle the mass with your hands to make a shape resembling a loosely tangled ball of yarn. Place it between the wired tea strainers. Close the strainers around the ball of dough, twisting the extension wire once. Set aside while you heat 4 to 5 inches of oil in a deep fryer or heavy pan until a deep-fry thermometer registers **365 degrees F.**

DEEP-FRYING

Holding the strainers by the extended piece of wire, lower the pastry into the hot oil, making sure the pastry is well submerged. Turn once or twice, cooking the Snowball until it is golden, approximately 1 minute. If not using an electric deep fryer, regulate the heat to keep the temperature even. If the first Snowball begins to color too quickly, lower the temperature of the oil to 360 degrees F. Lay out several thicknesses of paper towel. Remove the strainer from the oil, letting it drain on paper towels. Untwist the extension wire. Allow the Snowball to fall from the strainer onto a clean piece of paper towel.

FINISHING

While the Snowballs are still warm, dust them completely with powdered sugar, turning them so they are well coated all the way around. Continue with the remaining pastry.

If you don't use all the dough at one time, it can be wrapped well in plastic wrap and refrigerated for several days or frozen, to be used on another occasion.

Serve the Snowballs at room temperature. If not using immediately, wait until they have cooled completely before storing them.

STORING

If not eaten immediately, *Schneeballen* will remain crisp for 1 week in an airtight container at room temperature, in which case they will probably need to be dusted again with powdered sugar before serving.

APFELSCHEIBEN IM KÄFIG

APPLE SLICES IN CAGES

MAKES ABOUT
20–24 SLICES

2 cups all-purpose
   flour, sifted
¼ teaspoon salt
7 tablespoons un-
   salted butter,
   melted and com-
   pletely cooled
   but still liquid
⅓ cup plus 1
   tablespoon water
8 large Granny
   Smith or other
   tart apples
Vegetable oil for
   deep-frying
TO FINISH
½ cup granulated
   sugar
1 teaspoon cinnamon
Powdered sugar
TO SERVE
Heavy cream, lightly
   whipped to form
   soft peaks
EQUIPMENT
Pastry wheel
Deep fryer or heavy,
   deep pan
Slotted spoon
Deep-fry thermometer

This unusual recipe from Switzerland offers an attractive and tasty apple treat which can be used as a snack or full-fledged dessert. Wrapped with narrow crossed strips of pastry to resemble a flower or cage, thick slices of apple are deep-fried until golden, dredged with cinnamon sugar, and served with a dollop of whipped cream. They are best eaten while still warm, but can be made earlier in the day and rewarmed in a medium oven if not eaten immediately.

PREPARING THE DOUGH

For the pastry, sift the flour and salt together into a large mixing bowl. Mix the water together with the cooled melted butter. Pour the liquid ingredients onto the flour and beat with a wooden spoon until well blended. Pull together into a flat round. Wrap the dough tightly in plastic wrap and refrigerate for 1 hour or until firm. when the pastry is ready, peel and core the apples, and slice them into 1-inch rings.

MAKING THE "CAGE"

On a lightly floured board, roll out the pastry ⅛ inch thick. Using a pastry wheel, cut strips of pastry ⅜ inch thick and long enough to wrap around the apple slices, starting and ending in the center of the same side. For smaller slices, allow 3 strips per slice; for larger slices, 4 strips per slice. Wrap the strips around so they all meet in the center of on the same side and resemble

the spokes of a wheel. Brush the center point with a little water
as each strip is applied and press them in well so they stick
together. Lay out a double thickness of paper towels.

DEEP-FRYING

Heat 3 to 4 inches of vegetable oil in a deep fryer or heavy
pan until a deep-fry thermometer registers **360 degrees F.** Mix
the sugar and cinnamon together in a shallow bowl and set
aside. Fry the slices, 3 at a time, submerging them in the fat
with a slotted spoon. When the pastry is golden on the underside, turn the slices and allow the other side to color. When
done, remove the paper towels to drain. While still warm, roll
the slices in the cinnamon sugar, then dredge with sifted powdered sugar. Continue until all the slices are fried.

Serve while still warm with lightly whipped cream.

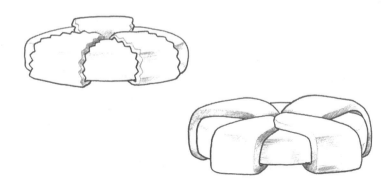

SCHENKELI (BERNESE MUTZENMANDELN)

SUGARED "THIGHS"

MAKES ABOUT 45

½ cup (1 stick)
   unsalted butter,
   softened
⅔ cup less 1 table-
   spoon superfine
   sugar
2 large eggs
1 tablespoon kirsch
   or light rum
Grated rind of 1
   lemon
2 cups all-purpose
   flour
¼ teaspoon salt
Vegetable oil for
   deep-frying
TO FINISH
½ cup sugar
1 teaspoon cinnamon
EQUIPMENT
Deep fryer or heavy
   pan
Slotted spoon
Deep-fry thermometer

A specialty from Canton Bern in Switzerland, these small pastries made at local fairs and occasionally at home are tapered at either end like a thigh (Schenkel) before they are deep-fried and sugared. When cooled, they will keep in an airtight tin for up to three days.

PREPARING THE DOUGH

Using an electric mixer, cream the butter and sugar together until light in color. Add the eggs, one at a time, beating well before adding the next. Beat in the kirsch or rum and grated lemon rind. Scrape down the beaters. Sift the flour and salt directly onto the butter mixture and fold it in with a spoon until well blended. Pat the dough into a flat round and wrap well in plastic wrap. Chill in the refrigerator for 1 hour or until it is firm enough to handle.

SHAPING THE DOUGH

Break off walnut-sized pieces of dough. On a lightly floured board, roll them back and forth into a fat cylinder, tapering the ends neatly with your fingers to produce the characteristic thigh shape. Continue until all the dough is shaped. Lay out a double thickness of paper towels. Mix the sugar and cinnamon together in a shallow bowl. Set aside.

DEEP-FRYING

Heat 3 to 4 inches of oil in a deep fryer or heavy pan until a deep-fry thermometer registered **360 degrees F.** Fry them three to four at a time, submerging them in the oil with a slotted spoon. When they are golden on the underside, turn them and cook the other side until golden. Remove them to paper towels to drain. Cut one in half to make sure it is cooked clear through. While the *Schenkeli* are still warm, roll them in the cinnamon sugar. It is normal for them to have a slight split down the center. Continue until all of the pastries have been fried, adding more oil if necessary and reheating to the proper temperature before frying the next batch.

SPRITZKRAPFEN
PUFF PASTE DOUGHNUTS

MAKES 12 TO 14

1 cup all-purpose
  flour, sifted
½ teaspoon salt
6 tablespoons un-
  salted butter,
  cut in pieces
1 cup water
3½ large eggs (Beat
  the fourth egg
  with a fork, using
  only half the
  beaten egg)
Vegetable oil for
  deep-frying
TO FINISH
Powdered sugar,
  sifted
EQUIPMENT
Pastry bag fitted
  with large star
  tip
Paper cut per the
  instructions in
  the introduction
Deep fryer or heavy
  pan
Slotted spoon
Deep-fry thermometer

Called *Spritstrauben* in Austria, these deep-fried pastries, made at fairs and throughout the year, are as popular in Vienna as they are in Berlin. The trick is to pipe the puff paste or *pâte à choux* onto a piece of paper only slightly larger than the diameter of the deep-fry pan. When the paper is held upside down above the hot fat, steam from the fat eventually causes the piped rounds to fall naturally into the fat. The paper should be just long enough so you can hold onto the ends out of range of the fat. If your deep fryer is 9 inches in diameter you should cut a rectangle or oval of paper 10 × 15 inches. You will need three to four pieces of parchment or wax paper cut to the proper size.

These pastries are best made shortly before they are to be served.

PREPARING THE PUFF PASTE

Sift the flour and salt together and set aside. Heat the butter and water in a heavy saucepan over high heat, stirring until the butter has melted. Allow the mixture to come to a full boil. Boil 10 seconds. Remove from the heat and immediately pour all the flour into the pan at once and stir vigorously until smooth. This is important if the mixture is to thicken properly. When well mixed, return to low heat and beat 3 to 4 minutes, or until the mixture no longer sticks to your fingers when pinched. Spread the mixture out on a plate to cool it. Wash out the

saucepan to remove any crust that has formed on the bottom and dry well. After 5 minutes, return the mixture to the pan. Off the heat, beat in one egg at a time with a wooden spoon until each egg is completely incorporated, using only half of the fourth lightly beaten egg. The mixture should be very glossy.
NOTE you can use a food processor for beating in the eggs if you have one with a large enough container.

PIPING AND DEEP-FRYING

Spoon the mixture into a pastry bag fitted with a large star tip. Lay out a double thickness of paper towels. Heat 3 to 4 inches of vegetable oil in a deep fryer or heavy pan until a deep-fry thermometer registers 360 degrees F. Pipe the pastry in 2½-inch wreaths onto the precut paper, leaving the ends free on either side so you can hold the paper. Pipe no more than four on a sheet. When finished piping, hold the piece of paper upside down several inches above the hot fat. After a few seconds, the pastry rounds will fall on their own into the fat. Adjust the heat if necessary to keep the temperature constant. When they are golden on the underside, turn them and allow them to color on the other side. Remove to paper towels to drain. While still warm, dust with sifted powdered sugar. Continue until all the pastries are fried.

M A S T E R   R E C I P E

YEAST-DOUGH PASTRIES

BASIC DEEP-FRIED YEAST DOUGH

¼ cup water, heated to 105 degrees
1 tablespoon sugar
2 packages dry powdered yeast
3 cups plus 2 tablespoons all-purpose flour
½ teaspoon salt
6 tablespoons un-salted butter, melted
¼ cup milk
2 large eggs at room temperature
½ cup superfine sugar
Grated rind of 1 lemon

Mix the water and sugar together. Sprinkle the powdered yeast over the warm water. Leave to rise in a warm place for about 10 minutes. Meanwhile, sift the flour and salt together into a large mixing bowl, and make a well in the center. When the yeast has risen and bubbled, melt the butter in a small saucepan. Add the milk and warm the two together until the mixture reaches 105 degrees. Mix together with the yeast and pour into the well you have made in the flour. Beat the eggs lightly with the ½ cup of sugar and grated lemon rind and add to the liquid ingredients. Using a wooden spoon (ideally one with a hole in the middle), gradually draw the flour into the liquid ingredients. When well mixed, continue beating with the spoon, then, eventually using your hand, pull the mixture up and throw it back into the bowl. Continue for 6 to 8 minutes, or until the dough is smooth. It is meant to be quite sticky and loose. Cover with a damp cloth and leave to rise in a warm place until doubled, about 1½ hours.

Use as required in the recipes.

HEFEKÜCHLEIN
Raisin Yeast Cakes

These small, raisin-filled yeast balls from Switzerland are sold at village fairs and are made in homes occasionally throughout the year. Similar deep-fried raisin-filled yeast pastries are made in Germany. Called *Kirchweihnudeln* or *Kirchweihküchel*, they are produced annually at *Kirchweihe*—a village festival that commemorates the dedication of the local church.

The yeast dough is sticky and loose enough to be scooped up with a metal spoon, after which it is dropped into hot fat. It is important to test the first one or two balls to make sure they have cooked clear through. Cut them in half to check. If they have not, the temperature of the fat should be lowered slightly so they cook more slowly, then test again.

Hefeküchlein are best served while still warm. However, if made earlier in the day they can be rewarmed in a hot oven (**425 degrees F.**) for several minutes before serving.

MAKES ABOUT 35

1 recipe Basic
  Deep-Fried Yeast
  Dough, facing page
½ cup raisins
2 tablespoons light
  rum, barely
  warmed
2 tablespoons all-
  purpose flour
Vegetable oil for
  deep-frying
TO FINISH
⅓ cup granulated
  sugar
1 teaspoon cinnamon
EQUIPMENT
Deep fryer or heavy
  pan
Deep-fry thermometer
Slotted spoon

1½ HOURS BEFORE DEEP-FRYING

Make the Basic Deep-Fried Yeast Dough and allow it to rise, approximately 1½ hours. While the dough is rising, soak the raisins in the rum. When the dough has risen, beat it down with a spoon. Drain the raisins and toss them together with 2 tablespoons of flour to help separate them. Mix them into the dough until well distributed. Lay out a double thickness of paper towels. Mix the sugar with the cinnamon in a shallow bowl or plate and set aside.

DEEP-FRYING

Heat 3 to 4 inches of vegetable oil in a deep fryer or heavy pan until a deep-fry thermometer registers **360 degrees F.** Dip a metal tablespoon into the hot fat, then into the dough, scooping up a heaping spoonful. Use a second metal spoon to help push the dough off into the hot fat. Working quickly, spoon up to four balls into the fat, pressing them under the fat with a slotted spoon. Cover the dough with a damp cloth when it is not being used. Turn the balls several times with a slotted spoon. When golden all over, remove to paper towels to drain, testing one ball from the first batch to make sure it is cooked through. When cool enough to handle but still warm, roll the *Hefeküchlein* in the sugar/cinnamon mixture. Continue until all the dough is used, adding more oil to the pan if necessary, and bringing it to the correct temperature before cooking the next batch of *Hefeküchlein*.

HAMBURGER APFELPFANNKUCHEN

HAMBURGER APPLE YEAST PANCAKES

Apple pancakes made in various ways are at local fairs throughout Germany. This version from Hamburg, made with a loose yeast dough, is traditionally baked in a pan with deep indentations which help give the *Pfann-kuchen* a regular shape. However, they can easily be shaped with spoons and deep-fried—the method given here, since the traditional pan is not widely available.

1½ HOURS BEFORE DEEP-FRYING

Make the Basic Deep-Fried Yeast Dough. While the dough is rising, peel, core, and quarter the apples. Cut across in thin slices, then coarsely chop. Toss the slices together with the lemon juice in a mixing bowl. Add the sugar, rum, and grated lemon rind and leave to steep 5 minutes. When the dough has risen, beat it down with a spoon. The dough should be loose and somewhat sticky. Add the apple mixture to the yeast dough, mixing well to distribute it evenly. Lay out a double thickness of paper towels. Mix the sugar and cinnamon in a shallow bowl and set aside.

DEEP-FRYING

Heat 3 to 4 inches of vegetable oil in a deep fryer or heavy pan until a deep-fry thermometer registers **360 degrees F.** Mix the sugar and cinnamon together in a shallow bowl and set aside. Dip a metal tablespoon into the hot fat, then into the dough, scooping up a heaping spoonful. Use a second metal spoon to help push the dough off into the deep fat. Work

MAKES ABOUT 40

1 recipe Basic Deep-Fried Yeast Dough, p. 200
2 pounds Golden Delicious apples (about 6 to 8)
Juice of ½ lemon
4 tablespoons sugar
2 tablespoons light or dark rum
Grated rind of 1 lemon
Vegetable oil for deep-frying
TO FINISH
⅓ cup granulated sugar
1 teaspoon cinnamon
EQUIPMENT
Deep fryer or heavy pan
Deep-fry thermometer
Slotted spoon

quickly and spoon three to four balls into the fat at once, pressing them under the fat with a slotted spoon. Turn several times. When golden on all sides, remove to paper towels to drain.

When the *Pfannkuchen* are cool enough to handle but still warm, roll them in the sugar/cinnamon mixture. Continue deep-frying until all the dough is used, adding more oil to the pan if necessary, and bringing it to the correct temperature before cooking the next batch of *Pfannkuchen*.

SCHMALZBREZELN
YEAST-DOUGH PRETZELS

MAKES
APPROXIMATELY
20

1 recipe Basic
Sweet Yeast
Dough, p. 217
Vegetable oil for
deep frying
TO FINISH
1 cup granulated
sugar, mixed
with
2 tablespoons
cinnamon
EQUIPMENT
Deep fryer or heavy
pan
Deep-fry thermometer
Slotted spoon

Large sweet yeast dough pretzels, deep-fried and sugared, are a specialty in Germany for New Year's Eve. They are best made the same day they are to be served. Like doughnuts in flavor, they can also be served for breakfast and make an unusual treat for children on Halloween. You will need to prepare the dough a day in advance of deep-frying the pretzels.

THE DAY BEFORE
PREPARING THE DOUGH

Make the Basic Sweet Yeast Dough. After it has risen, punch the dough down, wrap it well in plastic wrap, then in a heavy plastic bag, tightly knotted. Refrigerate overnight. An hour after refrigerating, punch the dough down—it will have expanded considerably.

The Following Day
SHAPING THE DOUGH

Leave the dough at room temperature 30–45 minutes, kneading it briefly after 20 minutes to help soften it. After it has warmed slightly, knead well and divide it into three parts. Wrap the dough not being used with plastic wrap and place in a plastic bag, knotting the bag well. Refrigerate until needed. Cut the dough in 1½-inch strips and roll them back and forth on a lightly floured board until they are ropes, 14 inches long and approximately ⅜ inch in diameter. Holding one end in each hand, cross them 2 inches before the ends. Twist the ends together twice. Pull the twisted ends back down to the center of the looped strip, moistening them lightly with water and pressing them well into the loop of dough. You should now have a figure resembling a twisted pretzel. Lay the finished pretzels on a baking sheet, 1½ inches part. As you finish each sheet, cover the pretzels with a damp towel and leave them in a warm place until they have risen noticeably, approximately 30 minutes.

30 Minutes Later
DEEP-FRYING

When the pretzels have risen, lay out a double thickness of paper towels. Heat 3 to 4 inches of vegetable oil in a deep fryer or heavy pan until a deep-fry thermometer registers **360 degrees F.** Fry two or three pretzels at a time, submerging them in the fat with a slotted spoon. When they are golden on the underside, turn them over and allow them to color on the other side. If they seem to color too quickly, lower the heat slightly. Remove from the fat with a slotted spoon and drain on paper towels. While still warm, dust on both sides with the mixture of sugar and cinnamon. Continue until all the pretzels have been fried, adding more oil if necessary, and bringing it back to the correct temperature before frying the next batch.

BERLINER PFANNKUCHEN
BERLIN JELLY DOUGHNUTS

MAKES ABOUT 40

*1 recipe Basic
Sweet Yeast
Dough, p. 217*
*3 cups (36 oz)
apricot or plum
jam*
*1 egg white, lightly
beaten*
*Vegetable oil for
deep-frying*
TO FINISH
Granulated sugar
*Powdered sugar,
sifted (optional)*
EQUIPMENT
*Deep fryer or heavy
pan*
Deep-fry thermometer
Slotted spoon
*2½-inch plain round
cookie cutter*

While *Pfannkuchen* in German means pancake, for Berliners it refers to a favorite carnival treat—deep-fried jelly doughnuts, similar to the version we eat in America. Traditionally eaten on Shrove Tuesday throughout Germany, and on New Year's Eve in some parts, this favorite specialty goes by different names in different regions: *Silvesterkrapfen, Berliner, Bismarcks, Fastnachtskuchen,* or *Faschingskrapfen,* to name a few. The product, however, is the same.

For best flavor, they should be deep fried the same day, or shortly before they are served. Plan to prepare the dough the day before the deep frying. This recipe makes about 40, but it can easily be cut in half.

THE DAY BEFORE
PREPARING THE DOUGH

Make up the Basic Sweet Yeast Dough, wrapping and refrigerating the dough overnight.

THE FOLLOWING DAY
ASSEMBLING THE DOUGHNUTS

Leave the dough at room temperature 45 minutes, kneading it after 20 minutes to help warm it through. Knead again and divide the dough in three parts (or two, if using half a recipe). Wrap and refrigerate the pieces not being used until needed. Roll out each piece on a lightly floured board until ¼ inch thick.

With the cookie cutter, cut out rounds from the rolled-out dough. Knead the scraps together and roll out again. On half of the rounds place a generous teaspoonful of jam in the center. Moisten the rim with lightly beaten egg white. Place a plain round on top and press the edges together well to seal the seam. Place the doughnuts on a baking sheet, cover them with a damp towel, and leave them in a warm place until they have noticeably risen, about 30 to 40 minutes. Continue with the remaining dough until all the doughnuts are cut and filled. Spread out a double layer of paper towels.

30–40 Minutes Later
DEEP-FRYING

Fill the deep fryer or heavy pan with enough oil that when the doughnuts are submerged, they will not be completely covered. This will produce the distinguishing line around the center of each. In a heavy pan, you will need approximately 1½ inches of oil; in a deep fryer, slightly more depending on the depth of the metal basket. Heat the oil until a deep-fry thermometer registers **360 degrees F.** Place two or three doughnuts in the fat at a time, adjusting the oil temperature if necessary, so it remains constant. With the hot oil in the pan, baste the tops and cover the pan with a lid for 3 minutes to help them to rise. When golden on the underside, turn them and cook uncovered until they are golden. Drain on paper towels. Test one doughnut from the first batch by cutting it in half to make sure it is cooked through. If not, the temperature of the fat is probably too hot, coloring them too quickly. Lower the temperature of the fat slightly and test again.

When the doughnuts are cool enough to handle but still warm, roll them in a shallow bowl of granulated sugar. If desired, you can dust the tops of the doughnuts with sifted powder sugar after they have been rolled in granulated sugar.

Continue until all the doughnuts are cooked, adding more oil to the deep fryer when needed and heating it to the correct temperature before frying the next batch.

GRIDDLE WAFERS

MASTER RECIPE

EISERKUCHEN

GRIDDLE WAFERS

*MAKES ABOUT
16–18 5-INCH
WAFERS*

*4 tablespoons
unsalted
softened
1 cup sugar
½ teaspoon vanilla
extract
2 large eggs, lightly
beaten
2 cups all-purpose
flour, sifted
1½ cups water
TO FINISH
Powdered sugar,
sifted
EQUIPMENT
Special 2-handled
embossed griddle
(Waffeleisen) or
electric model
(not a waffle iron,
which has too
deep a grid)*

Some years ago on a trip to Germany, I bought a beautifully embossed iron griddle for wafers with two long handles, meant to be heated on a normal gas or electric stove burner. Upon returning home, I found the griddle came, alas, without recipe or instructions. My mother's German housekeeper came to my rescue with the following family recipe, which makes thin, wonderfully crisp embossed wafers I normally curl into a cylinder and dust with powdered sugar. For a more elaborate dessert or teatime treat, they can be filled with lightly sweetened whipped cream piped with a pastry tube.

There are also electric embossed wafer griddles which can be used, following instructions from the manufacturer. Because of the time required, these wafers are generally made for special occasions. They are especially festive at Christmas when they make a beautiful centerpiece on a platter of assorted cookies and fruit breads.

½ Hour Before
PREPARING THE BATTER

Cream the butter until light, beating in some of the sugar, the vanilla extract, the eggs, a little at a time, and finally the remaining sugar. Gradually beat in the sifted flour, alternating with the water, until the batter is smooth. The batter should be moderately thin, flowing freely when poured. Alternatively, process the butter, sugar, liquid ingredients, and flour briefly in a food processor or blender until the batter is smooth. Allow to rest ½ hour.

MAKING THE WAFERS

Once the prepared batter has rested for at least ½ hour, brush both sides of the wafer iron with oil. Heat both sides of the griddle on a burner over medium heat until a drop of water on the griddle bounces. Over the sink or counter (rather than over the burner), pour a large spoonful of the batter on the center of one side of the preheated iron. There should be enough batter to spread just to the edges of the iron when it is closed without spilling out. Close the iron and heat on one side, directly on the burner, for approximately 45 to 60 seconds, or until it has browned. Repeat on the other side until it is golden in color and can be removed easily from the griddle. Cooking time on the second side will be shorter. The first wafer, which generally is not very pretty because of the oil on the griddle, should be used for a test. If it seems slightly thick, beat 1 to 2 teaspoons of water into the batter to thin it slightly. You shouldn't need to oil your griddle again after the first wafer has been cooked. Oil again only if the wafers begin sticking.

Proceed with the remaining batter until it is used up. If desired, curl the wafers into cylinder or cone shapes while they are still hot and dust them with sifted powdered sugar. They can be eaten as is or filled with whipped cream and a few fresh berries in season.

STORING

To store, place the wafers in a tin or jar with tight fitting lid. Store at room temperature for up to 10 days.

WASSERBRETZELI
WATER WAFERS

*MAKES ABOUT
16–18 LARGE OR
32 SMALL
WAFERS*

*1 large egg
2½ tablespoons heavy
   cream
2½ tablespoons
   vegetable oil
1 pinch salt
1¼ cups sugar
Grated rind of 1
   lemon
2 cups all-purpose
   flour sifted
1 cup water
EQUIPMENT
Special 2-handled
   embossed iron
   griddle
   (Waffeleisen—
   see Equipment) or
   electric model
   (not a waffle iron,
   which has too
   deep a grid)*

In Switzerland, a *Bretzeli* (not to be confused with *Brezel*—pretzel) is the word used for a griddle wafer. Where the German version uses butter, this Swiss recipe uses cream and vegetable oil. Lemon rind rather than vanilla gives the wafers a distinctive flavor. Swiss wafer irons, which also come in electric models, are often divided into four so that four small wafers can be made at a time instead of one large one. If small, these wafers are generally left flat and unsugared. On a Sunday afternoon, they make a delicate accompaniment to a fruity white wine or a pot of steaming tea.

½ HOUR BEFORE
PREPARING THE BATTER

In a medium-sized mixing bowl, beat the egg, cream, oil, salt, sugar, and lemon rind together until well blended. Gradually beat in the flour, alternating with the water until the batter is smooth. Alternatively, blend the liquid ingredients with the flour in a blender or food processor until smooth. Allow the batter to rest ½ hour before using.

MAKING THE WAFERS

Once the prepared batter has rested for at least ½ hour, brush both sides of the embossed wafer iron with oil. Heat both sides of the griddle over medium heat until a drop of water bounces on the griddle. Over the sink or counter, rather than over the stove, pour a large spoonful of the batter on the center of one side of the preheated iron. There should be enough batter to spread just to the edges of the iron when it is closed without spilling out. Close the iron and heat on one side, directly on the burner, for approximately 45 to 60 seconds, or until the wafer has browned. Repeat on the other side until it is golden in color and can be removed easily from the griddle. Cooking time on the second side will be shorter. The first wafer, which generally is not very pretty because of the oil on the griddle, should be used for a test. If it seems slightly thick, beat 1 to 2 teaspoons water into the batter to thin it slightly. You shouldn't need to oil your griddle again after the first wafer has been cooked. Oil again only if the batter begins to stick.

Proceed with the remaining batter until it is used up.

STORING

To store, place the wafers in a tin or jar with tight-fitting lid. Store at room temperature for up to 10 days.

KÜMMELBRETZELI
CARAWAY WAFERS

**MAKES ABOUT 50
2-INCH WAFERS**

2 cups all-purpose
flour
½ teaspoon salt
7 tablespoons un-
salted butter
1½ teaspoons (½
tablespoon) cara-
way seeds
1 large egg, lightly
beaten
3 tablespoons dry
white wine or
Vermouth
DECORATION IF
BAKED IN THE
OVEN (OPTIONAL)
¾ cup grated
Parmesan cheese
EQUIPMENT
Special embossed
iron griddle
(see Equipment),
or bake in
the oven.

These savory Swiss wafers made with white wine and caraway seeds make an unusual hors d'oeuvre or soup accompaniment. While they are generally made on an embossed iron griddle (see Equipment), because they are made of pastry dough rather than batter, they can also be baked on a cookie sheet in the oven. In this case, a small amount of grated Parmesan cheese could be sprinkled on each one to give them a more finished look and a richer flavor.

2–24 HOURS BEFORE
PREPARING THE DOUGH

Sift the flour with the salt into a large mixing bowl. Grate the butter on the coarse blade of a cheese grater into the flour, mixing it into the flour every so often before continuing. Cut the butter flakes into the flour with two round-bladed knives until the mixture resembles coarse meal. Blend briefly with your fingertips. Mix in the caraway seeds. Combine the lightly beaten egg with the wine. Add ¾ of the liquid and cut it into the mixture with a knife. Add only enough additional liquid so the dough will pull together into a ball. Knead briefly on a lightly floured board. Roll the dough into 2 logs, 1½ inches in diameter. Wrap tightly in plastic wrap and refrigerate several hours or overnight.

AFTER THE DOUGH HAS CHILLED
MAKING THE WAFERS

To cook, cut dough into thin, ⅛-inch slices. If using a wafer iron, oil the two griddle plates and heat on both sides until a drop of water bounces. Place one or more dough rounds on the iron griddle, depending on its size, and cook briefly—approximately 45 seconds—on each side until the wafer is golden. Remove immediately from the griddle and repeat with the remaining dough.

OVEN METHOD

If baking in the oven, place the dough slices on buttered, floured baking sheet. Sprinkle each one with grated Parmesan cheese is desired. **Preheat the oven to 375 degrees F.** and bake until golden. Remove the wafers to cooling racks and proceed with the remaining dough.

STORING

Store in an airtight tin at room temperature. The wafers will keep fresh for several weeks if stored as above, or they can be wrapped and frozen for up to 3 months. If frozen, crisp briefly on a baking sheet in a hot oven and cool before serving.

5

FESTIVE BREADS—FESTLICHE BROTE

The recipes in this chapter are guaranteed to give pleasure to the whole household when the wonderful aroma of freshly baked bread wafts from the kitchen. These breads for holidays and special occasions are generally richer than daily breads, and have a long tradition. In pre-Christian times bread was not just for sustenance, but was also a symbol of life and fruitful harvest in fertility rites. With the coming of Christianity, these rites were merged symbolically into the celebration of the Eucharist.

Today, many of the fancy breads are drawn from the earliest traditions, in particular the braided breads baked in different shapes. A plain braided loaf (*Zopf*), wheels symbolizing the sun, wreaths for eternity, and crescents for the moon. Others are tied more closely to later Christian tradition: Dresden Christmas Stollen—a rich fruit loaf—and Easter Carp (*Osterkarpfen*). In more recent years, a small number have been assimilated from other cultures—Easter Egg Nests (*Eier im Nest*) from Greece and Doves (*Tauben*) from Italy—or have been created by an imaginative baker: New Year's good-luck pigs (*Neujahrs-Glücksschweinchen*). They all have one thing in common: they are baked to commemorate and celebrate as well as to savor.

Since bread is a staple in all German-speaking countries, commercial bakers there are generally exceptionally skilled. Home bakers also are for the most part highly competent. While the daily bread is usually bought from the local bakery, it is not uncommon for people to bake specialty breads throughout the year using traditional family recipes: *Kugelhopf*, an unmolded raisin-filled round, for Sundays; fruit breads such as *Hutzelbrot*, a dark fruit loaf, and *Weihnachtszopf*, fruit-filled braided loaf, for Christmas; *Speckkuchen*, flat bread with bacon, for New Year's; and an assortment of fish, wreaths, Easter egg nests, and doves for Easter (*Oster-Hefegebäck*), to name just a few.

Because most of these breads are made with a rich yeast dough, similar to a brioche dough, in most recipes I have recommended making the dough a day before it is to be baked. Overnight refrigeration makes it much easier to work with and encourages the different shapes to rise instead of flattening out. While bread making is a pleasurable task, it's also a time-consuming one, best left for a day when it's no effort for you to stay home (or when the weather is miserable), since the bread must be watched closely during the proving and baking stages and, because of the quantities, will most likely have to be baked in batches.

Many of the fruit-rich breads, especially, have excellent keeping properties if well wrapped and stored in a cool place. The other breads, for the most part, can also be baked ahead when it is convenient, then well wrapped in aluminum foil and frozen for up to three months.

M A S T E R   R E C I P E

LEICHTER HEFETEIG
BASIC SWEET YEAST DOUGH

NOTE If using dry yeast, dissolve it with the 2 tablespoons sugar in the ⅓ cup water warmed to 90 degrees F. Allow to rise in a warm place for about 10 minutes or until bubbly. Proceed with the instructions below, remembering not to add the water again.

ACTIVATING THE FRESH YEAST

Crumble the fresh yeast in a small bowl and mash together with the 2 tablespoons sugar, using a spoon, until the yeast is liquid. Set aside for several minutes. Sift half the flour into a large mixing bowl and sift the other half onto a large piece of paper or into a bowl and set aside.

MAKING THE SPONGE

Make a well in the center of the flour in the bowl. Heat the milk—with the water if using fresh yeast—until just warm to the touch, 80 degrees F. Pour into the well along with the dissolved yeast. Draw in the flour with a wooden spoon, beating well to make a thick batter. Dust some of the reserved flour over the top, cover with a damp towel, and allow the "sponge" to rise in a warm place until bubbling and double in bulk, approximately 30 minutes.

MAKING THE DOUGH

Grate the lemon rind into a bowl with the eggs and beat together lightly with the salt and sugar. Add the melted butter which has been allowed to cool. Set aside. When the sponge has risen sufficiently, beat the batter briefly to deflate it. Add the egg and butter mixture, then gradually beat in enough of the

*1½ ounces fresh
yeast or 1½
tablespoons dry
yeast (see Note)*
*2 tablespoons granu-
lated sugar*
*6½ cups (2 pounds)
bread flour*
1¼ cups whole milk
⅓ cup warm water
*Grated rind of 1
lemon*
2 large eggs
1 teaspoon salt
⅓ cup superfine sugar
*½ cup plus 2
tablespoons (1¼
sticks) unsalted
butter, melted*

reserved flour until the dough becomes manageable enough to handle. Knead on a lightly floured board until smooth and shiny or use an electric kneader, adding more flour if necessary to keep the dough from sticking. You will probably need most or all of the reserved flour. By hand, kneading will take approximately 15 to 20 minutes.

RISING AND CHILLING

Place the dough in a clean, well-buttered bowl. Lightly butter the surface of the dough and cover with a damp towel. Allow to rise in a warm place until double in bulk, approximately 1½ hours. Punch the dough down with your fist and knead briefly. Wrap well in plastic wrap, then in a large, heavy plastic bag, tightly closed, and refrigerate. For best results, refrigerate overnight, if time permits. An hour after refrigerating, punch the dough down in the bag—it will have expanded considerably. Use as directed in the recipe, kneading again briefly. Although you can use the dough without refrigerating overnight, this step is a good idea if you are making a decorative bread, as it will hold the design better.

REMEDY FOR BREAD THAT
BROWNS TOO RAPIDLY

In any of the recipes, if this dough browns too rapidly before the bread tests done (when a wooden skewer inserted in the bread comes out clean), drape a piece of aluminum foil over the bread to keep it from browning further.

RICH SWEET YEAST BREADS

M A S T E R   R E C I P E

SCHWERER HEFETEIG
BASIC RICH SWEET YEAST DOUGH

NOTE If using dry yeast, dissolve it with the 2 tablespoons sugar in the ½ cup of water warmed to 90 degrees F. Allow to rise in a warm place about 10 minutes or until bubbly. Proceed with the recipe as follows, remembering not to add the water again.

ACTIVATING THE FRESH YEAST

Crumble the fresh yeast in a small bowl and mash together with the 2 tablespoons sugar, using a spoon, until the yeast is liquid. Set aside for several minutes. Sift half the flour into a large mixing bowl and sift the other half onto a large piece of paper or into a bowl and set aside.

MAKING THE SPONGE

Make a well in the center of the flour in the bowl. Heat the milk—with the water if using fresh yeast—until just warm to the touch, 80 degrees F. Pour in the well along with the dissolved yeast. Draw in the flour with a wooden spoon, beating well, to make a thick batter. Dust some of the reserved flour over the top, cover with a damp towel, and allow the "sponge" to rise in a warm place until bubbling and double in bulk— approximately 30 minutes.

1½ ounces fresh yeast or 1½ tablespoons dry yeast (see Note)
2 tablespoons sugar
7⅓ cups (2½ pounds) bread flour
½ cup warm water
1½ cups whole milk
Grated rind of 1 lemon
2 large eggs
1 teaspoon salt
⅔ cup superfine sugar
¾ cup (3 sticks) unsalted butter, melted

MAKING THE DOUGH

Grate the lemon rind into a bowl with the eggs and beat together lightly with the salt and sugar. Add the melted butter which has been allowed to cool. Set aside. When the sponge has risen sufficiently, beat the batter briefly to deflate it. Add the egg and butter mixture, then gradually beat in enough of the reserved flour until the dough becomes manageable enough to handle. Knead on a lightly floured board until smooth and shiny or use an electric kneader, adding more flour if necessary to keep the dough from sticking. You will probably need most or all of the reserved flour. By hand, kneading will take approximately 15 to 20 minutes.

RISING AND CHILLING

Place the dough in a clean, well-buttered bowl. Lightly butter the surface of the dough, and cover with a damp towel. Allow to rise in a warm place until double in bulk, approximately 1½ hours. Punch the dough down with your fist and knead briefly. Wrap well in plastic wrap, then in a large, heavy plastic bag, tightly closed, and refrigerate. For best results, refrigerate overnight, if time permits. An hour after refrigerating, punch the dough down in the bag—it will have expanded considerably. Use as directed in the recipe, rekneading again briefly.

CHRISTMAS BREADS

In addition to the fruit-filled Christmas breads included in this chapter, a wide assortment of shapes and figures are made from plain sweet yeast dough for the Christmas holidays, including Santa Claus figures (*Weihnachtsmänner*), braided Christmas stars (*Geflochtener Weihnachtsstern*), Swiss Christmas men (*Grittibänzen*), and New Year's goodluck pigs (*Neujahrs-Glücksschweinchen*). If not to be used within a few days, any of these breads can be wrapped in aluminum foil after baking and frozen for up to three months.

WEIHNACHTSMÄNNER
SANTA CLAUS FIGURES

MAKES APPROXI-
MATELY SIX
8-INCH FIGURES

1 recipe Basic Sweet
 Yeast Dough
 (p. 217)
1 egg, lightly beaten
Whole blanched al-
 monds, split
 (see Almonds)
Currants

ASSEMBLING

Prepare the dough the day before, according to the instructions in the master recipe, kneading it briefly before use. Butter and flour baking sheets. Roll out the dough ½ inch thick. Use a large Santa Claus cookie cutter or make an 8-inch stencil from cardboard, and cut out medium-sized or large Santa figures. Knead the scraps together and roll a piece of dough back and forth on a board into a long thin roll. Brush the Santa figures with lightly beaten egg. Wind a piece of the rolled dough around its middle for a belt, and other pieces around the bottom of the robe, on the cuffs and hat to simulate fur. Place a split almond on the top of the hat for a pompon and edge the bottom of the robe with split almonds. Use two currants or small pieces of dough for eyes. Cut out a large mustache and beard from scraps of dough. Brush the decorations with beaten egg.

RISING

Place the Santa figures 2½ inches apart on the prepared baking sheets. Leave in a warm place until they have risen noticeably—approximately 20 to 25 minutes. Refrigerate for 15 minutes to help them keep their shape during baking. In the meantime, **preheat the oven to 400 degrees F.**

BAKING

Brush the figures once more with beaten egg. Bake in the middle of the oven until golden. Cool on wire racks.

GRITTIBÄNZEN

SWISS CHRISTMAS MEN

Whimsical *Grittibänzen* figures are traditionally found in most bread bakeries in German-speaking Switzerland during the Christmas season. They make amusing gifts for children and can easily be baked at home using the master recipe for sweet yeast dough. Instead of the tiny white pipe that is usually placed in the figure's mouth (which would be difficult to find), a twig of evergreen can be placed in his arm.

MAKES 4 LARGE
OR 6 MEDIUM
FIGURES

1 recipe Sweet Yeast
   Dough (p. 217)
1 egg, lightly beaten
4 to 6 small sprigs
   of evergreen for
   decoration

ASSEMBLING

Prepare the dough the day before, according to the instructions in the master recipe, kneading it again briefly before use. Butter and flour baking sheets. Roll the dough out into a large rectangle ½ inch thick. Cut the dough into 4 or 6 rectangles, 8 to 10 inches long, depending on whether you are making large or medium-sized figures. Leave a small amount of dough to be used for decoration. Using a sharp knife, cut a round head. Make two slashes on either side of the head and cut away arms. Make one slash up the middle almost to the waist to make the legs. Roll a small piece of dough into a very thin strand. Cut off three small pieces and coil them to form two eyes and a nose. Brush the surface of the figure well with lightly beaten egg and apply the tiny rings to the face. Roll a slightly larger piece of dough into another thin strand twice the height of the figure. Double the rope and loop it around the head and neck of the figure. Twist it two or three times to secure it, like a tie, and trail the ends down the center of each leg. Trim off even with the feet.

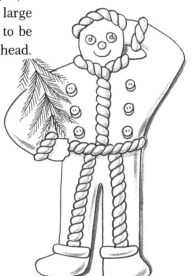

Make a similar strand and tie one piece around the waist for a belt, two small pieces above the feet to simulate the tops of boots, and two others at the wrists to make cuffs. Use a sharp knife to score a smiling mouth and to mark a double-breasted row of three buttons on either side of the tie. Or make the buttons from dough and press in well with the tip of a knife. Tuck one arm behind a hip and raise the other behind the head. Brush all the decorations with lightly beaten egg. Check to make sure all the decorations are firmly attached, pressing them onto the figure with the side or tip of a knife if necessary.

RISING

Place the *Grittibänzen* 2½ inches apart on the prepared baking sheets and leave in a warm place until they have risen noticeably—approximately 20 to 25 minutes. Refrigerate for 15 minutes to help them keep their shape during baking. In the meantime, **preheat the oven to 400 degrees F.**

BAKING

Brush the figures once more with beaten egg. Bake in the middle of the oven until golden, approximately 25 minutes. Cool on wire racks. Place a piece of evergreen in the arm of each.

GEFLOCHTENER WEIHNACHTSSTERN

BRAIDED CHRISTMAS STAR

ASSEMBLING

Prepare the dough the day before, according to the instructions in the master recipe, kneading it again briefly before use. Butter and flour baking sheets. Divide the dough to be used into six even pieces. Cut five of the pieces into three strands each. Roll the strands back and forth on a board until they are ropes 10 inches long, tapering to very thin at one end.

Braid the strands in threes to make tight braids. Brush the ends of each with lightly beaten egg and pinch together, pressing the tapered ends under. Each braid will form a point of the star, with the thicker part of the braids meeting in the center. Assemble the star, pressing the thick ends together in the center. Roll the sixth piece of dough until it is approximately ½ inch in diameter and 20 inches long. Starting from the center, coil it around to form a rosette. Brush the entire surface of the star with lightly beaten egg. Place the rosette in the center, pressing it down well to seal the seams. Brush the rosette with egg.

RISING

Place on the prepared baking sheet and leave in a warm place until it has risen noticeably—approximately 30 minutes. In the meantime, preheat the oven to 400 degrees F.

BAKING

Brush a second time with the beaten egg, making sure it gets well into the crevices. Bake in the middle of the oven until golden and until a wooden skewer inserted in the bread comes out clean—approximately 45 minutes. Carefully remove to a rack to cool before eating.

MAKES 1

1 recipe Basic Sweet Yeast Dough (p. 217) (You will need only three quarters of the amount for this recipe; the remainder can be used for one of the other figures suggested in this section.)

1 egg, lightly beaten

DRESDNER CHRISTSTOLLEN
DRESDEN CHRISTMAS STOLLEN

*MAKES 2 LARGE
OR 4 SMALL
LOAVES*

*1 recipe Basic Rich
Sweet Yeast
Dough, p. 219
1⅓ cups golden
raisins
1 cup currants
2 tablespoons light
or dark rum,
lightly warmed
2 teaspoons flour
1 cup mixed candied
orange and
lemon peel
1¼ cups blanched
almonds, coarsely
chopped
TO FINISH
¾ cup (1½ sticks)
unsalted butter,
melted
Superfine sugar
Powdered sugar*

Although different variations are baked in all parts of Germany, the stollen from Dresden, which generally comprises the richest mixture of butter and dried fruits, is the best-known. The traditional shape of stollen—tapered at each end with a ridge down the center—is meant to represent the Christ Child in swaddling clothes, thus the name Christstollen. It is a specialty of the Christmas season, and because of its good keeping properties is generally baked well in advance so that it can ripen.

Because it is so rich it is generally sliced thin, and is delicious for both breakfast and tea. It can be served at room temperature or slightly warmed (see the instructions at the end of the recipe).

THE DAY BEFORE

The day before making the stollen, soak the golden raisins and currants in a bowl with the rum. Prepare the dough according to the instructions in the master recipe.

THE FOLLOWING DAY
KNEADING

Butter and flour baking sheets. Knead the dough again briefly. Cut the round of dough into six pieces and place the pieces in a large mixing bowl. If the dough has been refrigerated overnight, cover with a damp towel for half an hour to allow to come to

room temperature. Drain the golden raisins and currants. Toss
them together with 2 teaspoons of flour to absorb the moisture
and keep them from sticking together. Combine them with the
chopped candied peels and coarsely chopped almonds. Sprinkle
some of the fruit and nut mixture over each piece of dough until
it is all used up. Knead the dough together with the fruit, first in
the mixing bowl and then on a lightly floured board. When well
blended, divide the dough into two (for large 14-inch stollen) or
four (for small 8-inch loaves). Roll each piece of dough into a
long, flat oval approximately 1 inch thick, using a rolling pin.
Wrap and refrigerate those pieces not being shaped.

SHAPING

With a rolling pin (preferably a long, narrow one), press a
firm indentation down the center of the dough. This will make
the stollen fold more securely. Fold one half of the stollen over
the other, lengthwise. Press the overlapping edge firmly to help
seal the seam. Taper the ends neatly to make slightly rounded
points. Use your hands to plump a small rounded ridge down
the center: place the side of each hand lengthwise on either
side of the visual center of the stollen, leaving a space of approximately 2 inches between your hands. Press them simulta-
neously into the soft dough, causing the ridge of dough to
protrude slightly. Continue down the length of the stollen. Place
it on a prepared baking sheet. If placing more than one on a
baking sheet, leave 3 inches between them. Brush with some of
the melted butter. Allow to rise in a warm place until double in
bulk—approximately 45 minutes. In the meantime, **preheat
the oven to 350 degrees F.**

NOTE. Keep in the refrigerator any stollen not being baked with
the first batch. Take it out to rise about 45 minutes before your
oven will be free.

BAKING

When the stollen has risen properly, bake, one sheet at a
time, in the middle of the oven. After 15 minutes, drape a large

piece of aluminum foil loosely over the stollen, covering the top, sides, and ends, to keep it light in color. Bake until lightly colored and a wooden skewer inserted in the stollen comes out clean, approximately 50 to 70 minutes, depending on the size.

When the stollen is done, remove it from the oven and brush generously with the remaining melted butter. Allow to cool for 5 minutes on the baking sheet. Dust first with superfine sugar, then with powdered sugar while the bread is still warm. Transfer to a wire rack to finish cooling.

When well wrapped in several layers of aluminum foil, stollen will keep in a cool place or in the refrigerator for as long as one month, or for up to three months if frozen after baking.

To refresh stollen that has been refrigerated, slice it thin, stack the pieces on top of one another, and wrap them in aluminum foil. Place in an oven **preheated to 375 degrees F.** and allow to warm through, approximately 10 to 15 minutes.

CHRISTSTOLLEN MIT MARZIPAN

CHRISTMAS STOLLEN WITH MARZIPAN

The following stollen variation is one that was baked by a German bakery in Colorado every Christmas and which I enjoyed as a child.

1 recipe Dresden Christmas Stollen

1 pound ready-made marzipan Powdered sugar

Prepare the loaves of stollen as described in the master recipe. Before folding them in half lengthwise, roll out the marzipan on a board lightly dusted with powdered sugar. Roll it out slightly shorter than the length of the stollen and wide enough to cut two or four 2-inch strips (depending on whether you are making two or four stollen). Cut the strips of marzipan to fit down the center of each loaf. Fold the loaf over the marzipan as described in the master recipe, tucking in any marzipan that protrudes. It should be completely covered. Press the edge down well to seal it. Then proceed as above.

WEIHNACHTSZOPF
CHRISTMAS BRAID

At Christmas time, the traditional Sunday braided bread is often made with a slightly richer dough and filled with nuts and fruit. In Germany it would be served, sliced thin, both at breakfast and as part of a selection of baked goods with afternoon coffee.

THE DAY BEFORE

The day before baking, soak the golden raisins and currants in the rum and prepare the dough according to the instructions in the master recipe.

THE FOLLOWING DAY
KNEADING

Remove the dough from the refrigerator ½ hour before use, covering it with a damp towel. Knead again briefly. Butter and flour a baking sheet.

Toss the golden raisins and currants together with a few teaspoons of flour to absorb the moisture and keep them from sticking together. Combine them with the chopped mixed peel and coarsely chopped almonds. Cut the round of dough into six pieces. Place the pieces in a large mixing bowl. Sprinkle the fruit and nut mixture over each piece until it is all used up. Knead the dough together with the fruit, first in the mixing bowl and then on a lightly floured board. When well blended, divide the dough in half for two loaves.

MAKES 2

1 recipe Basic Rich Sweet Yeast Dough (p. 219)
⅔ cup golden raisins
½ cup currants
2 tablespoons rum
2 teaspoons flour
½ cup mixed candied orange and lemon peel, chopped
¾ cups blanched almonds, coarsely chopped
TO FINISH
2 eggs, lightly beaten with a pinch of salt
Powdered sugar (optional)

SHAPING

Take one piece of dough and divide it into three even pieces. Wrap and refrigerate the piece of dough not being used. Roll each strip back and forth on a board to make long, narrow ropes approximately 14 inches long, tapering the ends slightly. Start the braid in the middle, braiding out to each end. Tuck the ends under, pressing them firmly to make sure they stick.

RISING

Place on a buttered and floured baking sheet and brush the surface well with beaten egg. Allow to rise in a warm place until double in bulk, approximately 1 hour. After 45 minutes, **preheat the oven to 375 degrees F.**

NOTE Unless you have two ovens, you will probably have to bake one loaf at a time. You can braid your second loaf, cover it with aluminum foil, and refrigerate it until you place the first one in the oven. Then remove the second braid and leave it in a warm place to rise as before.

BAKING

When the braid has risen sufficiently, brush once more with beaten egg. Bake just below the center of the oven until golden brown and a wooden skewer inserted in the bread comes out clean, approximately 1 hour. If the bread is browning too quickly, cover loosely with aluminum foil. Remove to a rack to cool. If desired, sprinkle a small amount of sifted powdered sugar just down the center of the loaf.

STORING

If wrapped in several layers of aluminum foil, the braid keeps well in the refrigerator for up to 1 month or in the freezer for up to 3 months.

WARMING

To refresh slices of Christmas Braid that have been refrigerated, slice the bread thin, stack the slices, and wrap in aluminum foil. Heat in a **preheated 375-degree F. oven** until warmed through, approximately 10 to 15 minutes.

BIRNBROT
SPICY PEAR BREAD

This lovely Christmas bread from Canton Glarus in Switzerland is traditionally made at home and in bakeries in large quantities (as much as twenty loaves) well in advance of the Christmas season, and the extra loaves are consumed during the cold winter months. The wonderfully spicy kirsch-laced filling is made with dried pears (pears are grown in abundance in the region), grapes, and nuts mixed with bread dough, and is cleverly concealed in a thin wrapper of plain bread dough. This wrapper helps to keep the bread moist and makes the loaf a great surprise for the uninitiated person who first cuts into it and finds the rich fruit interior. These loaves make ideal Christmas presents and can be kept for two or three months if well wrapped and stored. They are best made at least two weeks in advance to allow the flavors to ripen.

THE DAY BEFORE

Prepare the dough the day before, according to the instructions in the master recipe. Place the dried pears in a saucepan, cover them with 2 inches of water, and leave them to soak overnight.

THE FOLLOWING DAY
PREPARING THE FILLING

Pour off all but ½ cup of the water. Add the red wine and butter. Simmer, covered, over a low heat for 20 minutes or until tender, checking occasionally to make sure the pears are not sticking and the liquid has not evaporated. Add a little more

*MAKES 8 LOAVES
4 BY 10 INCHES*

*2 recipes Basic
  Sweet Yeast
  Dough (p. 217)*
*2 pounds dried
  pears*
⅓ cup red wine
*2 tablespoons un-
  salted butter*
2 cups sugar
*1¼ pounds grapes,
  preferably seed-
  less, coarsely
  chopped*
*1 cup candied lemon
  peel or mixed
  peel, finely diced*
*2 cups walnuts,
  coarsely chopped*
*6 tablespoons
  cinnamon*
*1½ tablespoons
  ground cloves*
*¾ cup kirsch or
  light rum*
TO FINISH
2 eggs, lightly beaten

water if necessary. When tender, most of the liquid should have evaporated or been absorbed. If not, turn the heat to high and, stirring, cook until you have a fairly thick mixture. The pears should have the consistency of a coarse puree. You should have approximately 7½ cups of pears. Mix the pears together with the sugar, grapes, candied peel, walnuts, cinnamon, ground cloves, and kirsch or rum. The mixture will be fairly moist.

Butter and flour baking sheets. Cut off one third of the dough, refrigerating the remainder. Cut this piece into six and place in a bowl with the fruit mixture. Using your hand, knead the fruit and dough together by squeezing it between your fingers until the two are well blended. The mixture will be sticky and moist. The pear filling should be thick enough to hold its shape. Test by spooning a mound onto a plate. If it flattens, add a few tablespoons of flour or as much as is needed to thicken it sufficiently to holds its shape.

PREPARING THE WRAPPER

Remove the reserved piece of bread dough from the refrigerator. Divide it into four pieces, refrigerating all but one until needed. Roll out each piece on a lightly floured board into a thin rectangle approximately 10 by 16 inches. Make sure there are no holes in the rectangle and if there are, knead and roll out the dough again. Cut the piece of dough in half, to make two rectangles. Take one quarter of the fruit/dough filling and divide it between the two rectangles, spooning it lengthwise down the center of each to within 1½ inches of each end. Fold the ends of the rectangle up and the sides over to cover the filling, so that it is like a wrapped parcel. Brush the edges with lightly beaten egg and press them together well to seal the seams.

RISING

Carefully place the loaves seam side down on one of the prepared baking sheets, leaving 2½ inches between them to allow for expansion. Brush the surface of each loaf completely with beaten egg and prick it decoratively twelve to fourteen times with the prongs of a fork. Leave the loaves in a warm place until they have risen noticeably—approximately 30 to 45 minutes. In the meantime, **preheat the oven to 400 degrees F.**

BAKING

Brush the loaves a second time with beaten egg. Bake in the middle of the oven until golden brown, approximately 45 to 60 minutes. The loaves will spread slightly because of the moist filling. Cool on racks when done. Wrap tightly in aluminum foil when cool and store in a cool dry place or in the refrigerator for up to two months, or freeze for up to four months.

Continue making and baking the remaining loaves in the same fashion, leaving them in the refrigerator before proving (the final rising) until approximately 1 hour before the oven is free.

HUTZELBROT
YEAST FRUIT BREAD

MAKES 6

1 pound dried pears
  (available at
  specialty grocers—
  see also Mail
  Order Sources)
1 pound prunes
8 ounces dried figs
1 ounce fresh yeast
  or 1 tablespoon
  dried yeast
  (see Note)
1 tablespoon sugar
3¼ cups (1 pound)
  bread flour,
  sifted, plus ap-
  proximately 9
  cups (2¾ pounds),
  as needed
1 cup soaking liquid
  drained from the
  fruit
⅔ cup mixed candied
  orange and lemon
  peel, finely chopped
2¾ cups (1 pound)
  golden raisins
1¼ cups unblanched
  almonds, coarsely
  chopped
1¼ cups walnuts,
  coarsely chopped
1 cup sugar

CONTINUED ON
FACING PAGE

Small flat loaves of fruit bread decoratively studded with split blanched almonds and an occasional candied cherry are traditionally found at Christmas markets, notably those of Nürnberg and Rothenburg ob der Tauber, as well as at commercial bakeries at Christmas time.

The loaves can be baked up to two months in advance; they keep well if wrapped in aluminum foil and stored in a cool place.

NOTE If using dry yeast, dissolve it with the 2 tablespoons sugar in ⅓ cup water warmed to 90 degrees F. Allow to rise in a warm place for about 10 minutes or until bubbly. Proceed with the recipe as follows, reducing the liquid used for the sponge to ⅔ cup.

THE DAY BEFORE
SOFTENING THE DRIED FRUIT

The day before baking, soak the dried pears in warm water to cover for 1 or 2 hours. Drain them, remove cores and stems, and cut pears into thin strips. Place in a saucepan and cover with 3 inches of water. Simmer, partially covered, over a medium heat until barely tender, about 15 minutes. While the pears are cooking, pit the prunes and cut into thin strips. Cut the figs into strips also. When the pears are tender, remove the pan from the heat. Add the prunes and dried figs. There should be at least 1½ inches of water covering the fruit. If not, add a little extra hot water. Leave the dried fruit to soak, covered, overnight at room temperature.

The Following Day
MAKING THE SPONGE

Drain the fruit, reserving 1 cup of the soaking liquid. Cream the fresh yeast with the sugar in a small bowl or cup. Heat the reserved soaking liquid to just warm, about 80 degrees F. Sift 3¼ cups flour into a large bowl and make a well in the center. Combine the creamed yeast with the soaking liquid and pour into the well. Beat in enough of the flour to make a thick batter—a sponge. Dust extra flour over the sponge, cover the bowl with a damp cloth, and leave in a warm place to rise until bubbly, 20 to 30 minutes. Beat down the sponge with a wooden spoon.

MAKING AND KNEADING THE DOUGH

Beat the remaining flour from the sides of the bowl into the sponge, adding the drained soaked fruit pieces, the mixed peels, golden raisins, almonds, walnuts, sugar, salt, and spices. Work the mixture together well for 4 to 5 minutes, first with a wooden spoon, then with your hands. It will be quite sticky. Begin adding the additional flour first by cupfuls, then smaller amounts, until the dough can be removed to a board for kneading. Flouring your hands well, knead on a lightly floured board, adding small amounts of the remaining flour and reflouring the board frequently. Do this until the dough becomes an easily kneadable mass which no longer sticks readily to your hands, approximately 10 minutes. Don't worry if there is a little flour left over from the measured amount. The dough should be soft and pliable. If it is too firm, it will make a dry loaf when baked.

SHAPING AND DECORATING

Butter and flour baking sheets. Divide the dough into six pieces. Form each into a somewhat flat narrow loaf 8 inches long with rounded ends. Place the loaves on the prepared baking sheets, leaving 2¼ inches between each to allow for expan-

½ teaspoon salt
2 tablespoons cinnamon
1½ teaspoons ground cloves
½ teaspoon allspice
1 teaspoon powdered anise
DECORATION
Split whole blanched almonds; 6 halved candied cherries
GLAZE
1 egg, lightly beaten

sion. Decorate just the corners with split blanched almonds, or place the almonds at intervals all round the edge with a halved candied cherry in the center.

RISING

If you don't have enough oven space to bake all the loaves at one time, refrigerate those that must be baked later, covering them with a damp towel. Take them out to rise shortly before the others are ready to go into the oven. Cover the loaves that are to be baked first with a damp cloth and leave to rise in a warm place until they have risen noticeably, approximately 2 hours.

BAKING

Preheat the oven to 350 degrees F. Brush the loaves with lightly beaten egg. Bake in the middle of the oven until golden brown, approximately 50 to 70 minutes. Remove the loaves to a wire rack to cool. Allow to cool completely before wrapping in aluminum foil and storing. Proceed with the remaining loaves in the same fashion.

DREIKÖNIGSKUCHEN
THREE KINGS CAKE

Twelfth Night, January 6, is celebrated in many regions of Germany and Switzerland with a wreath or round of rich yeast bread with a single almond or trinket baked inside. Whoever gets the piece with the token is king or queen for the day. The following version, a wreath with eight balls encircling it and topped with a gold foil crown, is typically found in Switzerland.

SHAPING THE WREATH

Prepare the dough the day before, according to the instructions in the master recipe. The next day, knead it again briefly before use. Butter and flour a baking sheet. Cut off two thirds of the dough. First roll it out in a long, narrow rectangle with a rolling pin to help soften it. Then, using your hands, roll the strip of dough back and forth on a board to form a narrow rope approximately 24 inches long. Curve the rope into a perfect circle on a buttered and floured baking sheet. Using your hand, press the rope slightly flat on the surface to make it easier for the balls to stick. Brush the ends of the rope and the surface with lightly beaten egg, pressing the ends together well to seal the seam. Smooth the seam with your fingers. Using the back of a knife, mark eight indentations around the ring at even intervals.

MAKES 1

*1 recipe Basic Sweet
  Yeast Dough
  (p. 217)*
*1 large unblanched
  almond*
1 egg, lightly beaten
TO FINISH
Granulated sugar
DECORATION
*A circular crown
  made of gold
  foil, decorated or
  not, slightly
  smaller in circum-
  ference than the
  wreath (optional)*

FORMING THE BALLS, ASSEMBLING AND RISING

Divide the remaining dough into eight even-size pieces. On a board or between the palms of your hands, roll each into a perfect ball. Press the unblanched almond into the center of one of the balls, smoothing over the hole. Place one ball at each marked indentation on the wreath, pressing them in well so they don't fall off. Brush the balls with lightly beaten egg. To prevent the balls from toppling off in the early rising stages, take a piece of aluminum foil and crumple it into a thick round about 1¼ inches high, which will fit in the center of the ring just touching the balls but well inside the rope base. Butter well the sides that touch the dough. Take another length of aluminum foil and crumple it into a rope approximately 1¼ inches high and long enough to wind around the outside of the wreath. As before, it should just touch the balls but not be pressed against the rope base. This is important since you will want to remove the foil supports partway through the baking to allow that part of the dough to brown. Butter well the inside of the foil that touches the dough. Leave the wreath in a warm place to rise until double in bulk, approximately 30 to 40 minutes. In the meantime, **preheat the oven to 400 degrees F.**

BAKING

Before baking, brush again with lightly beaten egg. Sprinkle each ball lightly with granulated sugar. Bake just below the center of the oven for about 20 minutes. Remove the outside foil support and, if you can do so with ease, the piece of foil in the center. If it is difficult to retrieve the center piece of foil, however, leave it until the wreath has finished baking. Bake until the wreath is golden and until a wooden skewer inserted in one of the balls comes out clean, approximately 35 to 45 minutes total baking time. Remove to a wire rack to cool. If the foil is still in the center, remove it while the dough is still warm. Before serving, if desired, place a decorated gold foil crown in the center of the wreath.

NEW YEAR'S BREADS

NEUJAHRS-GLÜCKSSCHWEINCHEN
NEW YEAR'S GOOD-LUCK PIGS

In Germany, pigs are symbol of good luck and make their appearance on cards as well as confections (pink marzipan pigs, for instance) and baked goods (cookies and breads). These amusing pig faces filled with marzipan make unusual gifts for children at Christmas time.

MAKES 5

1 recipe Basic Sweet Yeast Dough (p. 217)
2 eggs, lightly beaten
1 pound marzipan

MAKING THE FACES

Prepare the dough the day before, according to the instructions in the master recipe, kneading it again briefly before use. Butter and flour baking sheets. Roll out the dough ⅜ inch thick. Using a round lid 5 inches in diameter or a cardboard stencil as a guide, cut out ten circles. With a cookie cutter or a glass, cut out five circles 2½ inches in diameter. The smaller circles will be the snouts. From the scraps, cut out ten triangles 2½ inches long and 1½ inches wide. These will be the pigs' ears. Using a small round aspic cutter or thimble, cut out two small circles in the lower part of the small circles (the snouts) to make nostrils. Roll scraps of dough into small balls, cutting a "V" with the points of scissors in each to make the eyes. Brush half the large circles with lightly beaten egg. Place a nose almost at the bottom of each circle with the eyes above. Attach a triangular ear on each side, per the illustration, with the tips pointing down. Brush the decorations with lightly beaten egg.

ASSEMBLING

Roll out the marzipan on a board lightly dusted with powdered sugar until it is about ⅜ inch thick. Cut out five 4-inch circles using a lid or stencil made from cardboard and a sharp knife. Place a round of marzipan on the five undecorated circles. Brush the edges of the dough with lightly beaten egg. Top with the decorated faces, pressing the edge all around to seal the seam.

RISING

Place the faces on the prepared baking sheets. Leave in a warm place until they have risen noticeably, approximately 20 minutes. Refrigerate for 15 minutes to help them keep their shape during baking. In the meantime, **preheat the oven to 400 degrees F.**

BAKING

Brush the faces once more with lightly beaten egg. Bake one sheet at a time in the middle of the oven until golden, approximately 20 minutes. Remove to a rack to cool before eating.

NOTE Knead together any scraps that are left over and make another face or use for one of the other figures described in this section.

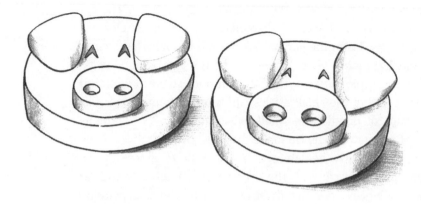

SPECKKUCHEN
BACON BREAD

In the town of Rothenburg ob der Tauber, Germany, the bakers make this specialty for New Year. The perfect preventive medicine against a hangover, the bread is traditionally eaten on New Year's Eve before the merrymaking begins, giving sustenance and a generous coating of bacon fat to an empty stomach. It makes a delicious snack or light luncheon dish served with a green salad.

Slab bacon, if available, is preferable to sliced bacon as it can be cut in thicker dice and the fat will better penetrate the dough as it bakes. However, sliced bacon can be used. Buy very fatty bacon for best flavor.

THE DAY BEFORE
PREPARING THE DOUGH

The day before baking, mix the sugar with ¾ cup warm water (90 degrees F.) and sprinkle the yeast over the top. Allow to rise in a warm place for about 10 minutes or until bubbly. In the meantime, sift half the flour into a large mixing bowl, making a well in the center. Heat the milk and butter to the same temperature as the water. Pour the yeast and milk mixture into the center of the flour, gradually beating in the flour to make a thick batter—a sponge. Lightly beat the eggs with the salt and add to the sponge. Gradually work in the remaining flour. Use just enough flour to prevent the dough from being sticky. Remove to a lightly floured board and knead for 10 minutes by hand or with an electric kneader until smooth and shiny. Wrap tightly in plastic wrap, place in a heavy plastic bag, close tightly, and refrigerate. After an hour check the dough. Unwrap it and punch it down with your fist. Rewrap it well and return it to the plastic bag, closing the bag tightly. Leave overnight.

*MAKES FOUR
10-INCH ROUNDS*

*½ ounce dry yeast
¾ cup water
1 tablespoon sugar
7½ cups (2¼
    pounds) bread
    flour, sifted
1½ cups milk
½ cup (1 stick)
    unsalted butter
3 large eggs
2 teaspoons salt
1½ pounds fatty
    bacon (see above),
    cut in ⅜-inch dice*

The Following Day
SHAPING

Butter and flour baking sheets. When ready to use, knead the dough again briefly and divide it into four. Roll out one piece of dough into a 12-inch circle, rewrapping and refrigerating the rest until you have room in the oven to bake the other rounds. Holding the outer edge, lift up the rolled-out dough and rotate it, letting its weight stretch it. Use your fist to stretch out the center. Roll once more to flatten the circle further. Place on a buttered and floured baking sheet. Stud evenly with one fourth of the diced bacon, pressing it well into the dough. Leave in a warm place, covered with a damp cloth, from 15 to 20 minutes or until it has risen noticeably. In the meantime, **preheat the oven to 400 degrees F.**

BAKING

Bake in the middle of the oven for 20 to 30 minutes or until golden. Brush the entire surface with the fat that has accumulated around the bacon. Proceed in the same fashion with the other three rounds, cooling them on a wire rack when they are done. The rounds will shrink to approximately 10 inches.

NOTE Bacon Bread can also be made in two large rectangles if desired. It is best eaten shortly after it is made or if baked ahead, can be wrapped in aluminum foil and warmed in a hot oven.

EASTER BREADS

While not celebrated with the intensity that it is in the neighboring Eastern European countries, Easter, which marks the end of the Lenten fast on the church calendar, is marked by bakers in German-speaking countries with an assortment of various rich yeast breads: *Bremer Osterklaben* (almost identical to *Dresdner Christstollen, Osterkarpfen* (rich yeast dough in a fish shape found in Switzerland); *Osterkranz* (braided rich yeast wreath); *Eier im Nest* (Easter egg nests); and *Tauben* (rich yeast doves), to name just a few.

OSTERKARPFEN

EASTER CARP

*MAKES 1 LARGE
 OR 2 SMALL
 FISH*

½ *recipe Basic
 Sweet Yeast
 Dough (p. 217)*
1 *egg, lightly beaten*
⅓ *cup whole blanched
 almonds, split
 (see Almonds)*

The fish, an early symbol of Christianity, is a shape seen frequently at Easter time, especially in France where it takes the form of chocolates made in special fish molds. Swiss bakers, no doubt influenced by this, have used the same shape with yeast bread to make charming glazed fish with almonds for scales, measuring anywhere from 5 to 14 inches in length.

SHAPING AND DECORATING THE FISH

Prepare the dough the day before, according to the instructions in the master recipe. Knead it briefly again before use. Butter and flour a baking sheet. Roll the dough into a large oval approximately 14 inches long if one fish is desired, or divide it in two, rolling out two ovals 7 to 8 inches in length to make two smaller fish. Roll out ¾ inch thick. If you are hesitant to cut out a fish freehand, make a cardboard stencil which should include indentations for fins and tail. Place the stencil on the dough and, using a sharp knife, cut out the fish shape. Brush the fish with lightly beaten egg. Knead together the scraps and roll out. Cut out fins and tailpieces. With the back of a knife, score them with parallel lines. Coil a small rope of dough to make an eye. Form another small crescent of dough for the mouth. Place the pieces of dough on the fish and brush each one with beaten egg. Using the points of sharp scissors, snip V-shaped gashes at 1-inch intervals, cutting only partway through the dough, on the upper two thirds of the fish to stimulate scales. Press a split almond into each gash, rounded side up, so that it lies flat with two thirds of the almond showing.

RISING

Place the fish on the prepared sheet. If there are two, leave 3 inches between them to allow for expansion. Cover the fish with a damp cloth and allow to rise in a warm place until double in bulk, approximately 40 minutes. In the meantime, **preheat the oven to 400 degrees F.**

BAKING

Brush the entire fish once again with beaten egg. Bake in the middle of the oven until golden and risen, approximately 30 to 40 minutes depending on the size of the fish. Remove to a rack to cool before eating. The fish can be wrapped in aluminum foil and frozen for up to three months.

OSTERKRANZ

EASTER WREATH

MAKES 1 WREATH

*1 recipe Basic Rich
Sweet Yeast Dough
(p. 219)
1 egg, lightly beaten*

MAKING AND DECORATING THE WREATH

Prepare the dough the day before, according to the instructions in the master recipe. Knead it again briefly before use. Butter and flour a baking sheet.

Cut off a small piece of dough (approximately ⅙ of the total) to be used for decoration. Roll the remainder into a rectangle 12 inches long. Cut the rectangle into three even strips. Roll the strips back and forth to round them and extend them another 8 inches. Brush the ends with lightly beaten egg and press them together. Braid the strands and form into a wreath, pressing the ends of the braid together to join them. Roll out the reserved piece of dough. Using a pastry wheel or a knife, cut out two large leaves and several flower shapes, scoring the leaves and flowers with the back of a knife to simulate veins. Brush the wreath well with beaten egg. Apply the leaves in bow-tie fashion where the ends of the braid join. Cover the seam with flowers. Brush the decorations with lightly beaten egg.

RISING

Place the wreath on the prepared baking sheet. Leave it to rise in a warm place until double in bulk, approximately 40 minutes.

BAKING

Preheat the oven to 400 degrees F. Brush the wreath again thoroughly with beaten egg. Bake in the middle of the oven until brown and risen, approximately 30 to 40 minutes. Remove to a rack to cool before serving. If desired, the Easter Wreath can be baked in advance, wrapped in aluminum foil, and frozen for up to three months.

EIER IM NEST
EASTER EGG NESTS

Traditionally found in Greece and Italy at Easter time, yeast dough nests with their colorful eggs have migrated north to the German-speaking countries. Hard-boil and dye your Easter eggs in advance. (For dying your eggs with vegetable dye and decorating with leaf and flower silhouettes, see instructions for the Swiss method at the end of the recipe.) The eggs will not actually be baked in the bread. Instead, aluminum foil eggs are placed on the bread during baking and replaced afterward by the real eggs.

MAKES 7

1 recipe Basic Sweet Yeast Dough (p. 217)
7 hard-boiled eggs, dyed in food coloring or in onionskin dye as described at the end of the recipe
1 egg, lightly beaten

MAKING THE NESTS

Prepare the dough the day before, according to the instructions in the master recipe. Knead it again before use. Butter and flour baking sheets. Crumple aluminum foil to the size and shape of an egg. You will need seven foil eggs.

Divide the dough into seven even-sized pieces, wrapping and refrigerating those not being used. Taking a little over half of each piece of dough, roll that piece into a small oval approximately 4 inches at the widest part and 4½ inches long. This should give you a rim of approximately 1 inch or more if an egg is placed in the center. Press one of the dyed hard-boiled eggs in the center of each oval. Brush the rim with lightly beaten egg. Taking the remaining small piece of dough, roll it back and forth to form a narrow rope slightly longer than is needed to go around the circumference of the oval, 14 to 15 inches. Twist the rope and wind it around the edge of the oval to form a rim or nest. Press it on well and trim the ends. Brush the twisted rope with beaten egg. Press the ends together well. Carefully remove the real egg and make a ball the same size from aluminum foil. Butter the bottom and sides of the foil egg with softened butter, rest it in the center of the nest, and place the nest on a buttered baking sheet. Place no more than four on a prepared baking sheet so that there is not a great differential in rising time between the first and last nest on each baking sheet. Continue with the remaining dough, working quickly, leaving at least 2 inches between each nest on the baking sheet to allow for expansion.

RISING

Cover with a damp cloth and leave in a warm place until they have begun to rise noticeably—10 to 15 minutes. Refrigerate for 15 to 20 minutes before baking. This will help them to keep their shape during baking, without rising too much, so that the foil egg can be easily removed and replaced.

BAKING

Preheat the oven to 400 degrees F. Glaze the dough once more with beaten egg. Bake one sheet at a time in the middle of the oven until golden, approximately 20 minutes. Remove nests from the baking sheet to wire racks to cool. Remove the aluminum foil eggs while the dough is still warm. Replace each with a colored hard-boiled egg.

VARIATION

Before baking, after the nests have been glazed for the last time, you can sprinkle finely chopped candied peel or coarse decorating sugar sparingly over the glazed rim of each nest.

DYING EGGS WITH VEGETABLE DYE

In Switzerland, an old-fashioned method of dying and decorating the eggs with vegetable dye is used which produces a beautiful, natural color. To make the dye, cook the skins only from 3 pounds of Spanish onions (the large yellow onions with brownish-yellow skins) in 1½ quarts of water for 1 hour, partially covering the pan while they simmer. At the same time simmer the eggs (use white eggs) in water, 10 to 11 minutes for eggs at room temperature, the time depending on the size of the eggs. Place them in a pan of cold water when done to stop the cooking.

TECHNIQUE FOR FLOWER
AND LEAF SILHOUETTES

When the onion skins have simmered for an hour, strain the liquid into a bowl, discarding the skins. Have ready small flowers, especially wild flowers if any are available, grass or small leaves, an old nylon stocking, and a piece of string. Dip whatever flower or green decoration you are using in water and press it against one of the hard-boiled eggs. One pretty flower or leaf can be sufficient. Cut the foot from the stocking to make a small sack. Carefully place the decorated egg in the toe of the stocking without losing any of the decorations. Using a piece of string, tie the egg tightly at the toe of the stocking so it can't move. Lower the egg in the stocking into the hot onion-skin dye, leaving it there from 1 to 5 minutes depending on whether you want a pale or dark tint. Remove the egg from the dye and take it out of the stocking. Remove the decorations, which should now appear as white silhouettes on the egg. Repeat with each egg. Reheat the dye if it becomes too cool. Allow the eggs to dry completely. To make them shine, rub them with a piece of bacon fat once they are dry.

TAUBEN
DOVES

Like the Easter egg nests, the rich yeast doves traditionally baked in Italy for Easter have crossed the border and are now a regular feature of the Swiss baking repertoire at this time of year.

Prepare the dough the day before, according to the instructions in the master recipe. Knead it again briefly before use. The doves can be prepared in two ways.

METHOD 1
MAKING THE DOVES

For a cutout version, divide the dough into four parts, wrapping and refrigerating those portions not being used. Butter and flour baking sheets. Roll the piece of dough into an oval approximately 9 inches long and 1 inch thick. If you are hesitant to cut out a dove freehand, make a cardboard stencil, giving the dove two wings and making indentations for the beak and tail. Place the stencil on the oval and cut out the dove with a sharp knife. Beat the egg white with a whisk or fork until frothy. Using a pastry brush, brush the dove completely with the egg white. Make an eye on the dove with a currant or a raisin. Using the back of a knife, score parallel lines on the wings and tail. Place flaked almonds neatly in overlapping rows on the ends of the wings and tail, beginning at the tip, to simulate feathers. Use them more sparingly in the center of the wings and tail, extending them slightly farther up the outside edges. Brush the almonds carefully with beaten egg.

MAKES 4 OR 5

1 recipe Basic Sweet Yeast Dough (p. 217)
1 egg white
4–8 currants or raisins
½ cup flaked almonds
Coarse decorating or granulated sugar

RISING

Place on the prepared baking sheet and leave in a warm place until the dove has begun to rise, about 20 minutes. Refrigerate for 20 minutes. This will help to keep the shape during baking.

BAKING

Preheat the oven to 400 degrees F. Brush the dove once more with egg white and sprinkle with sugar. Bake in the middle of the oven until golden and a wooden skewer inserted in the dove comes out clean, approximately 30 minutes. Remove to a rack to cool before eating. Continue with the remaining doves in the same manner.

NOTE Scraps left over from cutting out the doves can be kneaded together and used to make a fifth dove or one of the knotted doves described below.

METHOD 2
MAKING THE DOVES

In the second method, smaller, fatter doves are produced by knotting a rope of dough. Butter and flour baking sheets. Roll the Basic Sweet Yeast Dough out into a rectangle 13 inches wide and 14 inches long. Cut the dough lengthwise in strips 1½ inches wide. You should have nine strips. Roll the strips back and forth on the board several times to round them slightly. Tie each strip in a fat knot, slightly off center, plumping up the knot. The smaller end, which should just peek out, will be the head. Model it with your fingers, shaping it to a beak in the front. Use a pair of scissors to trim a neat, pointed beak. The tailpiece should extend about 2 inches. Cut several gashes in

the tail with the scissors. Use the back of a knife to make parallel lines on the tailpieces. Beat the egg white lightly with a wire whisk or fork until frothy. Using a pastry brush, brush the dove with the beaten egg white, getting it well into the crevices. Place a currant on the side of the head for an eye. Place no more than three doves at a time on the prepared baking sheet.

RISING

Leave in a warm place until they have risen noticeably, about 15 to 20 minutes. Refrigerate for 15 to 20 minutes before baking, to help them keep their shape.

BAKING

Preheat the oven to 400 degrees F. Brush the doves once more with the beaten egg white and sprinkle with coarse sugar. Bake in the middle of the oven until golden and a wooden skewer inserted in the middle of the dove comes out clean, approximately 25 to 30 minutes.

NOTE It is possible the heads and tails, which are not as dense as the body, will brown too quickly before the body is baked through. If so, cover them with aluminum foil, leaving the knotted portion exposed.

When the doves are done, remove them to a wire rack to cool. Continue with the remaining doves in the same manner, keeping the dough refrigerated until needed.

SUNDAY BREADS

ZOPF

BRAIDED LOAF

MAKES 4

2 tablespoons sugar
½ cup warm water
¾ ounce dried yeast
2 cups milk
4 sticks (1 pound
    unsalted) butter
3 teaspoons salt
2 cups sour cream
4 large eggs, lightly
    beaten
17 cups (5 pounds)
    bread flour,
    sifted, plus addi-
    tional flour as
    needed
2 eggs, lightly
    beaten, for glaze

Usually baked at home in Switzerland for Sunday, the baker's day off, braided bread—ranging from loaves knotted with one strand of dough to those plaited with up to twelve strands—is also a favorite in Austria and Germany, where at Christmas time extra fruit and nuts are sometimes added.

Some years ago, a German baker told me that the braided loaf was baked on Allerseelen (All Souls' Day, November 2) to commemorate the days when a warrior's wife would have her braid cut off before joining him in the grave.

Frau Gilgen from St. Gall, Switzerland, gave me this recipe—one I'd often sampled with relish in her home—which differs from other rich yeast recipes in this chapter because of the addition of sour cream, which makes the texture especially light.

Because this is not a sweet bread, it is equally good for sandwiches or served at breakfast, warm or toasted, with butter and jam.

PREPARING THE DOUGH

Mix the sugar with ½ cup warm water and sprinkle the yeast over the top. Allow to double in bulk in a warm place. Heat the milk almost to a simmer with the butter and the salt. Allow to cool for 5 minutes, stirring occasionally. Stir in the sour cream and the lightly beaten eggs. When just warm to the touch, stir in the yeast mixture. Pour the mixture into a large bowl and gradually beat in most of the sifted flour. Remove the dough to a lightly floured board and knead for 10 to 15 minutes by hand until smooth and shiny, or use an electric kneader. Add just enough extra flour to keep the dough from sticking. Place in a buttered bowl. Cover with a hot damp cloth and leave to rise in a warm place until double in bulk, approximately 1½ to 2 hours.

SHAPING

Butter and flour baking sheets. Divide the dough into four parts. Braid the loaves as diagrammed. Brush with lightly beaten

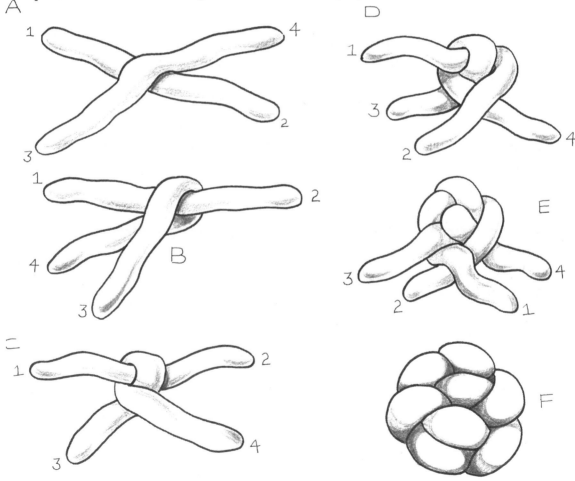

egg. Place the loaves 3 inches apart on prepared baking sheets. Keep the loaves refrigerated until 40 to 50 minutes before there is oven space available. Before baking, leave the loaves in a warm place, draped with a damp towel, until noticeably risen and almost double in bulk, approximately 40 minutes.

BAKING

Preheat the oven to 375 degrees F. Brush a second time with lightly beaten egg, getting the glaze well into the crevices. Bake one sheet at a time just below the center of the oven until golden and until a wooden skewer inserted in the bread comes out clean, 45 to 60 minutes. Remove to a wire rack to cool. Allow to cool completely before eating.

STORING

Zopf can be wrapped in aluminum foil and kept in the refrigerator for up to one week, or frozen, well wrapped, for up to three months.

KUGELHOPF
ALSATIAN COFFEE CAKE

*MAKES 2 SMALL
OR 1 LARGE
KUGELHOPF*

*FOR THE MOLD
¼ cup (4 table-
spoons) melted
unsalted butter,
cooled*

CONTINUED ON
FACING PAGE

In the Alsace and in the Black Forest of Germany, *Kugelhopf* is baked for breakfast on Sundays, the baker's day off, while in Austria, where it is known as *Gugelhupf*, a richer version is baked—sometimes with yeast, sometimes with baking powder—and served at teatime. Despite variations in the amount of eggs, butter, and sugar, and in the leavening agent used, *Kugelhopf* and *Gugelhupf* have more than shape in common. Traditionally baked in a round, decoratively fluted pan, this enriched yeast bread studded with raisins has long been a measure for judging a home baker's culinary skills. This is one yeast bread that, although available in bakeries, is baked at home as a matter of pride, with each housewife carefully guarding her own special recipe, generally passed on from mother to daughter.

While the Austrian version is rich with butter and perfect for an elegant tea, I am partial to the simpler Alsatian *Kugelhopf*, probably because I love eating it for breakfast and this version is lighter—suitable for early morning consumption.

Although it is never as good as when freshly baked, *Kugelhopf* will keep, well wrapped in the refrigerator, for three or four days, or it can be wrapped in aluminum foil and frozen for up to three months. And if you don't feel like rising at six in the morning to make a freshly baked *Kugelhopf* for Sunday morning breakfast, it is equally delicious baked in the afternoon and served at teatime or for an afternoon snack. To refresh *Kugelhopf* that has been refrigerated, slice it thin, wrap the slices, stacked, in aluminum foil, and heat them in a prepared 375-degree oven for about 15 minutes or until just warm.

The Alsatian recipe given below will make two small (1½-quart) or one large (3-quart) *Kugelhopf*. If you don't have a proper *Kugelhopf* mold, available in most specialty cookware shops, you can use any ring mold or Bundt pan. To determine the size of your mold see how many cups of water it holds.

2 teaspoons sugar
½ ounce dry yeast
½ cup (1 stick) unsalted butter, softened
½ cup sugar
2 large eggs
2 large egg yolks
Grated rind of 1 lemon
½ teaspoon salt
3⅓ cups (12½ ounces) all-purpose flour, sifted, plus up to 3 tablespoons additional flour for kneading
½ cup scalded milk (90 degrees F.)
⅔ cup raisins
TO FINISH
Powdered sugar, sifted
EQUIPMENT
1 3-quart Kugelhopf, ring mold or Bundt pan or
2 1½-quart Kugelhopf ring mold or Bundt pans

PREPARING THE MOLD

Prepare the mold pan by chilling it in the freezer for 15 minutes or in the refrigerator for 20 minutes. Brush every part of the mold well with the cooled melted butter. Return pan to the freezer or refrigerator briefly to set the butter. Remove and brush a second time so the mold is heavily coated. Chill until needed.

PREPARING THE DOUGH

Mix the sugar with ¼ cup warm water (90 degrees) and sprinkle the yeast over the top, leaving it in a warm place for about 10 minutes or until bubbly. Using an electric mixer, beat the butter and sugar together until light and creamy, about 3 minutes. Beat in the eggs and egg yolks one at a time, beating each well before adding the next. Beat in the lemon rind and salt. Beat in the flour and milk alternately, and then the bubbling yeast mixture, beating until all the flour and milk are added. Scrape down the beaters. Finally add the raisins and beat the mixture for several minutes with a wooden spoon. Begin working the sticky dough with your hand, flouring it lightly with up to 3 tablespoons of flour to keep it from sticking too much to your hand. Work the dough for about 4 minutes. The dough is meant to be sticky and moist, unlike bread dough.

RISING

If using two molds, divide the dough in two. Spread it evenly into the mold. Cover with a damp cloth and leave to rise in a warm place until it has doubled in bulk, approximately 45 minutes. After 30 minutes, **preheat the oven to 375 degrees F.**

BAKING AND FINISHING

Bake just below the center of the oven. After 25 minutes, check the *Kugelhopf*. It should be risen, golden and firm; a wooden toothpick inserted in the round should come out clean. Baking time will vary from 25 minutes for the small mold to 45 or 50 minutes for the large *Kugelhopf*, according to the depth and thickness of your mold. If not yet done, return it to the oven and test again in 10 to 15 minutes.

When done, rap the mold firmly on the counter. Invert the mold onto a wire rack and rap firmly again to unmold it. Allow the *Kugelhopf* to cool for several minutes, then sprinkle the top generously with sifted powdered sugar. Allow to cool before serving.

6

CAKES, PASTRIES, AND MEHLSPEISEN

Can anyone resist an exquisite cake or well-executed tart filled with fresh fruit and custard? Cakes and pastries are found in abundance in all three countries and are consumed throughout the year. At coffee hour, several different sorts might be sampled—more often than not with a healthy dollop of unsweetened whipped cream (or *Schlag*, as the Austrians call it). For the coffee ritual, it is the custom to dress in one's finery and go to one of the more prominent cafés in town (that is, one that serves good cakes and pastries), which are generally crowded by four o'clock.

On Sunday and on any holiday or special occasion, such as birthdays, first communion, or confirmation, a special cake or pastry is usually baked and eaten by the family at home.

Austrians also savor a lesser-known category of sweets called *Mehlspeisen*. Made with flour (*Mehl*) and eggs, and related to soufflés and crêpes, these warm desserts are often served in relatively substantial portions to be eaten as the main course for supper following a more substantial meal at lunch. Among the most popular *Mehlspeisen* are *Salzburger Nockerl* (Salzburg soufflé) and *Topfenpalatschinken* (crêpes filled with sweetened quark—similar to puréed cottage cheese—and baked in a creamy custard).

Multitiered wedding cakes as we know them in America are found in recent German cookbooks but rarely seen at weddings. For weddings in Switzerland and Germany, it is customary to buy the most distinctive cake produced by the best bakery in town. In Austria especially, home bakers often produce elaborate cakes (generally from a special recipe passed down through the family) for country wedding feasts and for Christmas.

The recipes in this chapter are a cross section of cakes and pastries that includes a few unusual Christmas and New Year's specialties, among them Pine Cone Cake (*Tannenzapfen*) and Lingonberry Meringue Cake (*Preiselbeerenschaumtorte*). Otherwise most of these recipes can be baked at any time of year for a special treat, with the exception of a few seasonal fruit tarts and strudels which are of necessity limited to the late summer.

While one cake in this section requires a special mold (*Rehrücken*, "saddle of venison" cake), most can be baked in ordinary baking pans or tart tins.

There are numerous complicated preparations in this chapter, among them Zug Kirsch Cake (*Zuger Kirschtorte*), Cardinal Slices (*Kardinalschnitten*), Chestnut Cream Slices (*Maronioberschnitten*) and Lingonberry Meringue Cake (*Preiselbeerenschaumtorte*). They are not easy to make, but the recipes are as specific as possible so that, despite the time they take to make, they can be produced successfully. For an easier selection, begin with Chocolate Almond Cake (*Schönbrunnertorte*), Cheesecake (*Käsekuchen*) and Apple Crumb Cake (*Apfelstreuselkuchen*).

REFERENCE SECTIONS

Before using these recipes you might find it useful to look again at the Baking Tips at the beginning of this book. That section covers such techniques as lining cake pans and using piping bags. It is important, especially with cakes, to organize all your equipment and measure your ingredients in advance, and preheat your oven.

STORING

Storing and freezing recommendations vary in some instances, but unless otherwise stated, most cakes can be made in advance and kept, loosely covered, in the refrigerator for four to five days or frozen for up to three months. If freezing, allow the cake to freeze overnight before wrapping it carefully in foil, making sure the foil doesn't touch any of the decorations.

CAKES

KASTANIENTORTE
CHOCOLATE CHESTNUT TORTE

Puréed chestnut gives this Austrian torte its moisture; chocolate, its richness; and chestnut cream, its extra bit of sin! Plan to make the torte at least one day prior to serving it. It will keep well in the refrigerator for up to one week or can be kept frozen for three months or longer. In the latter case, freeze the torte unwrapped for four hours before wrapping it well in aluminum foil.

THE DAY BEFORE
PREPARING THE CAKE PAN

Butter the cake pan well with softened butter. Cut out a piece of parchment paper that fits the bottom of the pan perfectly. Butter the paper well. Flour the bottom and sides of the pan, shaking out the excess. Set the pan aside.

PREPARING THE BATTER

Beat the sugar and egg yolks together with a wooden spoon until smooth and thick, approximately 3 minutes. Gradually beat in the chestnut purée, then the grated chocolate, until the mixture is well blended. Beat the egg whites with a pinch of salt until stiff. Stir a large spoonful of the egg-white mixture into the

CAKE
¾ cup sugar
6 large egg yolks
1 cup canned unsweetened chestnut purée (blended in a food processor for 20 to 30 seconds to smooth the texture)
4 ounces semi-sweet chocolate, finely grated
6 large egg whites
Pinch of salt
2½ tablespoons flour
CHESTNUT CREAM
2 cups heavy cream, chilled
⅓ cup sugar (or a little more, to taste)
1 cup chestnut purée, blended in a food processor as above
EQUIPMENT
9-inch springform cake pan
Piping bag with small star tip (optional)

chestnut mixture to lighten it. Spoon this mixture onto the egg whites, folding some of the mixture together with a large metal spoon. Sift the flour onto the top of the mixture and continue folding, gently, until no large streaks of white remain. Spoon the mixture into the prepared cake pan, spreading it evenly. Rap the pan on the counter several times to remove any air pockets.

BAKING

Preheat the oven to 350 degrees F. Bake in the middle of the oven until the cake is risen and firm to the touch, approximately 45 to 50 minutes. Remove from the oven and allow to rest 4 minutes. Using a table knife, carefully loosen the sides of the cake from the pan. Quickly invert the cake onto a wire rack and allow to cool completely. Cover loosely with aluminum foil and refrigerate overnight.

THE FOLLOWING DAY
MAKING THE CHESTNUT CREAM

Beat the cream with an electric mixer until it begins to thicken. Add the sugar and beat a few seconds longer. Add the chestnut purée and beat 20 to 30 seconds longer until the mixture is thick and well blended. The consistency should be that of very thick whipped cream. Refrigerate until needed.

NOTE If you want to decorate the cake once it is iced, reserve a small amount of filling, place it in a piping bag fitted with a small star tip, and refrigerate it along with the rest.

ASSEMBLING AND DECORATING

Cut the cake in half horizontally across using a serrated knife. Spoon ⅓ of the filling into the center of the cake and spread to just within the outside edge. The weight of the top layer will force some of the filling to spread, so it is important not to spread the filling clear to the edge. Cover with the top layer and place in the freezer for 15 mintes to help firm the filling. Remove from the freezer and spread the top and sides evenly with the remaining cream. You can either make swirls on the top of the cake, using a small metal spatula, or make the top and sides smooth by dipping the spatula into hot water, drying it, and smoothing it over the cream. If desired, you can pipe a frill or rosettes at even intervals around the outside edge of the cake using a piping bag. Refrigerate at least 4 hours before serving.

HASELNUSSTORTE
HAZELNUT TORTE

This delicious Austrian torte, combining hazelnut sponge cake with coffee butter cream, is impressive to serve and easy to make. I recommend using homemade bread crumbs since they have more flavor and a finer texture than the commercial product.

CAKE
5 large egg yolks
⅔ cup superfine sugar
1 cup plus 2
    tablespoons ha-
    zelnuts, skinned
    (see Hazelnuts)
    and finely ground
5 large egg whites
Pinch of salt
2 tablespoons all-
    purpose flour
½ cup fine bread
    crumbs
(see Baking Tips)

GLAZE
⅔ cup apricot jam
1 teaspoon lemon juice

ICING
½ cup (1 stick)
    unsalted butter,
    softened
1 cup powdered
    sugar, sifted
1½ teaspoons strong
    coffee (1 tea-
    spoon instant
    coffee dissolved
    in ¼ cup boiling
    water)
2 large egg yolks

DECORATION
¼ cup skinned
    hazelnuts, ground
5 skinned hazelnuts,
    whole (optional)

CONTINUED ON
FACING PAGE

PREPARING THE CAKE PAN

Butter the cake pan well with softened butter. Line it with a round of parchment paper that fits perfectly in the bottom. Butter the paper and dust the pan well with flour, shaking out the excess. Set aside.

PREPARING THE BATTER

Preheat the oven to 325 degrees F. Using a wooden spoon, beat the yolks and sugar together until thick and smooth, approximately 3 minutes. Beat in the ground hazelnuts and set aside.

Using an electric mixer, beat the egg whites with a pinch of salt until stiff. Stir ¼ of the egg whites into the yolk mixture to lighten it. Pour the mixture onto the remaining whites. Sift the flour on top. Fold several times with a large metal spoon. Sprinkle half of the fine bread crumbs on top and fold until half blended. Add the remaining bread crumbs and continue folding until all the ingredients are just blended, being careful not to overfold. Spoon the batter into the prepared cake pan, smoothing it evenly. Rap the pan several times on a counter to remove any air pockets.

BAKING

Bake in the middle of the oven until the cake is risen and firm to the touch, approximately 45 minutes. When done, allow to cool on a wire rack 2 minutes. Loosen the sides of the cake carefully, using a table knife or small spatula. Invert quickly onto a wire rack and remove the piece of paper from the bottom. Allow to cool completely on the rack. When cool, cut in half horizontally with a serrated knife.

EQUIPMENT
9-inch springform cake pan

GLAZING

For the glaze, heat the apricot jam with 1 teaspoon of lemon juice, stirring continually, and boil 1 minute. Press through a sieve into a bowl, placing the apricot pulp back in the jam jar. Using a pastry brush, coat the sides of both layers and the surface of the top layer generously with hot jam. Set aside.

MAKING THE ICING

To make the icing, beat the softened butter and powdered sugar together until light and creamy, approximately 4 minutes with an electric mixer. Add the strong coffee and finally the egg yolks, one at a time, beating well before adding the next. Beat at least 3 minutes longer to dissolve the sugar completely.

ASSEMBLING AND DECORATING

Assemble the cake. Remove the bottom layer of the cake to the base of the springform pan (turning the layer upside down so it has a flat surface). Spread the surface of the bottom layer with ¼ of the butter cream. Cover with the top layer. Spread the remaining butter cream evenly on the surface and sides of the cake. Warm a metal spatula in hot water, dry it, and run it across the top and sides of the cake to help spread the icing smoothly.

Press the ground hazelnuts well into the sides of the cake to cover evenly. If desired, decorate the top with 5 whole hazelnuts placed at even intervals around the edge of the cake.

STORING

Refrigerate for at least two hours or overnight. The cake can be frozen for up to three months, in which case it should be frozen for 3 to 4 hours before it is wrapped with aluminum foil.

FRANKFURTER KRANZ
RUM AND PRALINE CAKE

4 tablespoons (2
  ounces) melted
  butter, to grease
  the pan
CAKE
¾ cup (1½ sticks)
  unsalted butter,
  softened
1 cup superfine
  sugar
Grated rind of 1
  lemon
3 large eggs
¾ cup plus 1
  tablespoon all-
  purpose flour
⅔ cup plus
  1 tablespoon
  cornstarch
1 tablespoon baking
  powder
SYRUP
¼ cup water
1 tablespoon sugar
½ cup rum
ALMOND BRITTLE
  (KROKANT)
Oil for the baking
  sheet
1 cup granulated
  sugar
1 cup whole blanched
  almonds

CONTINUED ON
FACING PAGE

When I first lived in Frankfurt, the old Café Kranzler was still the most fashionable place to meet for a slice of *Kuchen*, a predinner glass of *Sekt* (German champagne), or a delicate post-theater supper of *Kalbslendchen* (veal fillet) or *Königinpastetchen* (*vol-au-vent* filled with creamed chicken, tongue, and mushrooms). With the construction of Frankfurt's underground went the refined dining area of the old Kranzler. Fortunately, the baking expertise of the Kranzler was preserved, though its walls were not.

On a recent trip, I was delighted to find their doors open once again and their *Frankfurter Kranz*, my favorite indulgence in that establishment, as delicious as before. A traditional Frankfurt specialty saved for special occasions, *Frankfurter Kranz* consists of a butter-rich cake baked in a round tin, split in layers which are laced with rum, sandwiched and covered with butter cream, and sprinkled with crunchy almond brittle (praline or *Krokant*).

It is best to bake the cake at least a day before you plan to eat it. Once it has been sandwiched and covered with butter cream, it should be refrigerated for at least four hours to firm the butter cream and make it easier to cut. For best appearance, use a plain 9-inch round tube pan or savarin mold rather than a fluted Bundt pan.

PREPARING THE CAKE PAN

Prepare a 9-inch plain tube pan by placing it in the freezer for 15 minutes or in the refrigerator for 20 minutes. While it is chilling, melt 4 tablespoons butter and allow it to cool. Remove the chilled pan and, using a pastry brush, coat the entire inner surface thoroughly with melted butter. Chill for another 10 minutes. Repeat with a second coating of butter. Dust the inside with flour (ideally using a flour dredger). Tip the pan around to coat it thoroughly. Tap out the excess. Refrigerate.

PREPARING THE BATTER

Using an electric mixer, cream the butter, sugar, and grated lemon rind together until the mixture is fluffy and light in color. Beat in the eggs one at a time, beating well after each before adding the next. Scrape down the beaters. Sift the flour, corn-starch, and baking powder together onto a piece of paper. Sift them a second time onto the butter mixture. Using a large metal spoon, fold the flour carefully into the butter until no visible pockets of flour remain. Spoon the batter evenly into the prepared pan, smoothing it to make it even. Tap the pan firmly several times on the counter to remove any air pockets.

BAKING

Preheat the oven to 350 degrees F. Bake in the middle of the oven until the cake has risen, is firm to the touch, and has begun to pull away slightly from the sides of the pan, approximately 40 minutes. Remove the cake from the oven and allow it to rest for 10 minutes. Loosen the cake from the sides of the pan with a knife. Holding a wire rack firmly against the top of the pan, quickly invert the cake onto the rack to unmold it. Allow to cool to room temperature. If time allows, wait 8 hours or more before slicing the cake. Using a serrated knife, cut the cake horizontally across twice to make three even layers.

8 HOURS LATER
MAKING THE SYRUP

For the syrup, boil ¼ cup water with the sugar for about 30 seconds, stirring until the sugar has dissolved. Remove the pan from the heat and add the rum, mixing it well.

BUTTER CREAM
4 sticks (1 pound)
* unsalted butter,*
* softened*
3 cups powdered
* sugar, sifted*
4 large egg yolks
3 tablespoons rum
TO FINISH
Candied cherries,
* cut in half*
EQUIPMENT
9-inch plain tube
* pan*
Pastry tube with
* small or medium*
* star tip*

Place the bottom layer of the cake on a serving plate. Pour half of the syrup mixture into a cup and spoon it slowly and evenly over the bottom of the cake.

MAKING THE KROKANT

Oil a large baking sheet and set it aside. Place the sugar in a heavy pan and cook over medium heat, stirring until it has completely melted. Then turn the pan from side to side a few times until the liquid is pale yellow. Add the whole blanched almonds, stirring to coat them well. Continue stirring until the sugar has turned a caramel color and the nuts have begun to crackle and give off an aroma. Immediately pour the mixture onto the oiled baking sheet, and using two forks, spread it out in a thin layer. Allow it to harden and cool at room temperature. When it is cool, break the *Krokant* into small pieces and pulverize them in a blender or food processor. Spread it out on a piece of aluminum foil and set aside.

MAKING THE BUTTER CREAM

Using an electric mixer, beat the butter until creamy. Gradually beat in the sifted powdered sugar and continue to beat for at least 8 minutes to dissolve the sugar. Add the egg yolks one at a time, beating well after each addition. Finally add the rum and beat for another minute. You will need about one third of the butter cream to fill the layers.

ASSEMBLING AND DECORATING

Spread about one sixth of the butter cream on the syrup-soaked bottom layer of the cake, spreading it evenly with a metal spatula. Place the second cake layer on top. Sprinkle this layer with the remaining syrup, spooning it slowly and evenly over the surface. Spread evenly with an equal amount of butter cream. Cover with the top layer. Spoon about ½ cup of butter cream into a piping bag fitted with a small or medium star tip.

Set it aside. Use the remaining butter cream to coat the top and sides of the cake completely. Smooth the icing with a metal spatula dipped in hot water.

Sprinkle the pulverized *Krokant* over the top and sides of the cake, pressing it on gently with your hands. Using a dry pastry brush, brush off any *Krokant* that has fallen on the rim of the plate and sprinkle it on top of the cake. Take a small piece of paper towel, twist it, and moisten the end. Carefully lower it into the center hole to pick up any *Krokant* that has fallen onto the plate. Using the butter cream in the piping bag, pipe eight tiny rosettes (or as many as you want) at even intervals on top of the cake. If desired, garnish each rosette with a halved candied cherry or just a sliver of cherry. Refrigerate for at least four hours to firm the butter cream before slicing.

SCHÖNBRUNNERTORTE

CHOCOLATE ALMOND CAKE

CAKE
3 ounces semi-sweet
  chocolate, bro-
  ken in pieces
4 large egg yolks
⅔ cup superfine sugar
¾ cup blanched
  almonds, finely
  ground (see
  Almonds)
3 large egg whites
Pinch of salt
GLAZE
⅔ cup red currant
  jelly
1 teaspoon water
ICING
4 ounces semi-sweet
  chocolate, bro-
  ken in pieces
½ cup plus 2
  tablespoons un-
  salted butter,
  softened
1 cup plus 1
  tablespoon pow-
  dered sugar, sifted
1 large egg, lightly
  beaten
1 tablespoon light or
  dark rum

CONTINUED ON
FACING PAGE

Named after Schönbrunn, the beautiful summer palace located on the outskirts of Vienna, *Schönbrunnertorte* is a delicious, flourless chocoalte almond cake which is split in half, glazed with red currant jelly, then sandwiched together and covered with chocolate butter cream. Much easier to make than most Viennese tortes, it freezes well (for up to three months) or can be refrigerated for up to four days.

PREPARING THE CAKE PAN

Butter an 8-inch springform pan well with softened butter. Cut out a piece of parchment paper that perfectly fits the bottom of the pan. Butter the paper well. Flour the bottom and sides of the pan, shaking out the excess. Set the pan aside.

PREPARING THE BATTER

Melt the broken chocolate in a double boiler or in a heatproof soup plate or shallow bowl placed over a saucepan filled with 2 inches of boiling water. Stir occasionally until the chocolate has melted. Remove from the heat and allow the chocolate to cool.

Beat the egg yolks and sugar together with a wooden spoon until pale and creamy. Beat in the cooled melted chocolate and finely ground almonds.

Using an electric mixer, beat the egg whites with a pinch of salt, beginning on moderate speed until they are frothy. Increase the speed and beat until they are stiff, scraping down the sides of the bowl several times.

Stir ¼ of the stiffly beaten egg whites into the chocolate mixture to lighten it. Pour this mixture onto the egg whites and fold them in carefully with a large metal spoon until no streaks of white remain. Spoon the batter into the prepared cake pan, smoothing it evenly.

TO FINISH
Cocoa powder
TO SERVE
*½ pint heavy cream,
   lightly whipped*
EQUIPMENT
*8-inch springform
   cake pan*

BAKING

Preheat the oven to 350 degrees F. Bake in the preheated oven until the cake is firm to the touch and has begun shrinking away from the sides of the pan, 30 to 45 minutes. Loosen the cake from the sides of the pan with a knife. Turn out onto a cake rack and remove the piece of paper from the bottom. Allow to cool completely. When cool, use a serrated knife to slice the cake in half horizontally.

GLAZING

For the glaze, heat the red currant jelly with 1 teaspoon of water, stirring continually until it comes to a boil. Strain through a sieve into another bowl or pan. Brush the top of the cake with the warm glaze; then brush the surface of the bottom half of the cake with the glaze.

ICING AND FINISHING

For the icing, melt the broken chocolate pieces as before and allow them to cool. Cream the softened butter together with the sifted powdered sugar. Beat for at least 5 minutes to dissolve the sugar. Beat in the melted chocolate. Scraping down the sides of the bowl, beat for another 2 minutes. Add the lightly beaten egg and the rum and beat until smooth. Using a metal spatula, spread one third of the butter cream on the bottom layer. Cover with the top layer. Spread the top and sides with the remaining butter cream. Dip the spatula in hot water and run it over the top and sides of the cake, redipping it when necessary, to produce a smooth surface. Dust the top of the cake with sifted cocoa powder.

Refrigerate the cake for at least three hours to firm the butter cream before serving. Serve with a dish of lightly whipped cream on the side.

ZUGER KIRSCHTORTE
ZUG KIRSCH CAKE

*JAPONAIS (ALMOND
    MERINGUE)
    LAYERS*
3 large egg whites
*⅓ cup plus 2
    tablespoons su-
    perfine sugar*
*¼ cup plus 2
    tablespoons
    blanched al-
    monds, finely
    ground (see
    Almonds)*
*1 tablespoon plus 1
    teaspoon all-
    purpose flour,
    sifted*
SPONGE
*½ cup all-purpose
    flour*
*2 tablespoons
    cornstarch*
1 pinch salt
2 large eggs
*⅓ cup plus 2
    tablespoons su-
    perfine sugar*
*KIRSCH BUTTER
    CREAM*
*1¼ cups (2½ sticks)
    unsalted butter,
    softened*
*1⅓ cups powdered
    sugar, sifted*
2 tablespoons kirsch

CONTINUED ON
FACING PAGE

Zug may be the smallest canton in Switzerland, but its reputation looms large among pastry-lovers. Its specialty, *Zuger Kirschtorte*, is a many-layered pale pink creation of almond meringue, kirsch-soaked sponge, and kirsch-flavored butter cream which together produce an unusual contrast of brittle and moist textures. It is one of Switzerland's greatest cakes.

Inspired by the famous Zug kirsch—a clear, unsweetened schnapps distilled from the abundance of special cherries harvested there—it is found in bakery shops throughout Switzerland and is distinguished by a simple presentation typical of Swiss baking: toasted almonds round the sides, a single halved cherry in the center, the pale pink icing dusted with powdered sugar and delicately cross-hatched in a diamond pattern. Its simple appearance, however, is deceptive, as it requires two different cake mixtures and is time-consuming to prepare. But, for a special holiday or birthday, it is well worth the effort. It is best made at least a day ahead to allow the butter cream to firm.

PREPARING THE CAKE PANS

Butter the cake pans and line the bottoms with a round of parchment paper cut just to fit. Butter the paper. Dust the pans with flour, shaking out the excess. Set aside.

MAKING THE JAPONAIS LAYERS

Preheat the oven to 325 degrees F. Using an electric mixer at medium-high speed, beat the egg whites until they just hold their shape but are not dry. Beat in the sugar by the tablespoon, beating for at least 20 seconds between each. When all the sugar has been added, beat for another 2 minutes. Carefully fold the ground almonds and sifted flour into the meringue with a large metal spoon. Divide the mixture evenly between two of the prepared cake pans. Bake on the second-lowest rack of the oven, with the handle of a wooden spoon propped inside the oven door to keep it slightly ajar, until golden and dry, 40 to 50 minutes. If the bottom of the meringue layers is still moist, turn them upside down, take off the paper, return to pans and place in the oven until dry, about 5 minutes. Set aside on a wire rack to cool.

MAKING THE SPONGE CAKE

Preheat the oven to 350 degrees F. Choose a crockery or glass bowl that will just rest in a saucepan. Pour 2 inches of water into the saucepan and bring to a boil. Sift the flour, cornstarch and salt onto a piece of paper. Remove the saucepan from the heat. Place the mixing bowl over the saucepan and add the eggs and the sugar, beating them together with an electric mixer or whisk until the mixture is thick and mousselike, about 3 minutes with an electric mixer. When ready, the mixture trailed from the beater will hold the shape of the letter M for 3 seconds on top of what is in the bowl. Check frequently to prevent overbeating. As soon as it reaches the correct consistency, sift the flour mixture onto the egg mixture. Fold in carefully with a metal spoon, turning the bowl slightly each time, until no pockets of flour can be seen. Pour into the prepared cake pan. Rap the pan firmly to remove any air bubbles. Bake in the middle of the oven for 15 to 20 minutes, or until the cake is golden and has begun to shrink away from the sides of the pan. Remove from oven and loosen the cake from the sides of the pan with a knife. Turn out onto a wire rack to cool, peeling off the paper.

MAKING THE BUTTER CREAM AND SYRUP

Beat the softened butter and powdered sugar together until light in color and creamy, about 8 minutes with an electric

2 *egg yolks*
2–3 *drops red food coloring*
SYRUP
3 *tablespoons warm water*
3 *tablespoons kirsch*
1 *tablespoon superfine sugar*
DECORATION
1 *cup flaked almonds, toasted on a baking sheet in a hot oven and coarsely chopped*
1 *halved candied cherry*
EQUIPMENT
3 *9-inch cake pans*

mixer. Add the kirsch according to taste, the egg yolks, one at a time, and finally a few drops of red food coloring to tint the icing a pale pink. Beat at least another 3 minutes to dissolve the sugar completely and to obtain a light, creamy icing.

Combine the syrup ingredients in a small bowl, mixing them well, and set aside.

ASSEMBLING THE CAKE

Place four strips of 3-inch-wide wax paper on a serving plate to form a square slightly larger than the cake. Place one japonais layer in the middle of the square and spread it with one quarter of the butter cream mixture. Top with the sponge layer. Prick the sponge with the prongs of a fork. Pour the syrup mixture over the cake, covering it evenly. Spread the surface with another quarter of the butter cream. Top with the second Japonais layer, the bottom side up. Spread the top and sides of the cake evenly with the remaining butter cream. Warm a metal spatula in hot water, dry it, and run it across the top of the cake to help spread the icing smoothly.

DECORATING

Coarsely chop the toasted almonds. Press them well into the sides of the cake to cover evenly. Refrigerate the cake for 30 minutes to firm the butter cream slightly. Using a metal spatula dipped in hot water and dried, make diagonal lines on the top of the cake at 1½-inch intervals, first in one direction, then in the other, to form a trellis pattern. Warm and dry the spatula each time you make a mark, barely pressing it into the icing. Dust the top of the cake with sifted powdered sugar. Place a halved candied cherry in the center. Remove the paper strips carefully and, using a dry pastry brush, dust off any fallen nuts or sugar.

STORING

Refrigerate for at least 2 hours or overnight. If desired, the cake can be frozen for up to 3 months, in which case you should dust the top with powdered sugar again before serving.

SACHERTORTE

Reputedly the only cake in the world that was ever the subject of a court case, this famous Viennese creation—a rich chocolate sponge cake glazed in apricot and iced in bittersweet chocolate—was first produced in 1832 by Franz Sacher, chef to Metternich. The court issue arose when Demel's, Vienna's most famous pastry shop, and the Sacher Hotel, owned by a branch of the same Sacher family, contested who had the right to call their product the genuine (*echt*) Sachertorte. Demel's case was based on the fact that the shop had bought the right to produce the genuine Sachertorte, stamped with an official seal of bittersweet chocolate, from Edouard Sacher, the grandson of the creator and the last scion of the dynasty. The Hotel Sacher based their case on the family connection with the cake's creator. The most discernible difference between the versions from the two establishments was in the placing of the apricot jam: should it be glazed on top of the cake and then covered with icing, as in the Demel's version, or should the cake be split in two and the jam spread between the layers, as in the Hotel Sacher's version? Seven years and no doubt many samplings later, the courts decided in favor of the Hotel Sacher. Demel's, however, did not sit quietly by. They announced they would simply market their torte as the *Ur*-Sachertorte, the very first version.

No doubt both establishments have a few tricks that are never disclosed in the recipes. The recipe below, however, is certainly closer to the real thing than most Sachertortes I have sampled in other countries. Because Demel's is probably my favorite pastry shop in the world, I have taken the liberty of going against the courts and *not*

BATTER
6 ounces semi-sweet chocolate, broken in pieces
½ cup (1 stick) plus 2 tablespoons unsalted butter, softened
¾ cup superfine sugar
6 large egg yolks
8 large egg whites
1 cup all-purpose flour
GLAZE
1½ cups apricot jam
1 tablespoon lemon juice
ICING
1⅔ cups sugar
½ cup water
8 ounces semi-sweet chocolate, broken in pieces
TO SERVE
1½ cups heavy cream, lightly whipped to form soft peaks
EQUIPMENT
9-inch springform pan or special cake pan with rounded edges (see above)

splitting my cake into two layers. However, if you feel otherwise inclined, you can move your apricot jam from the top of the cake to the middle.

Regardless, from a baker's standpoint apricot glaze has a function other than flavoring. When on top it provides a glassy, smooth surface on which to put the icing. This is certainly important in the case of Sachertorte, a cake with a smooth surface and well rounded edges, since the warm icing, worked to exactly the right temperature and consistency, must flow smooth and rapidly over the cake to give it its flawless chocolate covering. To produce slightly rounded edges on the cake, Viennese bakers' manuals recommend using a special cake tin with rounded edges manufactured specially for the purpose. I have a copper casserole that does this admirably. However, since few people are likely to have such a pan, glazing the tops, edges, and sides of the cake well with the hot strained jam helps to produce the rounded edges.

To ensure that the icing is well set, allow the iced cake to cool to room temperature first, then leave it overnight in a cool place or not-too-cold refrigerator before slicing it. In Vienna, Sachertorte is generally served with a dollop of unsweetened whipped cream which cuts the sweetness and marries wonderfully with the rich chocolate cake.

PREPARING THE CAKE PAN

Butter the cake pan well with softened butter. Line it with a round of parchment paper that fits perfectly in the bottom. Butter the paper and dust the pan well with flour, shaking out the excess. Set aside.

PREPARING THE BATTER

Place the broken chocolate pieces in a double boiler or in a heatproof soup plate or shallow bowl over a saucepan containing

2 inches of simmering water, stirring the chocolate occasionally until it has melted. Remove from the saucepan and allow the chocolate to cool.

Preheat the oven to 350 degrees F. Using an electric mixer, cream the butter with the superfine sugar until light in color, about 3 minutes. Beat in the egg yolks one by one, beating well between each. Wash the beaters and dry them well. Beat the egg whites with the electric beater until stiff. Stir one fourth of the egg white mixture into the yolk mixture to lighten it. Pour this mixture onto the egg whites. Sift part of the measured flour on top. Using a metal spoon, cut and fold the mixture, bringing the egg whites up from the bottom. Sift the remaining flour on top and continue cutting and folding until no pockets of flour remain and there are no large streaks of egg white. Spoon the mixture into the prepared cake pan, smoothing the batter evenly into the corners of the pan. Tap the pan several times on the counter to knock out any air pockets.

BAKING

Bake in the middle of the oven until the cake is firm to the touch and has begun to shrink away from the sides of the pan, approximately 50 minutes. Loosen the cake from the sides of the pan with a knife. Turn the cake onto a wire rack to cool and remove the paper from the bottom.

GLAZING

When the cake is cool, heat the apricot jam with the 1 tablespoon of lemon juice and allow to boil for 30 seconds. Strain the jam through a sieve, pressing well against the apricot pieces. Using a pastry brush, brush the top, edges, and sides of the cake thoroughly and evenly with the apricot glaze, making sure the cake is completely covered. Allow the glaze to cool and set.

PREPARING THE ICING

Meanwhile, make the icing. Heat the sugar and chocolate with ½ cup of water in a heavy saucepan, stirring constantly until the mixture comes to a boil. Stop stirring. Attach a candy thermometer to the side of the pan and use a wet pastry brush to brush down any sugar crystals that cling to the sides of the pan. When the mixture reaches 225 degrees F., remove the pan from the heat. Stir the icing with a wooden spoon constantly, bringing the hot chocolate up from the bottom to help cool the mixture evenly. After stirring for approximately 1 minute, test the icing. Pour a small amount onto a marble slab or clean work surface and work it with a metal scraper or spatula. When ready it will set quickly with a smooth surface. If it takes more than a few seconds to set, keep stirring to cool the icing a little more and test again. If the icing appears granular, it has been over-heated. To correct, add a few tablespoons of boiling water to the icing and return it to the heat briefly until the mixture is boiling and smooth. Then proceed as before.

ICING THE TORTE

When the icing has reached the correct temperature, place the wire rack with the cake over a marble slab or clean work surface. Pour all the icing at once directly onto the center of the cake, letting it flow in a steady stream and tilting the cake quickly if necessary to coax the icing over an uncovered side. You must work quickly before the icing sets. Once the icing has been poured on the cake, do not try to pour any remaining icing on a second time or use a brush or spatula to smooth it. That would mar the glassy surface of the icing which will have already begun to set. Allow the cake to rest until the icing has dried completely. Scrape up any icing that has overflowed and freeze (it will keep for up to three months; dilute with a little water when reheating it).

STORING AND SERVING

Store the cake in a cool place overnight before slicing. It keeps well for up to five days. Serve with a bowl of unsweetened, lightly whipped cream passed separately.

MARONIOBERSSCHNITTEN
CHESTNUT CREAM SLICES

*MAKES TWO 2-LAYER CAKES WITH A TOTAL OF 14–16 SLICES
SEE VARIATION AT END OF RECIPE FOR ONE 4-LAYER
CAKE*

In all the German-speaking countries in winter, vendors with charcoal-fired roasters attract customers with the aroma of their roasting chestnuts and the familiar cry, *"Heisse Maroni!"* (hot chestnuts). Perhaps chilled shoppers are drawn by the warmth of the fire and the thought of a bag of hot chestnuts to warm their hands even more than by the desire to consume them.

In both Austria and Switzerland, chestnuts make their way into many delicious desserts in the winter. The recipe below is a Viennese specialty. Layers of delicious Sachertorte mixture are baked in a sheet and cut into four strips. The strips are partially soaked in rum syrup, then sandwiched with chocolate cream, covered with whipped cream (*Obers*) and heavily sprinkled with tiny shreds of sweetened chestnut purée, called *Kastanienreis*.

The recipe makes two 2-layered rectangular cakes or, if a more elaborate cake is desired, one 4-layer cake, using the Variation noted at the end of the recipe. The cake and chocolate cream (*Parisercreme*) can be made and assembled with syrup up to two or three days ahead. However, for best appearance it is advisable not to finish the cakes with whipped cream and chestnut purée until the day it is needed. Chill the cakes for several hours before serving.

PREPARING THE BAKING SHEET

Prepare the baking sheet by buttering it well. Cut out a piece of parchment paper 4 inches wider and longer than the baking

1 recipe Sachertorte batter (preceeding recipe)
PARISERCREME
1 cup heavy cream
8 ounces semi-sweet chocolate, broken in pieces
RUM SYRUP
1/3 cup sugar
1/3 cup water
1/2 cup light or dark rum
TO FINISH
2½ cups heavy cream
4 tablespoons powdered sugar, sifted
1 teaspoon vanilla extract
KASTANIENREIS (RICED CHESTNUT PURÉE)
2½ cups sweetened chestnut purée (available in cans at grocery and specialty stores)
3–4 tablespoons light or dark rum, or to taste
1 teaspoon vanilla
Powdered sugar to taste (optional)
EQUIPMENT
Baking sheet with sides, 10 × 13 inches
Pastry bag fitted with a rosette tip

sheet and make a 3-inch diagonal cut at each corner. Place in the baking sheet, adjusting the corners so the paper stands up on the sides and the corners overlap neatly. If the sides of the pan are less than 2 inches, clip the overlapping corner points of paper with paper clips. This will secure the corners so that the sides stand up straight and high enough to hold the batter. Butter and flour the paper, tapping out the excess flour

PREPARING AND BAKING THE CAKE

Preheat the oven to 350 degrees F. Prepare the Sachertorte batter. Pour the batter into the prepared baking sheet, easing it into the corners and smoothing it with a metal spatula. Bake until the cake springs back to the touch, approximately 20 minutes. Prepare a clean towel or sheet of aluminum foil slightly longer than the baking sheet and sprinkled with sugar. When the cake is done, turn it out quickly onto the prepared towel or foil. When cool, cut off the crusty edges. Cut the cake across in 4 even strips, approximately 3 inches wide. This recipe will make two 2-layer cakes. Place two strips down on a flat surface to serve as bases.

MAKING THE *PARISERCREME* AND ASSEMBLING

Heat the cream in a saucepan with the pieces of chocolate and stir over low heat until the chocolate has melted. Place the saucepan in a pan of cold water and stir until cool, changing the water and adding ice cubes to speed up the process. Using an electric mixer, beat the cream until it is thick enough to spread. Divide the cream between the two cake bases and spread them evenly with a thick layer of chocolate cream. Place a second layer of cake on top of each base. Prick the top layers with the tines of a fork.

MAKING THE RUM SYRUP

Boil the sugar and water together until the sugar has dissolved. Remove from heat and add the rum. Slowly pour the mixture over the top cake layers, dividing it evenly between the two. Use a metal spatula to smooth the chocolate cream filling on the sides if it isn't even with the cake layers.

WHIPPING CREAM AND COATING

Beat the heavy cream until it beings to thicken. Gradually beat in the sifted powdered sugar and finally the vanilla. Beat until the cream is thick enough to hold its shape if piped. Set aside 1 cup of the whipped cream and spoon it into a pastry bag fitted with a star tip. Refrigerate until needed. Spread the remaining cream evenly over the two long sides and top of each cake, leaving the ends free.

PREPARING KASTANIENREIS

Using a food processor, mix the chestnut purée with the rum and vanilla. If desired, add a little powdered sugar to taste and process again until smooth. Press the mixture, a small amount at a time, through a coarse metal strainer over a piece of wax paper using a wooden spoon.

FINISHING

Sprinkle the "rice" lavishly over the cream, both top and sides. Using the cream in the pastry bag, pipe small single rosettes down the center of the cake with the reserved whipped cream; there should be one for each slice, estimating each slice at approximately 1¼ inches. If there is any *Kastanienreis* left over, it can be frozen and used for decoration when needed.

VARIATION

If desired, you can make a 4-layer cake instead of two 2-layer cakes. In this case, spread the chocolate cream between 3 layers— they will be slightly thinner layers of cream—and soak the second and third layers with rum syrup, leaving the bottom and top as they are. Since you will want to slice this cake thinner, simply pipe a decorative frill of cream down each side or the center, rather than attempting a rosette for each slice.

REHRÜCKEN

"SADDLE OF VENISON" CAKE

4 tablespoons melted
  butter, to grease
  the pan
CAKE
4 ounces semi-sweet
  chocolate, bro-
  ken in pieces
½ cup (1 stick) plus
  2 tablespoons
  unsalted butter,
  softened
½ cup superfine
  sugar
3 large egg yolks
1 cup unblanched
  almonds, finely
  ground (see
  Almonds)
1 cup fine bread
  crumbs (see
  Baking Tips),
  pressed through
  sieve
8 large egg whites
Pinch of salt
⅓ cup superfine sugar
GLAZE
1 cup red currant
  jelly
1 teaspoon water
CHOCOLATE ICING
8 ounces semi-sweet
  chocolate, bro-
  ken in pieces
1 cup heavy cream

CONTINUED ON
FACING PAGE

It is not surprising that the Austrians, who are especially fond of game and adept in its preparation, have chosen to honor one of the most popular dishes, saddle of venison, with a chocolate cake made in a special tin shaped like this cut of meat and studded with slivered almonds to simulate the *Speck*—bacon fat—used to lard the meat before it is roasted. The cake pan, which resembles a half cylinder with ridges along either side, is generally about a foot long and is sold in many specialty cookware shops outside Austria and Germany. However, if you cannot obtain one, use a 12- to 14-inch loaf pan instead. In this case, eliminate the slivered almond decoration and substitute a row of whole blanched almonds down either side, or a single row of blanched almonds down the center. The cake itself, made with butter, chocolate, eggs, and ground almonds, is flourless and quite delicious—well worth making with or without a *Rehrücken* pan.

This is an especially festive cake to serve at a dinner party in the autumn when game is in season. It can be made in advance and refrigerated, loosely covered with aluminum foil, for three or four days, or it can be frozen, loosely covered with aluminum foil, for a month or more.

PREPARING THE PAN

Place the *Rehrücken* pan in the freezer for 15 minutes or the refrigerator for 20. Using a pastry brush, brush the chilled pan well with the butter, which has been melted, then cooled. Chill and brush a second time, covering all the ridges well. Dust it with granulated sugar and flour, shaking out the excess. If using a loaf pan, line the bottom with a piece of buttered parchment paper before sugaring and flouring. Refrigerate.

PREPARING THE BATTER

Melt the chocolate in a double boiler or in a heatproof soup plate or shallow bowl placed over a saucepan filled with 2 inches of boiling water, stirring occasionally until the chocolate has melted. Remove the chocolate from the heat and allow to cool.

Using an electric mixer, beat the butter until creamy. Add the cooled chocolate and ½ cup of superfine sugar and beat the mixture for 2 to 3 minutes until it is smooth. Beat in the egg yolks, one at a time, beating well between each addition. Scrape down the beaters, and wash and dry them well for beating the egg whites. Stir in the finely ground almonds and the bread crumbs with a spoon.

Preheat the oven to 350 degrees. Using an electric mixer at medium-high speed, beat the egg whites with a pinch of salt until they just hold their shape but are not dry. Beat in the ⅓ cup of superfine sugar by the tablespoon, beating for at least 20 seconds between each. When all the sugar has been added, beat for a further 2 minutes. Using a large metal spoon, fold the stiffly beaten egg whites into the chocolate mixture until no streaks of white are visible. Spoon the cake mixture evenly down the length of the prepared cake pan, smoothing it into the corners and evening the top with a spatula. Tap the pan firmly on the counter several times to remove any air bubbles.

BAKING

Bake in the middle of the oven until the cake springs back to the touch, and has begun to shrink away from the sides of the pan—approximately 30 minutes. Remove the cake from the oven and allow it to cool for 5 minutes. Don't worry if it sinks slightly. Turn the cake onto a wire rack and allow it to finish cooling. If you are using a loaf pan, remove the piece of paper from the bottom of the cake. Place the wire rack on a clean work surface.

TO FINISH
1 cup slivered almonds (or if making in a loaf pan, ⅓ cup whole blanched almonds
TO SERVE (OPTIONAL)
Heavy cream, lightly whipped to form soft peaks
EQUIPMENT
12-inch Rehrücken pan or 4 × 12-inch loaf pan

GLAZING

For the red currant jelly glaze, heat the jelly in a saucepan with 1 teaspoon of water, stirring until the jelly comes to a boil. Remove the pan from the heat at once and strain the jelly through a sieve into a bowl. The cake can be glazed either while it is still warm or after it has cooled. Using a pastry brush, brush the entire surface of the cake evenly with the glaze.

ICING AND DECORATING

To make the icing, melt the broken pieces of chocolate with the cream in a saucepan, stirring continually. Heat until the chocolate has completely melted. Remove the pan from the heat and, stirring occasionally, let it cool to lukewarm. If you wish to accelerate the cooling process, place the saucepan in a bowl or sink filled with ice water which comes two thirds of the way up the sides of the pan. Stir the icing continually with a wooden spoon until it is lukewarm. (Stir rather than beat or whisk the icing, which would lighten its color.) When it is cool (not cold) to the touch and beginning to thicken slightly, pour the icing down the center of the cake, tilting the cake so that the icing runs down the sides. Use a pastry brush dipped in the icing to coat the ends and any part of the cake that is not already coated with the icing. Scrape up any icing that has fallen through the wire rack. Place it in a small container and freeze it to be used at a later date. Before the icing has completely set, stud the cake with slivered almonds if made in a *Rehrücken* pan. Pressing the almonds upright into the icing, place them in rows about 1 inch apart (use about eight slivered almonds per row) at even intervals on the sides and top of the cake. Let the cake cool completely before serving or refrigerate until needed. It can be served with lightly whipped cream.

BAUMKUCHEN

TREE CAKE

From Vienna to Berlin, a few specialty bakeries exhibit a prominent treat in their windows which compels aficionados to enter and sample to see whether they have at last found the definitive *Baumkuchen*. Up to 3 feet or more in height before greedy customers have reduced it, *Baumkuchen* is so called because of the concentric rings that appear in a cross-section of the cake, like those of an aging oak, and because of its treelike posture, characterized by indentations that resemble the shaft of a screw. Unlike most cakes, *Baumkuchen* is broiled, not baked, on a rotating rod that turns horizontally in front of a red-hot grill plate. Each time the preceding coating has caramelized, the baker applies a new layer of rich batter, which produces concentric rings. When the batter runs out, he presses a long wooden "comb" into the soft tree, giving it the characteristic indentations, before glazing it, first with apricot, then with a clear or chocolate icing. Proudly groomed, it is stood on end ready for the baker's window.

A typical *Baumkuchen* recipe in a baker's manual calls for, in addition to flavorings:

4½ pounds unsalted butter	*1 pound ground almonds*
48 egg yolks	*2 pounds, 10 ounces mixed cornstarch*
56 egg whites	
4 pounds sugar	*and plain flour*

It is obvious that the proportion of flour to butter, eggs, and sugar is extremely low, which accounts for the cake's richness.

Often given by guests invited to a German or Austrian home, several "rings" of Baumkuchen would be received by any hostess with relish. It is generally eaten at coffee hour, cut in paper-thin slices, though there's no need to confine its consumption to four o'clock in the afternoon.

While, alas, it is impossible to duplicate this great cake in its lofty form at home, the following Viennese recipe for *Baumkuchenschnitten* applies a similar technique and batter to a baking-pan version that can be made using a conventional broiler.

BAUMKUCHENSCHNITTEN
TREE CAKE SQUARES

*MAKES APPROXI-
MATELY 100
SQUARES*

BASE INGREDIENTS
*¾ cup plus 2
tablespoons
unsalted butter,
softened and cut
in pieces*
*5½-ounce block of
marzipan, bro-
ken in pieces*
*1 cup powdered
sugar, sifted*
*¾ cup plus 2
tablespoons corn-
starch, sifted*
*1 teaspoon vanilla
extract*
Pinch of salt
*Grated rind of 1
lemon*

CONTINUED ON
FACING PAGE

Baumkuchenschnitten, the home version of *Baumkuchen*, is made, layer upon layer, in a square cake pan under a hot broiler. It is ultimately cut in narrow strips, glazed with chocolate, and cut again in bite-sized pieces—perfect for a special after-dinner treat with coffee or as part of a teatime selection.

PREPARING THE CAKE PAN

Butter the baking pan, sides and bottom. Line the bottom with a piece of buttered parchment paper cut to size. Flour the pan, shaking out the excess. Set aside.

PREPARING THE BATTER

If you have a food processor, you can process all the Base Ingredients in the machine, first creaming the butter and marzipan together well before adding the other ingredients. The egg yolks should be added one at a time. Process until smooth.

Otherwise, cream the butter with an electric beater or wooden spoon until light and smooth. Crumble the marzipan, add, and beat for a few seconds. Add the powdered sugar, cornstarch, vanilla, salt, and lemon rind. Add one egg yolk at a time, beating it in well before adding the next. When all the yolks have been added and the mixture is smooth, set it aside. If you have used an electric beater, wash and dry the beaters well.

In a non-aluminum bowl, beat the egg whites until they just hold their shape but are not dry. Add the ⅔ cup of sugar by the tablespoon, beating at least 20 seconds before adding more. When all the sugar has been added, beat another 2 minutes. Using a large metal spoon or a rubber spatula, fold the meringue into the butter/yolk mixture, only partially folding it in. Sift the flour over the top and fold the flour and egg white together carefully until no more pockets of flour or clumps of meringue are evident.

Yolks of 3 large eggs
ADDITIONS
Whites of 6 large
  eggs
⅔ cup sugar
¾ cup all-purpose
  flour
CHOCOLATE GLAZE
8 ounces quality
  semi-sweet choco-
  late, broken in
  small pieces
2 teaspoons vegeta-
  ble oil
EQUIPMENT
Metal baking pan
  9 × 9 inches

BROILING THE LAYERS

Preheat your broiler. Adjust the broiler rack to the lowest level. Spoon the thinnest possible layer of batter into the paper-lined baking pan. You can use a pastry brush to brush batter into the corners covering the paper completely. Place under the broiler and cook until golden, 1 to 2 minutes, the amount of time depending on the intensity of your broiler. Brush the entire surface with another thin coating of batter, as before, and again place the pan under the broiler. Continue in this fashion until all the batter is used. Cool the cake completely before loosening the sides with a knife and unmolding it. Peel off the paper. Trim off the ragged edges of the cake with a sharp knife and set it aside.

GLAZING WITH CHOCOLATE

Heat the broken chocolate pieces with the vegetable oil in the top of a double boiler or in a heavy pan over low heat. Stir occasionally until the chocolate has melted. Place the pan of chocolate in a pan filled with several inches of hot water.

Return the cake to an upright position and brush the top—presumably the least attractive side—with an even coating of chocolate. This will eventually be the bottom of the cake. If the chocolate seems too thick, add a few more drops of vegetable oil, only enough to thin it sufficiently to brush it easily. Allow the chocolate to cool and set completely. Turn the cake over, chocolate side down. Cut the cake all the way through in narrow strips 1½ inches wide. You should have 6 strips. Brush the sides and top of each strip with chocolate, leaving the ends free. If the chocolate becomes too cool and thus too thick, replace the water in the outside pan with boiling water and stir the chocolate until it is rewarmed and fluid. When the glaze has set, cut strips in ½-inch bite-sized pieces, if using immediately or in the next few days.

STORING

If you wish to store the *Baumkuchenschnitten*, leave the strips uncut and slice them when needed. If well wrapped, the strips can be kept in the refrigerator for several weeks, or frozen and thawed as needed. Before cutting, bring the strips to room temperature. For neat slices, heat a sharp knife in hot water each time before cutting.

VARIATION

If you prefer to use the cake for a dessert rather than an accompaniment to tea or after-dinner coffee, you can glaze the top of the cake as described in the basic recipe. Then, when set, turn the cake over and cut it in half rather than in 6 strips. glaze the top and sides as before, leaving the ends free if you want the layers to show, or coating them if you desire. To serve cut in ½-inch slices and pass a bowl of lightly whipped cream separately.

KARDINALSCHNITTEN
CARDINAL SLICES

MAKES 8 TO 9 SLICES

MERINGUE
4 large egg whites
CONTINUED ON
FACING PAGE

This unusual Viennese cake, made of alternating rows of sponge and meringue, is baked in two layers in a long, rectangular shape, then sandwiched with coffee-flavored whipped cream or, in summer, with fresh fruit and whipped cream before it is cut into finger-width slices.

Because it needs a more complicated preparation than some cakes, it is best attempted by those with some baking experience. The delicate marriage of textures makes it a favorite dessert for any special dinner. If you use a coffee cream filling, it can be made and filled up to eight hours in advance. And if you are using a fresh fruit and whipped cream filling, the cake layers can be made the day before and filled no more than four hours before it is to be served. Refrigerate until ready to serve.

PREPARING THE MERINGUE

Butter and flour the baking sheet(s) and set aside.

Beat the egg whites with an electric mixer on a moderately low speed until frothy. Increase the speed and beat until the egg whites softly hold their shape but are not dry. Begin beating in the sugar, a tablespoon at a time, beating for at least 20 seconds between each addition. When all the sugar has been added, beat the meringue 3 or 4 minutes longer until the mixture is smooth and glossy. Spoon the meringue into a piping bag fitted with a plain ¾-inch tip and set aside.

PREPARING THE SPONGE BATTER

Sift the flour once onto a piece of paper and set aside. Choose a crockery or glass mixing bowl that will fit into a saucepan with its base resting well above the bottom of the pan. Bring 2 inches of water to a boil in the saucepan and remove the pan from the heat. Set the bowl over the pan, add the eggs and sugar to it, and use an electric mixer or whisk to beat the mixture rapidly until it is thick and mousselike, about 4 minutes. To test the consistency, use the beater to lift a little of the beaten eggs and sugar, then trail the shape of the letter M over the mixture in the bowl. If the shape holds for 3 seconds, the mixture is sufficiently beaten. If the shape dissolves, beat for a further seconds, then test again. Remove the bowl from the pan and beat in the vanilla for 10 seconds. Sift the flour a second time directly onto the whisked egg mixture. With a metal spoon, fold

⅔ cup superfine sugar
SPONGE BATTER
¾ cup plus 1
  tablespoon all-
  purpose flour
2 large eggs
3 large egg yolks
⅓ cup superfine sugar
1 teaspoon vanilla
  extract
FILLING A (COFFEE-
  FLAVORED
  WHIPPED CREAM)
2 teaspoons instant
  coffee granules
3 tablespoons boiling
  water
1½ cups heavy cream
3 tablespoons pow-
  dered sugar,
  sifted
FILLING B
  (WHIPPED CREAM
  AND FRESH
  BERRIES)
2 cups fresh raspber-
  ries or blueber-
  ries, or halved or
  quartered
  strawberries
4–5 tablespoons
  superfine sugar,
  or to taste
1½ cups heavy cream
TO FINISH
Sifted powdered
  sugar
EQUIPMENT
1 large baking sheet
  13 × 15 inches
  or 2 baking sheets
  at least 13
  inches long
Piping bag with
  ¾-inch plain tip

in the flour carefully, just sufficiently to break up any pockets of flour.

Using a large spoon and a metal spatula, spread half of the sponge mixture on the baking sheet in an even rectangle, approximately 6 × 11 inches, not quite to the edge of the baking sheet since it will expand slightly. If you are using one large baking sheet, leave space on it for the second rectangle. Spread out a second rectangle the same as the first. Smooth and even them with the spatula.

PIPING THE MERINGUE

Twist the top of the piping bag tightly and pipe a cylinder of meringue down the center of each sponge rectangle. Pipe a matching border down each edge on top of (not on the side of) the sponge rectangles. There should be three even ridges of meringue resting on the rectangles. Dust the sponge and meringue well with sifted powdered sugar.

BAKING

Preheat the oven to 325 degrees F. Bake on the oven rack below center. If the oven is not big enough to hold two baking sheets at the same level, bake for 6 to 7 minutes, one sheet on the rack below, until the top sheet begins to color lightly, then switch their positions. Bake until the sponge mixture is firm, approximately 12 to 14 minutes. The meringue should be allowed only to color slightly. Immediately after removing from the oven, loosen the bottom of each sponge with a metal spatula to prevent it from sticking. Allow to cool on the baking sheet(s). Cut one layer, which will be the top, vertically all the way through in 1¼-inch slices while still warm.

FILLING A

When the cake has cooled completely, make the filling. If you are using Filling A, dissolve the coffee granules in the 3 tablespoons boiling water. Whip the cream with chilled beaters until almost stiff. Add the powdered sugar and 1½ tablespoons of the coffee mixture and beat until stiff. Spread the cream evenly along the length of the uncut sponge base.

FILLING B

If you are using Filling B, sprinkle the sugar over the berries and crush them slightly. Add more sugar to taste. Whip the cream with chilled beaters until stiff. Fold the berries into the cream. Spread the fruit cream evenly along the length of the uncut sponge base.

FINISHING

Using a wide spatula, carefully lift the cut sponge layer and arrange on top. Cut two strips of wax or parchment paper 1½ inches wide and several inches longer than the cake. Place them lengthwise at intervals just inside the outside ridges of meringue. Dust the top of the cake with powdered sugar. Remove the paper strips carefully. Refrigerate until serving time, at least 2 hours.

TANNZAPFEN
PINE-CONE SPONGE CAKE WITH BUTTER CREAM

CAKE
½ cup all-purpose
  flour
3 large eggs
1 egg yolk
½ cup superfine
  sugar
½ teaspoon vanilla
  extract
2 tablespoons un-
  salted butter,
  melted and cooled
DECORATION
1¼ cups whole
  blanched al-
  monds, split (see
  Almonds)
BUTTER CREAM
1 teaspoon granu-
  lated instant
  coffee
2 tablespoons boiling
  water, or a few
  drops more as
  needed
1½ cups (3 sticks)
  unsalted butter,
  softened
2 cups powdered
  sugar, sifted
3 egg yolks
TO FINISH
Powdered sugar,
  sifted

CONTINUED ON
FACING PAGE

A special Swiss dessert for Christmas, this giant pine cone cake is studded with toasted split almonds and garnished with a branch of evergreen. It is made by cutting a sheet cake of thin sponge into 4 cone-shaped layers of graduating size, sandwiching and covering them with mocha butter cream, and inserting toasted split blanched almonds all over the surface to simulate the scales of a pine cone.

To make the cake, you will need a 12 × 16-inch baking sheet with sides and several pieces of cardboard to make the cone stencils. If the cake is made in advance and frozen, place in the refrigerator 3 hours before it is needed, then leave at room temperature 1 hour before serving. Dust again lightly with powdered sugar before serving.

MAKING THE STENCILS

Fold the pieces of paper in half before cutting so that the cone is symmetrical. In total, you will have 4 stencils: 1 large cone that will be the layer second from the bottom; 2 equal medium-sized cones which will go on either side of the large cone; and 1 small cone which will go on top. The large cone should measure 10 inches from tip to end, and 5 inches across at its widest part. The 2 medium-sized cones should measure 9 inches long and 4 inches across. The smallest cone should measure 8¼ inches long and 3¼ inches across. The ends of the cones can be perfectly straight except for the corners which should be slightly rounded.

PREPARING THE BAKING SHEET

Butter the baking sheet well with soft butter. Cut out a piece of greaseproof or parchment paper the exact size of the bottom and place in the pan. Butter it well. Dust the pan with flour and shake out the excess. Set aside. **Preheat oven to 325 degrees F.**

Twig of evergreen
Satin or silver
*   ribbon for a*
*   bow, if desired*
EQUIPMENT
Cardboard for
*   stencils*
12 × 16-inch baking
*   sheet with rim*

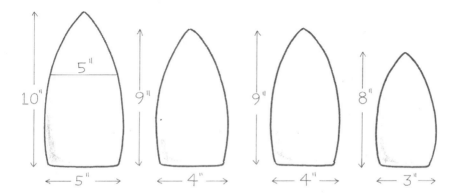

PREPARING THE BATTER

For the cake, sift the flour once onto a piece of wax paper and set aside. Choose a crockery mixing bowl that will fit into a saucepan with its base resting well above the bottom of the pan. Bring 3 inches of water to a boil in the saucepan, then remove the pan from the heat. Set the bowl over the pan, put the eggs, egg yolk, and sugar into it, and use an electric hand mixer or whisk to beat the mixture rapidly until it is thick and mousselike, about 4 minutes. To test the consistency, use the beater to lift a little of the beaten eggs and sugar, then drizzle the shape of the letter M over the mixture in the bowl. If the shape of the letter holds for 3 seconds, the mixture is sufficiently beaten. If the shape dissolves, beat 20 seconds longer and test again. Remove the bowl from the pan and beat in the vanilla, beating for 10 seconds. Sift the flour a second time directly onto the whisked-egg mixture. Using a metal spoon, fold in the flour carefully. Halfway through the folding, pour on the cooled melted butter and continue folding until the butter is blended and no pockets of flour remain.

BAKING

Spoon the batter evenly onto the prepared baking sheet, using a spatula to spread it evenly to the edges and into the corners. Bake in the middle of the oven until golden and the cake springs back to the touch, about 13 minutes.

While the cake is baking, lay out a clean dishtowel or cloth slightly larger than the baking sheet and sprinkle it evenly with granulated or superfine sugar, which will help keep the cake from sticking to it. When the cake has finished baking, remove it from the oven and invert it quickly onto the prepared cloth. Peel off the paper from the bottom of the cake. Trim off the crusty edges of the cake on all sides with a long knife.

CUTTING OUT

Arrange the paper stencils on the cake so that all of them fit. (If you have difficulty fitting one of the stencils, one of the medium-sized cone layers can be cut out in 2 pieces, later to be sandwiched back together with a little butter cream.) Using a sharp knife, cut out all of the cone shapes and set them aside.

TOASTING THE ALMONDS

Preheat the oven to 425 degrees F. Place the split almonds in a single layer on a baking sheet. Bake them in the middle of the oven until lightly browned, about 5 to 7 minutes. (Watch them carefully, as they color rapidly.) Remove the baking sheet from the oven and allow the almonds to cool.

MAKING THE BUTTER CREAM

Stir the instant coffee into 2 tablespoons of boiling water, stirring and mashing it until the coffee is dissolved. If necessary, add a few more drops of boiling water to dissolve the coffee completely. Set aside.

Using an electric mixer, beat the butter until it is well creamed. Gradually beat in the sifted powdered sugar. Continue beating for at least 8 minutes to dissolve the sugar completely. Beat in the egg yolks one by one, beating well after each addition. Beat in the dissolved coffee and beat another minute, scraping down the sides of the bowl and blending the coffee thoroughly.

ASSEMBLING

Place a medium-sized cone layer on a serving plate. Reserve half of the icing for covering the cake. Divide the remaining icing among the layers, spreading all but the smallest layer evenly with icing. Place the largest cone on top of the one already on the plate. Place a medium-sized cone on top of that. Cover with the un-iced small cone. Spread the top, sides, and end of the cone with the remaining butter cream, smoothing it into the ridges to give the cone a rounded appearance. Dip a metal spatula in hot water and glaze it over the icing to smooth the surface.

DECORATING

Begining at the point of the cone, insert toasted split almonds, curved side out, pointed end showing, so they lie almost flat. Continue up the top and sides of the cone, completely covering the cake and slightly overlapping the almonds so they resemble the scales of a real cone. Taper the almonds to follow the curve of the cone shape.

Dust a tiny amount of sifted powdered sugar just down the center of the cone to resemble snow. Refrigerate the cake at least 4 hours or overnight to firm the icing. Just before serving, place a twig of evergreen at the top of the cone and, if desired, finish with a small bow made of festive ribbon, arranging the streamers decoratively.

Slice in no thinner than half inch slices; wider slices can then be sliced in half.

PREISELBEERENSCHAUMTORTE
LINGONBERRY MERINGUE TORTE

CONTINUED ON
FACING PAGE

CAKE

1 cup (2 sticks) unsalted butter, cut in pieces and softened

1¼ cups superfine sugar

1 teaspoon vanilla

4 large eggs at room temperature (cover them with hot tap water for 2 minutes if they come straight from the refrigerator)

1¾ cups plus 2 tablespoons all-purpose flour

1½ teaspoons baking powder

3 tablespoons milk

SYRUP

½ cup water

4 tablespoons sugar

½ cup light or dark rum

FILLING

1¾ cups lingonberry preserves, preferably; otherwise, you can substitute raspberry jam, though it's somewhat sweeter. Reserve one fifth of this amount for garnish.

This decorative meringue-covered torte from Vienna is made up of rum-soaked layers of pound cake coated with lingonberry preserves. The small red berries, resembling red currants or small cranberries, are fuller-flavored than cranberries and thinner-skinned than either currants or cranberries.

Because they are especially tart, they harmonize well with the sweet meringue. While good-quality raspberry jam can be substituted, the lingonberries produce greater contrast in flavor and are readily available in grocery and specialty food stores, imported from Germany, Sweden, and Eastern Europe.

Because of its spectacular appearance—a decorative meringue coating embellished with tiny meringue cups filled with crimson lingonberries and toasted flaked almonds—this torte makes an impressive finish for a holiday dinner. I can see it, especially, ending a feast on New Year's Eve.

Because it takes several hours and a certain amount of patience to prepare, the recipe has been worked out so that it can be made up to two weeks in advance and frozen. The Italian meringue (meringue made with a boiled sugar syrup) holds up perfectly in the freezer. The cake can be placed in the refrigerator the day of the dinner and keeps well, refrigerated, if not all of it is eaten at once.

Because it is so rich, the cake can be cut in relatively thin slices.

EQUIPMENT

The base of a springform pan is called for, since when placed under the cake, it facilitates moving it from wire rack to baking sheet to cake plate—a task that would otherwise be extremely difficult owing to the weight and size of the cake.

PREPARING THE CAKE PAN

Butter the cake pan. Line it with a round parchment paper the same size as the bottom. Butter the paper and flour the pan, knocking out the excess flour. Set the pan aside. **Preheat oven to 350 degrees F.**

PREPARING THE CAKE BATTER

Using an electric mixer, cream the butter and sugar together until light and fluffy. Beat in the vanilla. Add 1 egg at a time, beating well after each addition. This is necessary to keep the mixture from curdling. Sift the flour and baking powder together. Pour the flour mixture onto the cake batter and fold it in thoroughly using a large metal spoon. Add the milk and fold it into the batter. Pour the batter into the prepared cake pan and spread it evenly with a spatula. Tap the pan firmly several times on a counter to knock out any air bubbles.

BAKING

Bake until the cake is golden and springs back to the touch, approximately 35 minutes. Loosen the edges of the cake with a sharp knife. Unmold it onto a cake rack to cool, peeling off the paper. When cool, cut the cake horizontally across to make 2 layers. Remove the bottom from the springform pan, wash and dry it, and place it under the bottom half of the cake. Place this, in turn, on a wire rack.

MERINGUE
7 large egg whites (approximately 1 cup), at room temperature
Pinch of salt
⅔ cup superfine sugar
MERINGUE SYRUP
1½ cups plus 2 tablespoons granulated sugar
⅓ cup water
GARNISH
⅓ cup flaked almonds
Reserved lingonberry preserves
TO SERVE
1½ cups heavy cream, lightly whipped
1 cup lingonberry preserves, to be passed separately (optional)
EQUIPMENT
1 9-inch springform cake pan
1 rimless baking sheet or the underside of a baking sheet with rim
Pastry bag fitted with plain ⅜-inch tip
Candy thermometer

MAKING THE SYRUP AND FILLING
THE CAKE

For the syrup, stir the water and sugar together until the mixture comes to a boil. Boil for 2 minutes, then remove from the heat and add the rum. Prick the surface of the cake base and the top of the lid numerous times with the tines of a fork. Slowly spoon the rum syrup over the base of the cake. Reserve the other half for the top layer. Set aside one fifth of the lingonberry preserves for garnish. Divide the remainder in half. Spread the base of the cake evenly with half of the lingonberries, reaching not quite to the edge. Cover with the top half of the cake. Spoon the remaining syrup slowly over the surface of the cake. Coat it evenly with the remaining half of the lingonberries, reaching not quite to the edge. Set the cake aside. **Preheat oven to 450 degrees F.**

MAKING THE MERINGUE

Place the ingredients for the meringue syrup in a heavy-bottomed pan and set aside. Using an electric mixer, beat the egg whites in a large bowl with a pinch of salt. Begin with the mixer on a moderately low speed. When the egg whites are foamy, increase the speed to moderately fast and beat until they softly hold their shape but are not dry. Begin adding the ⅔ cup of superfine sugar by the tablespoon, beating 20 seconds after each addition. When all the sugar has been added, beat another 3 or 4 minutes to make a thick, glossy meringue. Immediately heat the meringue syrup ingredients over high heat, stirring constantly, until the mixture comes to a boil. Wash down any sugar crystals with a wet pastry brush. Allow the syrup to boil until it reaches the hard ball stage, 248 degrees F. on a candy thermometer. Pour the hot syrup in a slow, steady stream onto the meringue, beating all the time. Beat at high speed until the meringue is cool, approximately 4 minutes. Coat the sides of the cake evenly with a thick layer of meringue, being careful not to mix in any of the lingonberries. Dip a metal spatula in hot water repeatedly and smooth the sides evenly.

DECORATING

Place the remaining meringue in a large pastry bag (or refill several times if the bag is small) fitted with a plain ⅜-inch tip. Beginning on the outside edge of the top, pipe a spiraling circle into the center of the cake, completely covering the lingonberries. If it isn't perfect, don't worry since it spreads slightly when baked and the flaked amonds cover up mistakes. On the sides, pipe straight up and down waves all the way around the cake. Pipe them as if you were handwriting an uninterrupted chain of U's, reaching up to the top edge of the cake and curving back down to the bottom of the cake, continuing the up and down motion to cover the outside of the cake all the way around. On top of the cake, mark off eight evenly spaced points. Pipe eight small cups, approximately 1¼ inches in diameter, going around in a double circle so the cups will be deep enough to hold the lingonberry garnish. Placing them on one at a time, decorate the top of the cake sparingly with flaked almonds. Slide the cake carefully onto a rimless baking sheet or the underside of a baking sheet with rim.

BAKING THE MERINGUE

Bake the meringue-coated cake in an oven **preheated to 450 degrees F.** until the meringue is lightly browned, watching it carefully. If your oven is hotter in the back than the front, turn the cake once before it is browned all over. Remove the cake from the oven and allow to cool to room temperature before moving.

FINISHING

When cool, loosen the meringue from the baking sheet carefully with a sharp knife. When you're sure it isn't sticking, slide the cake, including the metal base from the springform pan, onto a cake plate. Refrigerate until ready to serve. Before serving, fill the meringue cups with the reserved lingonberries.

Serve with lightly whipped cream and, if desired, extra lingonberries passed separately.

FREEZING INSTRUCTIONS

If freezing, allow the cake to cool completely before placing it in the freezer. Whether freezing it or not, it is especially important to cool the cake on the baking sheet before attempting to move it. Then loosen the meringue from the baking sheet, using a sharp knife. By baking the meringue-coated cake on a rimless baking sheet or on the underside of a baking sheet, as is recommended in the recipe, you can then slide it easily to a cake plate.

If freezing, or refrigerating it for more than a day, place 5 toothpicks or wooden skewers in the top of the cake to stick well above the meringue cups. Then drape the cake loosely with aluminum foil resting on the wooden picks so it doesn't touch the meringue.

The lingonberry garnish should not be placed in the tiny cups until just before serving time, to avoid the danger of its bleeding.

KÄSEKUCHEN

CHEESECAKE

While *Käsekuchen*, creamy rich cheesecake baked in a springform pan, would normally be considered everyday baking, like *Kugelhopf*, this is one item against which most German home bakers measure one another's skill. For this reason, I feel it merits elevation to the realm of specialty baking.

The recipe I have chosen is especially rich and creamy but less dense than most. It is also quick and easy to make. So that it can ripen properly, it is best to make it a day before it is needed. When covered with plastic wrap or aluminum foil it keeps well in the refrigerator for at least 8 days.

2 tablespoons un-salted butter, softened, for greasing the pan
5 tablespoons dry bread crumbs (see Baking Tips)
1 teaspoon sugar
½ teaspoon cinnamon
16 ounces cream cheese, softened
¾ cup superfine sugar
3 large eggs
1 cup heavy cream
2 tablespoons all-purpose flour, sifted
1 teaspoon vanilla extract
EQUIPMENT
8-inch springform pan

PREPARING THE CAKE PAN AND CRUMB CRUST

Grease an 8-inch springform pan well with 2 tablespoons of softened butter. Combine the bread crumbs with the sugar and cinnamon and sprinkle well over the sides and bottom of the pan, pressing them to make them stick. **Preheat the oven to 350 degrees F.**

PREPARING THE FILLING

Using an electric mixer, beat the cream cheese with the sugar until creamy, about 2 minutes. Add the eggs, one at a time, beating well after each addition. Beat in the cream, adding it gradually, and finally the flour and vanilla. When well blended, pour the mixture into the prepared pan.

BAKING

Bake in the middle of the oven for 45 minutes. Turn off the oven, leaving the cake inside. Wedge the handle of a wooden spoon between the door and the oven at the top, to keep the door slightly ajar. Leave the cake in the oven for 1 to 1½ hours, or until cool.

FINISHING

Remove cake and place in the refrigerator until fully chilled, preferably overnight. To serve, carefully loosen the sides of the cake with a knife and remove the sides of the springform pan.

PASTRIES

BASIC STRUDEL

Influenced by the paper-thin Turkish pastry used for baklava, the Hungarians were the first to put strudel on the food map, sprinkling their huge paper-thin round of pastry with butter-toasted bread crumbs, then wrapping it around a filling of juicy apples. The art perfected by the Hungarian bakers soon made its way to Vienna where strudel became a favorite treat at *Jause* (afternoon tea), filled with apples, sour cherries, plums, ground nuts, or ground poppy seeds. When filled with curd cheese (*Topfenstrudel*) or sour cream and milk (*Rahmstrudel*), it became a more substantial way to end the evening meal.

The Viennese learned from the Hungarians the importance of using the right flour—one with plenty of gluten—so that the pastry would develop enough elasticity to be stretched to transparent thinness without tearing. For this reason bread (hard wheat) flour high in protein (gluten), has been called for in the recipe, rather than pastry (soft wheat) or all-purpose flour. If making your own pastry, you will need a large table and a clean sheet or cloth to put over it so the pastry can be easily rolled when finished. If you don't feel ambitious enough to try your own pastry, at the end of the recipe is a method for using sheets of prepared phyllo dough—the Middle Eastern thin pastry sheets sold in the freezer sections of specialty groceries.

A good Viennese friend, Frau Meyer, who comes from a long line of accomplished bakers, told me she thought that since the war, with the exception of Demel's, Vienna's famous pastry shop, few commercial bakers made a strudel to surpass the traditional Viennese housewife's.

¾ cup lukewarm water
1 large egg, at room temperature, lightly beaten
1 teaspoon lemon juice
2 tablespoons melted unsalted butter
2½ cups bread flour
½ teaspoon salt
2 tablespoons vegetable oil
FILLING
Choose apple, cherry or plum from the section at the end of the recipe
CRUMB MIXTURE
1½ cups fine bread crumbs (see Baking Tips)
¾ cup (1½ sticks) butter
½ cup slivered blanched almonds, coarsely chopped
TO FINISH
¾ cups (1½ sticks) butter, melted
Powdered sugar
Heavy cream, lightly whipped
EQUIPMENT
Large (4 × 5-foot) table
Clean cloth to cover (an old sheet is ideal; otherwise use 2 large overlapping tea towels)

The missing ingredient? Butter, was her reply, lots and lots of butter, used both to toast the bread crumbs and to coat the thin pastry. Following Frau Meyer's advice, the recipes that follow are well fortified with this favorite Austrian ingredient.

To be at its best, strudel should be eaten as soon as it comes out of the oven or at least before it has completely cooled. At this stage the leaves of pastry are crisp and separate. Once it has steamed and cooled, the pastry becomes soggy. Not that the strudel isn't delicious even then, but it is no longer the same refined pastry.

For fillings, choose from the apple, sour cherry, or plum fillings that follow.

PREPARING THE DOUGH AND FILLING

To make the dough, mix the water, egg, lemon juice, and melted butter together in a small mixing bowl. Sift the flour and salt together into a large mixing bowl and make a well in the center. Pour the liquid ingredients into the well. Using a wooden spoon, gradually beat in the flour until it is all incorporated. The dough will be sticky at this point. Knead the dough on an unfloured board until it is smooth and elastic and comes away from your hands easily, approximately 7 minutes. Pat the dough into a flat round. Brush the surface with vegetable oil. Cover the dough with a mixing bowl and leave to rest at room temperature for 30 to 40 minutes. While the dough is resting, make one of the fillings at the end of the recipe.

PREPARING THE CRUMB MIXTURE

In a large skillet, cook the bread crumbs in butter until golden. If they are especially dry, you may want to add a little more butter. If desired, you can lightly roast the almonds on a baking sheet in a **preheated 425-degree oven** for approximately 5 minutes to give them a roasted flavor, although this is just a personal preference and isn't necessary. Set the almonds and browned crumbs aside.

When the crumbs, almonds, and filling are prepared and the dough has rested sufficiently, prepare to assemble your strudel.

ROLLING OUT AND STRETCHING THE DOUGH

Cover your table with a clean cloth and dust the cloth lightly with flour. Place the dough on the cloth and, using a rolling pin, roll it in all directions as thin as possible. It will be quite resistant. When it will stretch no farther with the rolling pin, brush the surface of the dough with the vegetable oil. This will keep it from sticking together if it folds on top of itself. Lightly flour your hands. Slip them underneath the dough, palms down, and beginning in the middle of the dough, start pulling gently with the back of your hands first, then with your thumbs rather than your fingers, always stretching from the middle outward to the edges. Rotate the dough over your hands to stretch it evenly all over until the thick ends finally drape over the sides of the table and the dough is paper-thin. Work gently and carefully but if the dough tears, don't worry. It won't ruin the strudel. Moistening your fingers, pinch the hole together as best you can and just be extra careful when you roll the strudel.

When the dough is thin enough, cut off the thick edge all the way around with scissors. This excess can be cut into thin noodles and simmered in a pot of soup, if desired. Brush the surface of the dough evenly with melted butter.

ASSEMBLING

Scatter the browned bread crumbs and chopped almonds evenly over the surface of the dough, leaving a 2-inch rim free all the way around. Spoon the prepared filling in a long loaf shape near the edge of pastry closest to you, leaving a 3-inch rim free between the edge and the filling and 3 inches free at either end of the filling. Now pick up the cloth under the strudel beginning at the edge closest to you and roll the strudel jelly roll fashion. (The cloth will help coax the strudel to roll.) Tuck the ends of the rolled pastry in neatly. Brush the roll well with butter. Place on a large buttered baking sheet, curving it around in a horseshoe shape to make it fit.

BAKING AND FINISHING

Preheat the oven to 400 degrees F. Bake the strudel just below the center of the oven until crisp and brown, brushing it once generously with butter toward the end of the baking. Baking time will be approximately 35 to 40 minutes. When done, remove the strudel from the oven and after 5 minutes, dust it with powdered sugar. Serve while still warm, with lightly whipped cream.

QUICK PHYLLO PASTRY STRUDEL

Prepared phyllo dough, which is available in the freezer section of most supermarkets, comes in sheets slightly larger than standard typewriter paper. The instructions given are for phyllo sheets approximately 10–12-inches wide and 13–14 inches long. Occasionally the pastry comes in huge sheets. In this case, you will not need to piece as many sheets together as instructed here.

Cover a large table with a clean cloth. Use 6 sheets of pastry. With the short side facing you, place 3 rectangles of pastry side by side with the edges slightly overlapping. Brush the overlap with melted butter to help seal it. Extend the size of the pastry by building on another 3 sheets of pastry, allowing a 1½-inch overlap. Again, brush the overlap with melted butter to seal. You should have a large, almost square patchwork of pastry. Then brush the entire surface of the pastry with butter. If there are no tears, you can stop here. If it is too thin and if there are any tears, sprinkle the first layer with some of the browned bread crumbs (if making apple or cherry strudel). Then place another layer of pastry on top, using 6 sheets, in the same manner as before. Brush this layer with butter. Then proceed as directed in the appropriate filling and basic strudel recipe.

APFELSTRUDEL

APPLE STRUDEL

1 recipe Basic Strudel

FILLING
3½ *pounds Granny Smith apples, peeled, cored, and thinly sliced*

Juice of 1 lemon
Grated rind of 2 lemons
½ cup golden raisins
¾ cup sugar

To make the filling, squeeze the lemon juice over the apples once they are sliced, and mix together with the grated lemon rind and golden raisins. Just before filling, mix in the sugar. Fill strudel dough, then roll and bake per the instructions in the master recipe.

VARIATION 1

I prefer the lemon flavor dominating this filling. However, if you like, you can add 1½ teaspoons of cinnamon to the apple mixture.

VARIATION 2

Another variation I've enjoyed in the Tyrol, obviously of Italian influence, is adding ½ cup of pine nuts to the apple filling.

KIRSCHENSTRUDEL

CHERRY STRUDEL

1 recipe Basic Strudel

FILLING

3 pounds tart red pitted cherries (fresh or canned sour cherries can be substituted; they must be well drained and the sugar should be decreased by half)

Grated rind of 2 lemons
1 cup sugar

Mix the cherries together with the grated lemon rind. Instead of spooning all the cherries in one mound, scatter them evenly over the pastry on top of the crumbs and almonds, leaving a 3-inch rim free all the way around. Sprinkle the sugar over the cherries. Then roll and bake per the instructions in the master recipe.

ZWETSCHGENSTRUDEL

PURPLE PLUM STRUDEL

In the late summer when purple plums are on the market, a *Zwetschgenstrudel* makes a delicious change from the apple or tart red cherry fillings more often seen.

1 recipe Basic Strudel Dough, eliminating the slivered almonds

FILLING

3 pounds purple plums, pitted   *½ cup sugar*
   and quartered (or if espe-   *1½ teaspoons cinnamon*
   cially large, cut in sixths)

Prepare the basic strudel dough and browned bread crumbs per the master recipe, eliminating the slivered almonds. Scatter the crumbs over the buttered strudel dough. For the filling, mix the above ingredients together. Instead of spooning all the plums in one mound, scatter them evenly over the pastry on top of the crumbs, leaving a 3-inch rim free all the way around. Then roll and bake per the instructions in the master recipe.

APFELSTREUSELKUCHEN

APPLE CRUMB CAKE

**MAKES 1 8-INCH
CAKE**

APPLE FILLING
2 *pounds green or
yellow apples,
peeled, cored, and
thinly sliced*
¼ *cup water*
⅓ *cup sugar, or
more to taste if
you prefer a sweet
filling and if the
apples are very
sour*
*Grated rind of 1
lemon*
Juice of ½ lemon
½ *teaspoon
cinnamon*
⅓ *cup golden raisins*
2 *tablespoons un-
salted butter*
PASTRY
½ *cup (1 stick)
chilled unsalted
butter*
1 *large egg*
½ *cup sugar*
1½ *teaspoons bak-
ing powder*
1¾ *cups all-purpose
flour*
TO FINISH
Powdered sugar

CONTINUED ON
FACING PAGE

For many years, whenever I've visited my friends in Rothenburg ob der Tauber, Germany, we've always made a Sunday coffee outing to the tiny village of Freudenbach, a half hour's drive away, where Annie Gramm, proprietress of the Gasthof Sonnenhof, bakes her delicious *Apfelstreuselkuchen*. While normally *Streuselkuchen* would be thought of as an everyday cake not worthy of any great excursion, Annie's cake has always been much lighter and more crumbly than anyone else's. After eating many cakes, we finally asked her for the secret, and learned that she mixes the baking powder with the egg before adding it to the butter and flour. Since baking powder is activated immediately when it is mixed with liquid ingredients and since the pastry isn't allowed to rest before baking, the leavening agent goes to work with full force, producing this especially light crumb.

For a filling, Annie cooks the apple mixture first, then spoons it on top of the bottom layer of pastry, covering it with pastry crumbs. She also recommended rhubarb as an excellent filling, on which I heartily concur.

Once you have cooked the filling, this is a very fast and easy cake to prepare.

PREPARE THE FILLING

Mix all the filling ingredients together in a heavy saucepan. Cook the mixture, covered, over medium-low heat, stirring occasionally to make sure the apples aren't sticking to the bottom of the pan. If necessary, add a few more drops of water. Cook until the apples are almost puréed but still have some texture, about 15 minutes. If there is excess liquid, turn the heat to high and simmer, uncovered, stirring so the apples don't stick to the pan. When the mixture is quite thick, remove from the heat and cool to room temperature or refrigerate until needed. The filling can be prepared several days in advance if desired.

Heavy cream (optional)
EQUIPMENT
8-inch springform pan

PREPARE THE PASTRY

Using the coarse blades of a hand grater, flake the chilled butter into a large bowl. In a small bowl or cup, mix the egg together with the sugar and baking powder using a fork. Pour the egg mixture onto the butter, stirring it in slightly just to help separate the flakes. Sift the flour on top of the butter and egg. Using your fingertips, work the flour into the other ingredients to make a crumb-like texture.

Lightly butter the springform pan and press a little over half of the crumb mixture into the bottom. Pat it in evenly with lightly floured hands. It should resemble a normal rich pastry, having lost its crumblike texture. Prick the pastry with the tines of a fork. **Preheat the oven to 350 degrees F.**

ASSEMBLING

Spoon the cooled apple filling evenly over the pastry. Crumble the remaining pastry mixture over the filling, distributing the crumbs evenly.

BAKING AND FINISHING

Bake the cake in the middle of the oven for about 45 minutes, or until risen and golden. Remove from the oven and allow to rest several minutes. While still hot, dust with sifted powdered sugar. Serve warm or at room temperature. If you like, serve thick unwhipped or lightly whipped cream with the cake.

RHABARBERSTREUSELKUCHEN

RHUBARB CRUMB CAKE

Using the pastry and basic instructions for *Apfelstreuselkuchen* (previous recipe), substitute the following rhubarb filling for the apple filling.

5 cups washed rhubarb, cut in
 1½-inch pieces
¾ cup sugar, or more to taste
⅓ cup golden raisins
2 tablespoons light or dark rum

Mix all the ingredients but the rum together in a heavy saucepan. Cook the mixture, covered, over medium-low heat, stirring occasionally to make sure the rhubarb isn't sticking to the bottom of the pan. If necessary, add a few tablespoons of water. Cook until the rhubarb is tender, 15 to 20 minutes. If there is excess liquid, turn the heat to high and simmer the rhubarb uncovered, stirring all the time, until the mixture is thick. Stir in the rum and simmer 1 minute longer. Allow the rhubarb to cool to room temperature or refrigerate before using.

   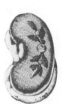

ENGADINER NUSSTORTE
ENGADINE NUT CAKE

Almost like a confection, this nut cake from the canton of Engadine is one of Switzerland's truly great pastries. For the uninitiated, however, this cake would probably pass unnoticed in a pastry shop window, as it has a very plain exterior: simple mahogany-brown sweet butter pastry on the sides, top, and bottom—no decorations, sugar, or icing. The filling is equally unpretentious, nothing more than caramel cream and walnuts. But when the cake is at room temperature, the liquid filling solidifies to a soft, nutty toffee. The marriage of flaky pastry and soft filling makes this unusual and special.

One cautionary note: make sure to use a large, deep, heavy-bottomed pan for caramelizing the sugar, and add the cream slowly. Even though heating the cream as instructed reduces the bubbling reaction, once mixed, the cream and caramel always bubble up. If the pan is too shallow, the mixture will run over the top.

This cake is best made at least one day in advance to allow the caramel to firm and the pastry to soften. The cake will then cut neatly. It is the perfect dessert or gift for caramel-loving friends. It is also useful for taking on picnics or long car rides as it is not at all fragile.

PREPARING THE PASTRY

Butter the sides and bottom of an 8-inch springform pan. Sift the flour and salt together into a large mixing bowl. Coat the stick of butter with flour from the bowl to make it easier to handle. Grate the butter directly into the flour, using the coarse

---

PASTRY
1¾ cups all-purpose
    flour
⅛ teaspoon salt
½ cup (1 stick)
    unsalted butter
⅔ cup superfine sugar
Grated rind of 1
    large or 2 small
    lemons
1 large egg
1 egg yolk
FILLING
1 cup heavy cream
2¾ cups powdered
    sugar, sifted
1⅓ cups walnuts,
    coarsely chopped
GLAZE
1 egg yolk beaten
    with 1 table-
    spoon cream
EQUIPMENT
Large, deep, heavy-
    bottomed saucepan
8-inch springform
    pan

blades of a grater. As the butter is grated, mix in the flakes with the flour occasionally before grating more. Add the sugar and lemon rind. Using 2 knives, cut the butter into the flour until the texture resembles coarse meal. Using your fingertips, blend the butter and flour for another 60 seconds. Mix the egg and yolk lightly with a fork and poor over the flour mixture. Using the fork, mix the egg into the flour mixture until well distributed. Then, with your hand, pull the dough together into a ball. Knead it lightly on a floured board until it forms a cohesive mass. Pat into a flat round. Wrap tightly in plastic wrap and refrigerate at least 1 hour before using.

ROLLING AND CUTTING OUT THE PASTRY

On a lightly floured board, roll out the dough ⅛ inch thick in a large rectangle approximately 19 inches long and 12 inches wide. (For more detailed notes on handling pastry, see Baking Tips.) Using the base of the springform pan as a stencil, cut out 2 circles. Place one circle on a piece of parchment or wax paper that has been laid on a baking sheet and freeze. This will be your lid. With the sides of the pan removed, place the other pastry circle in the bottom of the springform pan. From the remaining dough, cut out a strip 1½ inches wide and long enough to extend around the circumference of the pan. You can use 2 or 3 strips and piece them together once they are inside the pan. Place the ring (the sides of the pan) back on the base. Run the strip of dough along the sides, joining with the base by pressing the seam together well.

Refrigerate while making the filling.

MAKING THE FILLING

Heat the cream in a small pan until almost simmering. Cover and remove from the heat. Sift the powdered sugar into a large, deep, heavy-bottomed pan and stir constantly over medium low heat. The sugar will first form into small, crusty lumps. Keep stirring and soon they will begin to melt. The mixture will be a caramel color. Stir until the white lumps are dissolved and re-move from the heat. Immediately add the hot cream in a slow stream. The mixture will boil up so add only a small amount at first, then the remainder. Add the chopped walnuts. Stir briefly over medium heat to dissolve any bits of caramel that have solidified. Cool to room temperature before proceeding.

NOTE To speed the cooling process, place the pan of caramel filling in a bowl of very cold water and stir, changing the water if it becomes too warm.

FILLING AND FINISHING FOR OVEN

Preheat the oven to 375 degrees F. Remove the pastry-lined springform pan from the refrigerator. Spread the cooled filling evenly over the bottom. Remove the lid from the freezer, peel off the paper, and place the pastry circle on top of the filling. Use a pastry wheel or small knife to trim the side rim of pastry evenly so there will be a ½-inch overlap when the pastry is folded over the lid. Mix the egg yolk and cream with a fork to produce the glaze mixture. With a pastry brush, apply the glaze evenly over the lid. Loosen the side rim of pastry with a table knife. Carefully fold it over the lid, smoothing out any seams, and press it carefully into the lid to seal. Brush the overlap with egg glaze. With the tines of a fork, prick decorative markings at even intervals just inside the overlapping edge. Prick another circle of tiny holes toward the center.

BAKING AND SERVING

Bake in a preheated oven until a russet gold, approximately 40 to 50 minutes. Allow the torte to cool completely to room temperature and store in a cool place overnight. If the nut torte is refrigerated, allow it to come to room temperature before serving. The next day, or before serving, run a knife around the edge of the cake pan to release the pastry. Remove the sides of the springform. Loosen the pastry from the bottom of the pan and transfer it to a serving plate.

M A S T E R   R E C I P E

Süsser Mürbeteig
Basic Sweet Rich Pastry Dough

*1½ cups all-purpose
flour*
⅛ teaspoon salt
*6 tablespoons (¾
stick) unsalted
butter, well chilled*
*½ cup superfine
sugar*
*1 teaspoon grated
lemon rind*
*1 large egg, lightly
beaten*

This pastry is suitable for all dessert tarts, especially those with fruit or custard filling: the sugar in the pastry helps produce a crusty pastry without the need for "blind" baking—a partial baking ahead of time—normally required of unsweetened pastries when a juicy or liquid filling is used. The amount given is enough for a 10- or 11-inch tart tin.

Sift the flour and salt together into a large mixing bowl. Coat the stick of butter with flour from the bowl to make it easier to handle. Grate the butter directly into the flour, using the coarse blades of a hand grater. As the butter is grated, mix in the flakes with the flour occasionally, using your fingertips, before grating more. Add the sugar and lemon rind. Using 2 knives, cut the butter into the flour until the texture resembles coarse meal. Shake the bowl to cause any larger pieces of butter to rise to the surface and quickly rub any larger bits of butter into the flour. Continue until the butter is well blended but not greasy, 40 to 60 seconds.

Mix the egg lightly with a fork and pour over the flour mixture. Using the fork, mix the egg into the flour mixture until well distributed. Then, using your hand, pull the dough together into a ball. Knead the dough lightly on a floured board until it forms a cohesive mass. Pat it into a flat round. Wrap tightly in plastic wrap and refrigerate at least 1 hour before using. Use as directed in recipe.

ZWETSCHGENWÄHE
PLUM TART

In Swiss German, the word *Wähe* means tart, which can be filled with everything from cheese (*Käsewähe*) and any number of vegetables (*Gemüsewähe*) to simple egg, cinnamon, and sugar (*Zuckerwähe*) or one of many fruits (*Fruchtwähe*), such as purple plum, apple, apricot, or cherry. Most frequently the cheese, vegetable, and fruit tarts are made with a rich short-crust pastry and baked with a cream custard mixture that sets with the solid ingredients when baked. While rich yeast dough is also sometimes used for Swiss *Wähe*, both sweet and savory, it is more commonly used in Germany for their fruit tart equivalents (*Obstkuchen*) which, for the most part, are not baked with custard. The recipes below are based on the typical Swiss technique.

In the late summer throughout Switzerland when the small purple plums (*Zwetschgen*) are harvested, simple, custard-filled plum tarts appear in bakery-shop windows and farmhouse kitchens. The housewives in the Jura region, where I've often consumed this great treat, generally use enormous fluted black steel tart tins, either round or oval, which conduct the heat rapidly to produce an especially crusty pastry. Any kind of tart tin can be used, however, to produce this delicious sunburst of plums. It is best eaten the same or next day, warm or at room temperature, and should not be frozen.

1 recipe Basic Sweet
  Rich Pastry
FILLING
2 pounds purple
  plums, stoned
  and sliced in
  quarters or, if
  large, in sixths
3 tablespoons super-
  fine sugar
2 teaspoons
  cinnamon
2 tablespoons butter
CUSTARD
1 cup heavy cream
1 teaspoon
  cornstarch
2 large eggs
1 egg yolk
4 tablespoons super-
  fine sugar
TO FINISH
Heavy Cream
EQUIPMENT
10-inch tart pan,
  preferably metal

LINING THE TART PAN

Make the pastry per the instructions in the master recipe. Wrap well and refrigerate at least 1 hour. **Preheat the oven to 375 degrees F.**

On a lightly floured board, roll the dough out into a thin round 3 to 4 inches larger than the tart pan. See Lining Tart Pans. Lift the pastry round with your rolling pin and lay it over the pan. Press the pastry well into the sides of the pan, easing some of the excess dough down into the fluted sides to reinforce the edge. Run your rolling pin across the top of the top of the tart to cut off the excess pastry.

FILLING AND BAKING

Beginning on the outside edge and working toward the center, place the plum slices in concentric circles on top of the pastry, skin side down. Dust them with the sugar and cinnamon. Flake the butter on top with the coarse side of a hand grater. Bake in a preheated oven for 15 minutes. Combine the cornstarch with 3 tablespoons of the heavy cream and whisk into the remaining custard ingredients. Let stand 15 minutes. Pour the custard over the top of the tart, making sure to add only as much as the tart can hold. Return to the oven to finish baking until the pastry is golden and the custard is set, approximately another 30 to 35 minutes. Serve warm or at room temperature. Serve with lightly beaten whipped cream.

FRUCHTWÄHEN

FRUIT TARTS

Besides plums, which have such a short season, both apples and fresh or dried apricots—available year-round—are used in fruit tarts with a custard topping. Using the recipe and instructions for *Zwetschgenwähe*, make the following changes for apples and apricots.

APFELWÄHE

APPLE TART

Use the same recipe for *Zwetschgenwähe*, using 2 pounds of golden delicious apples instead of plums, and adding 6 tablespoons of finely ground blanched almonds and the grated rind of 1 lemon.

Line the tart pan with the pastry and sprinkle the bottom with the ground almonds. Peel, core, and quarter the apples. Slice them very thin and toss them in a mixing bowl with the sugar, cinnamon, and lemon rind. place them on top of the almonds, arranging the top layer in neat concentric circles. Flake 2 tablespoons of butter on top. Bake for 15 minutes before pouring the custard mixture over it. Bake until the pastry is golden and the custard set.

APRIKOSENWÄHE

APRICOT TART

If using fresh apricots, stone and quarter 2 pounds of them and prepare the tart exactly like the *Zwetschgenwähe*, eliminating the cinnamon. If using dried apricots, (approximately 1 pound), soak them overnight in warm water and drain well on paper towels before using. Prepare the tart as above.

LINZERTORTE

*1½ cups all-purpose
  flour
⅛ teaspoon ground
  cloves
¼ teaspoon
  cinnamon
1 cup unblanched
  almonds, finely
  ground (see
  Almonds)
½ cup superfine
  sugar
Grated rind of 1
  lemon
1 cup (2 sticks)
  unsalted butter,
  softened
2 egg yolks, lightly
  beaten
1 teaspoon vanilla
  extract
1½ cups raspberry
  jam
TO GLAZE
1 egg yolk
1½ tablespoons heavy
  or light cream
TO FINISH
Powdered sugar,
  sifted
EQUIPMENT
9-inch springform
  pan*

Oddly enough, my first taste of Linzertorte was actually in Switzerland—proof enough that this delicious Austrian specialty merits notice, since the Swiss have enough of their own delectable pastries to know what's worth importing. Named after the city—Linz—where it was first created, this torte looks less spectacular than the many multilayered Austrian creations. However, one should not judge pastries by height. Made with a butter-rich ground almond dough, it is distinguished by a grillwork of pastry covering a raspberry jam filling. Because the dough is very rich, it is more difficult to work, so it is important to have the dough well chilled and to work quickly when rolling out. Linzertorte is best baked a few days in advance so the flavors have time to mellow and the pastry can be cut easily without crumbling.

PREPARING THE PASTRY

Sift the flour, cloves, and cinnamon into a large bowl. Stir in the ground almonds, sugar, and grated lemon rind until well blended. Beat in the butter, lightly beaten egg yolks, and vanilla extract using a wooden spoon. Scrape the mixture onto a large piece of plastic wrap. Pull the sides of plastic up and around the dough and shape into a flat, rectangular loaf. Seal the ends and refrigerate 1½ hours or until firm.

LINING WITH PASTRY AND FILLING

Slice off ¾ of the dough and return the remainder, well wrapped, to the refrigerator. Cut ⅜-inch slices of dough from the loaf. Using your fingers, press the dough into the bottom and around the sides of the pan, extending a 1-inch rim of pastry around the inside edge of the springform pan. Smooth the pastry to a thickness of approximately ¼ inch, filling in holes with additional pieces of pastry. Attempt to have the thickness as even as possible so the torte will bake evenly. Using a pastry wheel or a knife, evenly trim the edge of the pastry rim that extends up the sides of the pan and remove the trimmings. Spread the bottom of the pastry evenly with the raspberry jam. Place in the refrigerator.

BEFORE BAKING

On a lightly floured board, roll out the pastry remaining in the refrigerator into a rectangle, approximately 6 by 9 inches. Make sure it doesn't stick to the board. If it should stick, loosen with a metal spatula, scrape off any pastry from the board, and flour the board again before you begin rolling again. Using a pastry wheel, cut out six strips ½ inch wide. You will need two that are 9 inches long, with the other four 8 inches or less in length. Remove the prepared shell from the freezer or refrigerator. Lay one 9-inch strip across the middle, placing one parallel strip on either side. Trim off the ends of the strips to meet the edges of the pan. Repeat with the other strips, laying them lattice-fashion across the other strips at an oblique angle so that the raspberry jam shows through in diamond shapes. Using a sharp knife, loosen the rim of pastry extending up the sides of the pan. Press it down onto the torte to cover up the ends of the strips. Using the back of a knife, make parallel markings at ¼-inch intervals all around the rim. Stir the egg yolk together with the cream and brush the exposed pastry with the glaze, making sure to get into the crevises where the pastry strips overlap. Refrigerate for 20 to 30 minutes.

BAKING AND FINISHING

After the Linzertorte has been refrigerated 15 minutes, **preheat the oven to 350 degrees F.** Bake in the middle of the oven until lightly browned, 45 to 50 minutes. Place on a large can and carefully release the lock on the springform pan, allowing the rim to slip off. Allow the torte to cool for 5 minutes, then dust with powdered sugar (using a dredger, if available).

SERVING AND STORING

Linzertorte should be eaten at room temperature, ideally after it has ripened for a few days. It will keep for over a week and can be stored in a cool place or in the refrigerator, loosely wrapped with aluminum foil, or it can be frozen, well wrapped, for three months or longer.

Mohnkuchen
Poppyseed Tart

Poppyseed pastries are such a common fixture in the Austro-Hungarian baking repertoire, it would be unfair not to offer one recipe made with this delicious ingredient. The one difficulty, however, is that the poppy seeds must be ground. Although I have seen several methods for grinding them at home using a blender, I have not found blender methods successful and have always resorted to specialty food shops (found especially in ethnic German or Hungarian neighborhoods) which sell and grind poppyseeds. The other alternative is to grind them in an electric coffee grinder, washing it well after the seeds are ground. The grinding process is essential, not only releasing their flavor, but allowing them to soften with the other ingredients when baked.

Used in everything from breakfast pastries and strudel to cakes and yeast dumplings, poppyseeds are a favorite ingredient taken over by the Austrians from their Eastern European neighbors. This unusual preparation combines a crisp, sweet pastry crust with a moist filling flavored with candied peel and raisins. It has wonderful keeping properties (up to two weeks, well wrapped in the refrigerator) and can also be frozen for three months or longer.

1 recipe Basic Sweet Rich Pastry Dough (p. 318)

FILLING
3 large eggs, separated
⅔ cup superfine sugar
1½ tablespoons candied peel, finely minced
1½ tablespoons raisins, chopped
Grated rind of 1 lemon
⅔ cup poppyseeds, ground (see recipe introduction)
Pinch of salt

TO FINISH
Powdered sugar, sifted

EQUIPMENT
10- or 11-inch tart pan

LINING THE TART PAN

Prepare the pastry per the directions in the master recipe. Wrap well and refrigerate for at least 1 hour.

Preheat the oven to 375 degrees F. On a lightly floured board, roll the dough out into a thin round 3 to 4 inches larger

than the tart pan. (See Baking Tips for additional reference.)
Lift the pastry round with your rolling pin and lay it over the
pan. Press the pastry well into the sides of the pan, easing some
of the excess dough down into the fluted sides to reinforce the
edge. Prick the bottom and sides with the prongs of a fork. Run
your rolling pin across the top of the tart to cutoff the excess
pastry.

PARTIAL BAKING

Butter a piece of aluminum foil and place it smoothly into the
pastry bottom, pressing the foil well into the sides of the rim.
Partially bake the pastry in the middle of the oven for approximately 15 minutes, or until the foil will remove easily without
tearing the pastry. Set aside to cool.

MAKING THE FILLING AND FINISHING

For the filling, beat the yolks together with the sugar using a
wooden spoon. Beat until thick and smooth, approximately 3
minutes. Stir in the minced candied peel, raisins, lemon rind,
and poppyseeds and set aside. Using an electric mixer, beat the
egg whites with a pinch of salt until stiff. Stir a large spoonful of
whites into the poppyseed mixture to lighten it. Pour this mixture
back on top of the egg whites. Fold in carefully using a large
metal spoon until no large streaks of white remain. Pour the
mixture into the cooled pastry shell. Bake in the middle of the
oven until the filling is set and the pastry is golden, approximately 20 to 25 minutes. Remove to a rack to cool. After 5
minutes, dust with powdered sugar. Serve at room temperature.

MEHLSPEISEN

SALZBURGER NOCKERL
SALZBURG SOUFFLÉ

In my student years, I had the opportunity to study one summer in the magic city of Salzburg. In sampling the regional culinary delights, I became addicted to *Salzburger Nockerl*—a delicate soufflé mixture made without milk and with hardly any flour. Setting out to find the city's best, I finally found the ultimate preparation at the Peterkeller, a charming vaulted restaurant/wine cellar built into the rocks near the opera. Besides its light, delicate texture, the Peterkeller's version didn't collapse like the others once it was brought to the table. The chef's secret? A little bit of baking powder sifted into the flour.

In Austria, this delicious treat is often eaten as a light supper dish. It makes a delicious light dessert, although not traditional, served with a bowl of fresh sugared berries. One advantage it has over most dessert soufflés, is that even though it must be prepared at the last minute, it only takes 8 to 10 minutes to bake. As a light supper dish, the following recipe would serve one (or two people, if they weren't terribly hungry). As a dessert offering, the recipe serves three. The recipe can be doubled and prepared according to the directions below, with the mixture mounded into two oven-proof dishes rather than one large one.

FOR THE BAKING DISH
3 tablespoons unsalted butter, softened
¼ cup whole milk or cream
SOUFFLÉ
3 egg yolks
1 teaspoon vanilla extract
Grated rind of 1 lemon
1 teaspoon baking powder
2 tablespoons all-purpose flour
5 egg whites
Pinch of salt
3 tablespoons sugar
TO FINISH
Powdered sugar, sifted
EQUIPMENT
1 oval (traditional) or oblong ovenproof baking dish, preferably crockery or glass, approximately 14 inches long and 3 inches deep

PREHEATING

Preheat the oven to 450 degrees F. Have all your ingredients ready. Spread the softened butter in the baking dish, add the milk or cream, and place in the preheated oven.

MAKING THE SOUFFLÉ MIXTURE
AND SHAPING

Working quickly, beat the egg yolks together with the vanilla extract and grated lemon rind using a wooden spoon. Sift the baking powder and flour together onto the yolk mixture. Set aside. Beat the egg whites with a pinch of salt, using an electric mixer, until they form soft peaks. Beat in the sugar a tablespoon at a time, beating well after each addition, until the whites are stiff. Stir a heaping tablespoon of whites into the egg-yolk mixture to lighten it. Using a rubber spatula, scrape the yolk mixture onto the whites. Fold the mixtures together, using a large metal spoon, until blended, being careful not to overfold. Remove the preheated baking dish from the oven (the butter/milk mixture should be steaming). Using a rubber spatula, dollop 3 large even mounds of the mixture into the dish. Use the spatula to smooth the sides and shape them like 3 ridged peaks.

BAKING

Bake in the middle of the oven until lightly colored, approximately 8 to 10 minutes. The *Nockerl* should be slightly firm on the outside but still very soft inside. Dust with powdered sugar and serve immediately.

KAISERSCHMARREN
EMPEROR'S PANCAKE

Emperor Franz Josef I was lucky indeed the day his entourage landed on a poor country farmer whose larder was bare but for eggs, butter, milk, and flour. This famous dish, supposedly created for the occasion, appears in most Austrian menus in the section called *Mehlspeisen* (See Chapter Introduction). Like *Salzburger Nockerl*, it would be eaten as a light supper dish or as a substantial dessert. Traditionally, *Kaiserschmarren* is served with a compote of plums or apricots. However, I generally serve it simply, as is.

PREPARING THE BATTER

Soak the raisins 30 minutes in the lightly warmed rum to soften and flavor them. Place the egg yolks, sugar, and milk in a blender and process at high speed for a few seconds. On medium speed with the lid removed, gradually add the sifted flour and process until smooth. Drain the raisins and stir into the batter. Beat the egg whites with the salt until stiff, using an electric mixer. Stir a large spoonful of the whites into the yolk/flour mixture to lighten it. Pour this mixture onto the whites and fold together with a metal spoon until no large dollops of white remain.

COOKING THE PANCAKE AND FINISHING

Heat a large skillet for 20 seconds over medium heat. Add 2 tablespoons of butter and heat until the foam on the butter is just disappearing. Pour the batter into the skillet to a depth of approximately ½ inch. If you are using a smaller skillet, you can

THIS RECIPE SERVES 1 FOR A MAIN COURSE OR 2 FOR DESSERT.

2 tablespoons raisins
2 tablespoons light or dark rum, lightly warmed (optional)
4 large eggs, separated
2 tablespoons sugar
1 cup milk
1 cup all-purpose flour, sifted
¼ teaspoon salt
4 tablespoons unsalted butter
EQUIPMENT
14- or 15-inch large skillet

make the *Kaiserschmarren* in two batches. Cook the pancake partially covered until it is puffed up in the middle and golden underneath. It should loosen easily from the skillet when golden. Invert onto a plate. Heat another 2 tablespoons of butter in the skillet and return the pancake to cook on the other side. When golden underneath, remove the pancake to a plate and shred with two forks into 1-inch ragged pieces. Return the pancake to the skillet and toss the pieces over medium heat for a few minutes, adding a little more butter if necessary. Remove to a platter, dust with powdered sugar, and serve immediately.

TOPFENPALATSCHINKEN
COTTAGE CHEESE CRÊPES

**MAKES APPROXI-
MATELY 16
FILLED CRÊPES**

PALATSCHINKEN
2 large eggs
1 egg yolk
3 tablespoons sugar
¼ teaspoon salt
1 cup milk (plus a
  little more if
  needed)
1 teaspoon vanilla
  extract
2 cups flour, sifted
1 tablespoon
  unsalted butter
FILLING
5 tablespoons un-
  salted butter,
  softened

CONTINUED ON
FACING PAGE

Palatschinken—thin pancakes similar to crêpes—are a favorite Austro-Hungarian dessert and are filled with everything from walnut cream and apricot jam to apples and vanilla soufflé. However, the most delicate and interesting preparation, in my opinion, is this one, in which the pancakes are filled with a souffléd cottage cheese mixture (in Austria, *Topfen* or *Quark*—a grainy, slightly tart milk product—is used), cut in half, covered with a rich cream custard mixture, and baked. They take some time to prepare but you'll find, once you've eaten them, they're worth every bit of the effort involved.

PREPARING THE BATTER

Make the batter in a blender. First process the eggs, egg yolk, sugar, salt, milk, and vanilla extract together for a few seconds.

With the blender on medium speed and the lid removed, gradually add the sifted flour. Process the batter for approximately 30 seconds, stopping the blender several times, until the mixture is smooth. Allow to rest at room temperature for ½ hour. Process once more for a few seconds in the blender.

MAKING THE PALATSCHINKEN

Heat the crêpe pan over high heat for approximately 30 seconds. Add 1½ teaspoons butter and roll it around in the pan to melt. Using a ¼-cup measuring cup or a ladle, pour enough batter into the hot pan to coat the bottom completely, pouring off any excess into the measuring cup to be used again. Cook over medium heat until golden on the bottom, approximately 1 minute. The pancake should release easily from the pan when it is done. Taking an edge of the pancake in your fingers, flip over and cook the other side for approximately 40 seconds, or until brown spots appear. Remove from the pan and repeat. Usually the first crêpe is not quite perfect in texture because the pan has to become perfectly seasoned. If the pancake seems too thick, thin the batter with a tablespoon or two of milk. Once the pan has become seasoned, you will generally not need to add more butter before cooking the next pancake. Continue with the remaining batter until it has all been used, stacking the pancakes on top of one another.

MAKING THE FILLING

Using an electric mixer or wooden spoon, cream the butter and powdered sugar together. Add the egg yolks one at a time, beating well between additions. Gradually beat in the cream, puréed cottage cheese, salt, vanilla extract, and grated lemon rind. Stir in the raisins. If an electric mixer was used, wash and dry beaters thoroughly before proceeding. Using an electric mixer, beat the egg whites until they form soft peaks. Begin adding the sugar by the tablespoon, beating well before adding more. When all the sugar has been added, beat another minute or two. Stir a large spoonful of stiff egg whites into the cottage cheese mixture to lighten it, then pour this mixture onto the

⅓ cup powdered sugar, sifted
4 large eggs, separated
⅓ cup cream
1 pound small-curd cottage cheese, processed quickly in a food processor (3 seconds with quick on/off control)
¼ teaspoon salt
1 teaspoon vanilla extract
Grated rind of 1 lemon
½ cup raisins, soaked in warm water ½ hour and drained
½ cup superfine sugar
FOR THE DISH
3 tablespoons un-salted butter, softened
CUSTARD
1 cup heavy or light cream
2 large eggs, lightly beaten
½ cup milk
3 tablespoons sugar
EQUIPMENT
8-inch crêpe pan with sloping sides
Large oval or oblong ovenproof baking dish, approximately 14 inches long and 3 inches deep

egg whites. Using a large metal spoon, fold the whites into the cheese mixture until no large streaks of white remain.

FILLING AND BAKING

Preheat the oven to 325 degrees F. Butter the ovenproof baking dish generously with butter and set aside. Lay the crêpes out flat on a work surface and spread each with approximately 2 tablespoons of the filling. Roll them without tucking in the ends. Cut each one in half across. Overlap the crêpes in the baking dish. Bake in the middle of the oven for 8 minutes.

PREPARING THE CUSTARD AND FINISHING

Mix the cream, eggs, milk, and sugar together with a whisk until smooth. Remove the baking dish from the oven and cover the crêpes evenly with the custard. Return to the oven and continue baking until the crêpes are beginning to brown and the custard is barely set, approximately 20 minutes. Dust with powdered sugar and serve warm.

GIFT IDEAS

Giving something home-baked on a special holiday or occasion is an American tradition. A gift of attractively packaged baked goods is personal and practical, a solution for large numbers at holdiay time that is equally suitable for the person who has everything.

Here are suggestions for both large-scale baking for the holidays and baking for a special occasion. Although there are numerous alternatives in the book, these selections will give you ideas for choosing what to bake and how to present it.

Presentation can be simple and inexpensive or more elaborate, involving a container that would constitute a gift in its own right. To accommodate your budget and requirements, the packaging reference is broken into two categories: Simple Container and Gift Container.

CHRISTMAS

Mixed Cookies

For each group I have selected three recipes which, when packaged together, make a varied and attractive presentation, in terms of color, shapes, and texture. At least one recipe in each group is based on a Basic Dough (indicated by BD) and you can therefore increase the variety of your selection by making a double batch of one of the Basic Doughs, preparing it in different ways. Choose one or more of the following groups, depending on how many different cookies you want to bake.

Vanilla Crescents
Basel Browns
Basic *Lebkuchen* (BD), cut out and decorated after baking with piped icing.

Chocolate Pretzels (BD)
Honey Cake Squares (BD)
Bethmanns

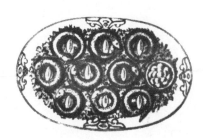

Meringues (BD) piped in wreaths
Marzipan-filled *Lebkuchen* Hearts (BD)
Florentines

Spitzbuben (BD)
Almond Sticks
Oktoberfest *Lebkuchen* Hearts (BD), made 2 to 3 inches in size

Cinnamon Stars
Lebkuchen Good-Luck Pigs (BD)
Milanese Butter Thins (BD)

SIMPLE CONTAINER

- Large red, green, or patterned *paper plates*. Many card/party supply shops also carry lines of paper plates that copy famous porcelain patterns. These make very attractive containers, as do the imported German paper plates available at specialty stores, with traditional German village and Christmas scenes.
- *Straw baskets*. These can be found at a reasonable price in many houseware departments and in import bazaars. Flower/plant stores are another good source. I always line straw baskets with a piece of colorful cotton fabric printed with small flowers. Although one cannot generally find Austrian or Bavarian fabrics in this country, many of the Laura Ashley prints have an Austrian look, particularly those with a dark red, dark green, or bright pink background. I don't bother hemming the fabric, but simply cut out a square with straight sides using a sharp pair of scissors or pinking scissors. Cut the square large enough so that when pressed into the basket, some of the fabric falls over the rim. The cookies are then placed on top of the fabric.
- *Decorative metal containers with lids*. Inexpensive selections are available in houseware departments and in card stores and party supply stores.

GIFT CONTAINER

- A porcelain, wooden, or glass *bowl* (new or antique)
- A red metal *strainer*. (There are models available now in most of the houseware stores that are like bowls made of mesh, without handles; later, they make an attractive container for fruit)
- *Cookie jar* or attractive *glass storage jar*
- 10-inch *bamboo steamer rack* (the kind used in woks). Although these usually come in sets of two or three with a lid on the top rack, you can give one each as a gift to a friend with a wok, using the lid on only one of the packages. A single steamer rack without a lid can be used perfectly by the recipient to steam vegetables or fish in a wok covered with its own lid. Although this container may seem odd in combination with traditional German cookies, the natural color of the wood and bamboo attractively set off their folk-art quality.
- A decorative porcelain, tin, or copper *pudding mold* (new or antique)

FINISHING

Fill the container with a variety of cookies. If the cookies have been baked in advance and stored, they should be packaged no more than a few days before presenting since, in most cases, they will no longer be in an airtight storage container and with time, will be subject to the effects of temperature and humidity. In the case of metal tins, close the lids. Cut a piece of cellophane large enough to wrap completely around the container. You will need a little extra length so that the ends of the cellophane can be gathered together in a plume in the center of the container and fixed securely with ribbon or cord. I prefer clear cellophane, but you can also use colored (generally available in yellow, green, and red). Any colorful ribbon or cord can be used, such as ½- or ¾-inch red, green, or striped grosgrain; red satin ribbon; gold, silver, red, or green metallic cord. Use a long enough length for you to tie a bow. If desired, you can tie a small sprig of evergreen into the bow, or thread a Christmas decoration, small pine cone, or chocolate heart covered in red foil, through the tie. If you buy the decorations in a Christmas tree ornament department, they will already have loops or strings attached.

LARGE COOKIES AND HOLIDAY BREADS

Lebkuchen Good-Luck Pigs 10 or 12 inches long
Gingerbread House
Oktoberfest *Lebkuchen* Hearts
Lebkuchen Star Candle Holders
Piped Cookies (piping the butter dough in the initials of the recipient, 6 to 7 inches long)
Santa Claus figures or Swiss Christmas men
Braided Christmas Star
New Year's Good-Luck Pigs
Spicy Pear Bread
Three Kings Cake
Dresden Christmas Stollen
Christmas Braid
Yeast Fruit Bread

SIMPLE CONTAINER

• For large cookies and delicate flat breads, buy Red *poster board*. Using a matting knife (available in art supply stores) and ruler, cut out a square or rectangle slightly larger than the size of the baked goods you are giving and center the cookie or bread on top. For other holiday breads, a poster-board base is not necessary.

GIFT CONTAINER

• A marble or wood *pastry board* (for large breads) or *cheese board* (for smaller breads and oversized cookies)

FINISHING

Finish per the instructions under Mixed Cookies.

Holiday Cakes

Pine-Cone Sponge Cake with Butter Cream, decorated per the instructions in the recipe.

VALENTINE'S DAY

- Bake a selection of heart-shaped cookies cut out or piped in hearts: *Lebkuchen* decorated with a halved candied cherry; butter cookies, iced or decorated; and meringues, piped in hearts and dusted with powdered sugar. Also see Marzipan-Filled *Lebkuchen* Hearts. For a *simple container,* place in a heart-shaped box or in a large red paper plate. For a *gift container,* buy a white porcelain *coeur à la crème* mold (with holes in the bottom) and fill with the cookies. To finish, wrap in cellophane and tie with ribbon, following the finishing instructions under Mixed Cookies.
- Oktoberfest *Lebkuchen* Hearts. Make one large heart per person, place on a square or heart cut from red poster board per the previous instructions for large cookies and Holiday Breads, and finish as above.

EASTER

Bake one of these Easter breads:

Easter Carp
Easter Wreath
Easter Egg Nests
Doves

Wrap larger loaves in clear cellophane and tie with a ribbon. Place the smaller figures in an *Easter basket* filled with artificial grass. Sprinkle colored jelly beans or small Easter eggs in the grass. If the basket has a handle, make a bow of pastel-colored satin ribbon for the handle. Just before presenting, you can thread a sprig of spring flowers through the bow.

HALLOWEEN

Prepare one of the deep-fried pastries from Chapter 4. Especially suitable are:

Bern Funnel Cakes

Mardi Gras Pastries

Slip-Knot Crisps

Sugared "Thighs"

Deep-Fried Puff Paste Doughnuts

Deep-Fried Raisin Yeast Cakes

Berlin Jelly Doughnuts

Offer to trick-or-treaters who come to your door, or serve on a buffet table to guests at a Halloween party (see Entertaining).

BIRTHDAYS, ANNIVERSARIES, MOTHER'S AND FATHER'S DAY, GRADUATION, HOSTESS GIFT, AND OTHER SPECIAL OCCASIONS

Prepare one of the cakes from Chapter 6, chosen to appeal to the recipient's taste.

FOR CHOCOLATE LOVERS

Schönbrunn Cake

"Saddle of Venison" Cake

Sachertorte

Chestnut Cream Slices

Tree Cake Squares

Chocolate Chestnut Torte

FOR NUT LOVERS

Rum and Praline Cake

Engadine Nut Cake

Linzertorte

OTHER FESTIVE CAKES INCLUDE:

Cardinal Slices

Lingonberry Meringue Torte

ENTERTAINING

To give you a better idea of how to incorporate some of these recipes into your own home entertaining, I offer the following suggestions according to the holiday or occasion.

CHRISTMAS

SUNDAY AFTERNOON OPEN HOUSE

In my childhood, my mother's friends always gave elaborate teas at holiday time, offering a vast selection of Christmas cookies, fruit breads, candied peels, and nut brittles. In the past I have used the same food formula, serving chilled German or Alsatian wine instead of tea and coffee. Because many people have a late breakfast or brunch on Sunday, skipping lunch, I've always scheduled my open house on a Sunday from four to six in the afternoon—a time when appetites are awakening. For serving the wine, I use a half barrel, lined with black heavy-duty garbage-can liners and filled with ice. (Half barrels are often available from country landscape gardening shops to be used for planting.) The wine bottles are opened in advance and recorked, with the neck of each tied with a red satin bow. As both Mosel and Alsatian wine comes in tall green bottles, either makes an attractive presentation at Christmas Time. Have a quality wine merchant make recommendations from his stock, select several, and try them before ordering for the party. On German wine labels, look for the phrase in small print near the bottom, *Qualitätswein mit Prädikat*, permitted only on wine meeting official control board standards of high quality and purity.

For a nonalcoholic beverage, I make a spicy chilled red fruit punch. To make, up to one week before the party, steep 1 gallon of cranberry-apple juice with the peel of 1 orange and 2 lemons, 6 cinnamon sticks, and 12 whole cloves in a large covered pot over low heat. After one hour, turn off the heat and allow to cool to room temperature. Strain out the flavoring ingredients and pour the punch into bottles. Cap or cork the bottles and refrigerate until needed. Serve chilled.

I prefer an open house to a tea since I like to invite men as well as women and children and most men traditionally feel out of place at a tea. However, if you prefer to give a holiday tea, the selection of baked goods that follows is equally appropriate. All of the items given are finger food, easy to eat and small or, in the case of the bread and cake selection, of a texture and finish that allow them to be cut in small pieces suitable for finger food.

BUTTER COOKIES

Vanilla Crescents
Spitzbuben
Ginger Cookies
Almond Sticks

LEBKUCHEN

Honey Cake Squares
Molasses Crisps
Basel Spice Cookies

WHISKED-EGG COOKIES

Spice Nuts
Cinnamon Stars
Bern Hazelnut Spice Cookies
Almond Meringue Kisses

CONFECTIONS

Date Macaroons
Bethmanns
Königsberg Hearts
Florentines

FRUIT BREADS

Dresden Stollen
Yeast Fruit Bread
Spicy Pear Bread
Alsatian Coffee Cake

CAKES

Tree Cake Squares
Linzertorte (cut in narrow wedges)
Engadine Nut Cake (cut in narrow wedges)
Pine-Cone Sponge Cake (not right for finger food; see Variation below)

VARIATION

Have one table with a selection of hot and cold finger food and another with a small selection of baked goods from the above list, with a Pine-Cone Sponge Cake as the centerpiece—to be cut in 1-inch slices with the broader slices cut again in half, and served on small dessert plates.

DECORATING THE CHRISTMAS TREE WITH COOKIES

The Christmas tree plays a major role in setting the holiday mood for home entertaining, and many of the cookie recipes in the book make attractive decorations. The tree can be simply decorated in the German style, with different gingerbread and whisked-egg cookies, small red apples, straw or wooden cut-out stars (available in specialty stores), and white lights. You can combine cookies hung from red cord or ribbon with your own collection of decorations.

Cookie recipes in the book that lend themselves well to tree decorating include:

Decorated *Lebkuchen*

Printed *Lebkuchen*

Old-Fashioned Zurich Molded Wafers

Lebkuchen Good-Luck Pigs

Printed Anise Cookies

Printed Red Christmas Cookies

Meringue Christmas Tree Wreath
    Ornaments

CHRISTMAS TABLE DECORATION

An amusing and decorative addition to your Christmas table setting, *Lebkuchen* Good-Luck Pigs can be piped with the name of each guest and used as place cards, propped against a glass at each place setting.

CHRISTMAS AND NEW YEAR'S FESTIVE DESSERTS

As dessert for a holiday dinner, either of the following makes an impressive display and a festive finish:

Lingonberry Meringue Torte

Pine-Cone Sponge Cake

NEW YEAR'S EVE

LATE NIGHT SNACK

If you give a New Year's Eve party that goes on into the early hours of the morning, bring out rounds of warm **Bacon Bread**, cut in finger-size pieces. The bread can be baked in advance and frozen. Before serving, thaw several hours at room temperature, then reheat in aluminum foil at 400 degrees F. for approximately 15 minutes.

VALENTINE'S DAY

Using the recipe for **"Saddle of Venison" Cake**, eliminate the almond decoration. Bake the cake in a 12-inch heart-shaped pan (measured from the top of the heart to the tip). Ice as directed. To finish, decorate per the instructions for *Oktoberfest* Lebkuchen *Hearts*.

EASTER BRUNCH

An **Easter Wreath** or **Alsatian Coffee Cake**, surrounded by colorful Easter eggs and spring flowers, would be the perfect sweet bread to accompany your favorite egg dish at an Easter brunch.

VARIATION

If you are serving a more substantial lunch entrée such as chicken or fish, half of the **Braided Loaf** *recipe could be used, transforming the dough into an* **Easter Wreath** *per the "Shaping" directions in that recipe. The dough in the Braided Loaf recipe is less sweet and therefore a more appropriate accompaniment to a meat or fish entrée.*

HALLOWEEN

Whether you invite people for a buffet dinner or an open house (where you would have more finger food—savory and sweet), a stack of sugar-dusted **Mardi Gras Pastries** makes a wonderful centerpiece and a delicious sweet snack that can be carried around and broken off in pieces.

DESSERTS FOR OTHER SPECIAL OCCASIONS

Bake one of the cakes suggested in the Gift Ideas section for other special occasions.

MAIL ORDER SOURCES

BALDUCCI'S
424 Avenue of the Americas
New York, NY 10011 (212) 673-2600

Specialty food store for both fresh and preserved foods; good source for candied and dried fruits, nuts, marzipan, chestnut purée

CHEF'S CATALOG
3915 Commercial Avenue
Northbrook, IL 60062 (312) 480-9400

Professional and everyday cooking equipment

CRATE AND BARREL
P.O. Box 3057
Northbrook, IL 60665 (312) 272-2888

Kitchenwares and housewares

GREAT VALLEY MILLS
687 Mill Road
Telford, PA 18969 (804) 357-6648

A variety of flours and grains

KITCHEN BAZAAR
4455 Connecticut Avenue, N.W.
Washington, D.C. 20008 (202) 363-4600

Cooking equipment of all sorts

MAID OF SCANDINAVIA
3244 Raleigh Avenue
Minneapolis, MN 55416 (612) 927-7996

Excellent source of hard-to-get baking and confectionery supplies, both equipment and ingredients

MISSOURI DANDY PANTRY
212 Hammons Drive East
Stockton, MO 65785 (417) 276-5121

Fresh nuts of all types

PAPRIKAS WEISS
1546 Second Avenue
New York, NY 10028 (212) 288-6117

My best source for hard-to-find ingredients and specialty baking equipment. Ground hazelnuts and almonds here are vacuum-sealed for freshness and, unlike many packaged ground nuts, can be recommended.

WILLIAMS-SONOMA
P.O. Box 7456
San Francisco, CA 94120 (415) 652-1515

A large selection of all cooking and baking equipment

ZABAR'S
2245 Broadway
New York, NY 10024 (212) 787-2000

Vast selection of specialty ingredients; selection of cookware

INDEX